BABYSHOCK

Editor
Dr. John Cobb   Consultant Psychiatrist

Contributors
Dr. Andrea Pound   Clinical Psychologist
Valerie Grove   Journalist
Leslie Garner   Journalist
Dr. Harvey Marcovitch   Consultant Paediatrician
Anne Petter   Social Worker
Joanna McNally   Health Visitor
Dr. Sol Goldenberg   General Practitioner and Obstetrician
Dr. Peter Hill   Child Psychiatrist
Dr. Stuart Lieberman   Family Therapist and
                        Consultant Psychiatrist
Susan Oliver   Fashion Consultant
Gina Carminati   Dance Instructor

Smoking During Pregnancy
Dr. Michael Russell   Psychiatrist

Interviewers
Dee Dudgeon
Marie Cobb
Anne Petter
Joanna McNally

Line illustrators
Viv Quillin
Nick May
Rob Shone

BABYSHOCK

A Mother's First Five Years

John Cobb

HUTCHINSON
London Melbourne Sydney Auckland Johannesburg

IM

Produced by
Pilot Productions Ltd
178-180 Wardour Street
London, W1V 3AA

First published 1980 by
Hutchinson & Co. (Publishers) Ltd
An imprint of the Hutchinson Publishing Group
3 Fitzroy Square
London, W1P 6JD

Hutchinson Group (Australia) Pty Ltd
30-32 Cremorne Street, Richmond South, Victoria 3121
PO Box 151, Broadway, New South Wales 2007

Hutchinson Group (NZ) Ltd
32-34 View Road, PO Box 40-086, Glenfield, Auckland 10

Hutchinson Group (SA) (Pty) Ltd
PO Box 337, Bergvlei 2012, South Africa

Set in Bembo by V & M Graphics Ltd, Aylesbury, Bucks

Printed in Great Britain by Anchor Press Ltd., Tiptree, Essex
and bound by William Brendon & Son Ltd., Tiptree, Essex

British Library Cataloguing in Publication Data
Cobb, John
Babyshock
I. Mothers
I. Title
301.42'7   HQ759

ISBN 0 09 140830 X

for Dee, who gave birth to the idea
and Carol, who gave it life

Contents

BABYSHOCK

Introduction

Introduction

"Motherhood is a high-risk profession".   Elaine Hefner.

Life is full of surprises. One of the most powerful of these is the change involved in becoming a parent. The impact of change is felt most by the mother, who may well find her life turned upside down. The less she anticipates this upheaval, the more of a shock it will be. Rather like riding a machine at the fun-fair, some will find the sensation exhilarating and others frightening. At the fun-fair you have some idea of what you are in for before the machine starts up. You also know in advance that the ride is only going to last a few minutes. Motherhood is very different. Several surveys carried out in the last ten years have shown that most women, before the birth of their first child, have little or no idea what to expect.

"I just don't think you have any idea of what motherhood is like until it happens – the total lack of privacy or time to be alone . . . also the sheer responsibility of it all."

"People and books tell you how to look after the baby lik ̄ they tell you how to drive a car. But no one tells you what state you'll be in when you're driving!"

"It is such a different experience to what I had imagined it would be. There's much more physical work involved. I didn't expect so many constantly broken nights and didn't anticipate the effects of such sleep loss. Nor did I anticipate how tense night crying would make me and how that would interfere with our sex life. . . ."

"I never thought I'd enjoy being a mother. I'm the most unmotherly person I've met. I'm quick-tempered. But it's those little hands going round my neck when she's tired that thrills me."

Nor is it just the quality of the experience that may be different, you are also likely to underestimate the time it may take to readjust. Present-day emphasis on ante-natal care and the delivery itself gives the impression that it is the physical stress of being pregnant and of going through childbirth that is crucial – that once the baby is born, the most difficult time is over. Experienced mothers know that nothing could be further from the truth. Childbirth is a beginning not an end in itself. The birth of a baby is a milestone in a woman's personal development – life will never be the same again – but the emotional growth which begins with the slow changes of pregnancy and leads up to the blood, sweat and tears of the delivery itself takes months, years even, to complete.

BABYSHOCK

"Having children has made me feel more mature, more of a person. It gives me a sense of responsibility. Motherhood is a marvellous thing."

Change and re-adjustment are not restricted to mothers. Increasingly, fathers are becoming more involved in the birth of their children (although not fast enough in some families; one still hears the aggravating male chauvinist comment, *"My wife has given up work to have a baby."*) One recent study showed that one half of fathers were 'highly participant' in the care of their children, while only one in five took no part at all. The traditional clear-cut distinction between the man, who was expected to 'go out and earn the money' and the woman who was expected to 'stay at home and look after the children' is becoming blurred. Some fathers find this hard to accept particularly if the mother has a career and enjoys a higher earning power. But others do make a substantial contribution to the mothering of their children, with the result that they experience at first hand the impact of the baby's arrival. One writer, possibly with his tongue in his cheek, has suggested that fathers have been neglected by experts because most of the research on child rearing, on which their opinions are based, is done during office hours when most men are at work.

This book is about this period of change and adjustment. It looks at the events surrounding conception, pregnancy, childbirth and the first few years of motherhood as they influence both partners, but especially the mother. It is *not* a guide to pregnancy, nor a child-care manual in the accepted sense. Many excellent books on these subjects already exist.

Traditionally, child-care literature has taken the child as a focal point, and has dictated what parents ought or ought not to do *for the sake of the child*. It is time to redress the balance, particularly since research during the past twenty years has shown that much so-called 'advice' created more problems than it solved.

Babyshock takes parents as the focal point, and it is intended as a companion and prop in times of stress. Our aim is to provide the framework through which a new mother will feel her life enriched by the experience of birth, which can lead to emotional growth as described here:

"I am pleased with how well I adapted and how enjoyable I find my child, and the general reduction in tension as to what to do with myself. In fact, I do more in my own right now than before."

Our theme is shared by Rhona and Robert Rapoport who in a more academic book *Fathers, Mothers and Others*, encapsulated the point:

"Parents are not only vehicles for the care of their children. They were persons before the

child arrived; are persons while they are parents; and will be after the children leave . . . 'Children first, last and always is no longer a tenable maxim for family life, on anyone's account."

The way mothers are neglected by members of my own profession first came home to me one November morning nearly two years ago. It was my wife's first visit to the ante-natal department of a London Teaching Hospital which has the reputation of being one of the most enlightened in its views on pregnancy and childbirth. Probably because of my status as a Consultant in the National Health Service, we only had to wait an hour and a half to be seen, instead of the usual three hours. After the preliminaries, she was shown into a small, white cubicle, given a gown – at least two sizes too small – and told to strip off, lie on a hard couch and wait. Fifteen minutes elapsed before four jolly young men in white coats and two nurses squeezed into the cubicle. The briefest introduction established that two of the men were doctors and the other two medical students. While they were in the midst of a none too gentle examination, one of the nurses whispered, *"Aren't you lucky, dear, having so many doctors looking after you?"*

The irony of the nurse's comment lies in the obvious fact that the doctors were not interested in looking after *her* at all. The focal point of their interest was the baby – extending their interest to my wife only to ensure that she was physically capable of producing a healthy child.

No wonder, when visiting ante-natal clinics, many women complain of feeling like cows; they are in fact treated like cows! As for fathers, they might as well not exist. It is easy to blame doctors and midwives for their mechanistic approach. Their training has in the past concentrated on reducing rates of death or physical damage both to mother and baby. They have been taught to be concerned with a woman's blood pressure and the size of her pelvis, but not taught to deal with a woman's natural anxieties, attitudes and expectations.

In former years, mothers as part of extended families received help from their own mothers or other experienced female relatives. If assistance was not available from these sources, there were probably friends or neighbours, known and trusted by the family for a number of years, or a local doctor, midwife or district nurse with time to stop and chat.

Today, increased mobility has led to scattered families. People stay less and less in one area and tend not to develop close trusting friendships with neighbours or local professional medical staff. People are forced to rely on self-help, in the shape of books, magazines, and other media, which prescribe child-care rules, but show little practical regard for the emotional support a mother needs.

BABYSHOCK

Just how inefficient experts have been in preparing parents for their new roles, is illustrated by a number of recent studies, one of which took the form of following a group of couples through pregnancy to six months after delivery. Among its conclusions, the study showed that the initial elation of having a baby – when it was present at all – was short-lived, that the fathers began to get anxious about careers and salaries, that new conflicts arose between the mothers and fathers, and that all the parents studied were dismayed and taken unawares by the drastic reduction in freedom and leisure time.

This situation is further influenced by the changing role of women in our society. Whereas most women used to view motherhood as a *primary* role, even as the sole reason for existence, there are many and increasing choices open to today's woman. Women are no longer single-mindedly preparing themselves for motherhood. In Britain employment rates for married women show that in 1950 about one in five were working full- or part-time. By 1970, this figure had risen dramatically and more than doubled. Furthermore, statistics show that many of these working women are mothers with young children. Attitudes have also changed, as a recent study by the Government Office of Population Censuses and Surveys shows. Only one woman in three agreed that 'a woman's place is in the home', and the number of husbands who actively discouraged their wives from working fell from fourteen per cent in 1965 to two per cent in 1978.

Clearly it is no longer possible to cling to the traditional split in sex roles, whereby the man is seen as provider – with prime responsibility to earn money, and the woman is cast as the home-maker – responsible for domestic work and care of children. Massive social changes are rather like fundamental changes in climate. It is tempting to strive to continue life as though nothing had happened and ignore increasing discomfort. In practical terms it is quite impossible. People will have to face the fact that they are not living in the 'good old days' and adjust their way of life accordingly.

If one looks at our society's approach to child-care over the last century, two major stages can be identified. Traditionally, the way a child developed was reckoned to be due to character. Character, it was said, is largely inborn and not made, though behaviour might be moulded or restrained by discipline and education. Schooling children was seen as a process akin to 'breaking in a colt' – a task which could be carried out as effectively by teachers as by parents. Good or bad children either came from 'good or bad stock' or were the product of good or bad training and education.

In the 1900s, some radical re-thinking took place. A number of experts challenged the traditional views. One of the most famous of these, Sigmund

Freud – the founder of psychoanalysis – saw the process of child development as *dynamic*. He argued that it is through the child's interaction with his mother that personality and character is formed. In his view all new born babies possess the same drives. The way these drives are satisfied or frustrated, particularly during the first three years of life, determine what sort of adult will result – good or bad, happy or unhappy, normal or neurotic, and so on.

From our point of view the significance of Freud's ideas is that they influenced not only the experts, but also generations of parents, who were led to believe that responsibility for the way a child develops lies solely with the mother. What matters is the way a child is loved and nurtured during the first three years. Instead of having 'good and bad' children, there were now 'good and bad' mothers. Freud emphasised the latter by spending much more time writing about a mother's power to do harm, than in describing the positive contribution she could make to her child's development.

The spirit of Freud's work was continued in the influential studies of John Bowlby just after the Second World War. He demonstrated the importance of early attachment between mother and baby, and showed that if this was severely disrupted the child's character could be scarred for life. His 'continuous presence' theory put still more responsibility on a mother's shoulders. Faced with this burden, it was natural for mothers to look to experts to guide them in the so-called 'craft' of motherhood. Though advice differed from one expert to another, and though the same expert might change his mind from one edition of his book to another, all shared a common theme. They assumed that no one could be a substitute for the baby's natural mother, who should be available twenty-four hours a day for the first three years. Dire warnings of lasting damage to the developing personality were stated or implied if women ignored their responsibilities. The baby's demands were to come first and second; the mother's needs, if considered at all, came a very poor third. Fathers were viewed as shadowy figures suitable for occasional support to mothers in their supreme task, but unsuitable for caring directly for children.

These views did have some valuable results. For example, attitudes towards the visiting of children in hospital changed dramatically. Whereas visiting used to be allowed only once a week, most hospitals created mother and baby units and permitted mothers to stay twenty-four hours a day with their children. But on the adverse side, many mothers, the competent as well as the less capable, were made to feel guilty, inadequate and anxious. "Am I doing enough?"; "It must be my fault that . . ."; "I must be a bad person to resent my baby at times . . ." were all common preoccupations. As far as children were concerned, constant attention, excessive permissiveness – 15 *don't at all costs frustrate a child's drives*-and lack of structure in the first three years could foster a type of adult who lacks self-control, purpose, and who insists that the world owes him a living – the so-called 'Spock-marked generation'.

More recent research has shown that Freud and his followers had been correct in their general approach. Mothers *are* important and personalities are formed as well as made. However, they were incorrect in detail and emphasis. Mothers are not *all*-important (grandparents, fathers, brothers and sisters can 'mother' as well as the natural mother herself). Mothers need not be present all the time. Short periods of intense and intimate interaction with their children are probably more helpful than endless days of just being together in the same room or house. Finally, babies are born with very different characteristics, some are easier than others not because of the way they are mothered but because of their inborn tendencies.

Opinion having swung as far as it could in the direction of mothers taking sole and all-consuming responsibility for their children, one might expect the pendulum to have swung in the other direction. In fact, it has started off in a new direction altogether.

The women's movement exposed the inequality that persists in society between men and women, and many of its arguments found support in the microcosm of the family. Giving births is no longer seen as a primary goal. Rather, it is presented as one of a variety of goals which a woman might have. More hardened advocates of women's liberation have stressed the stultifying aspects of bringing up a child. A sentiment clearly summarised in this poem:

> *Baby-minder, sock-finder, bacon-fryer, dish-dryer,*
> *Floor-sweeper, light-sleeper, brow-smoother, mend the Hoover,*
> *Nappy-folder, hand-holder, onion-chopper, mess-mopper,*
> *Button-sewer, to-and-froer, tidy-upper, what's for supper?*
> *Oh, I don't work – I'm nothing but a housewife.*

Pressure was on women to cast off the manacles of full-time motherhood and emerge from 'generations of slavery' to take more fulfilling roles in the outside world. In interviews with women, particularly middle-class women who had enjoyed successful careers prior to their having their first children about five years ago, we were told of the psychological pressure to go out to work and divest themselves of the *chore* of child-rearing. If Freud made mothers feel guilty and inadequate, the women's movement could be seen as making them feel irrelevant.

"I still feel slightly guilty at enjoying being a full-time mother. It's awful that society should make you feel like that. The other night we went out with a couple who are both

16

journalists. They said, 'Don't you get awfully bored; don't you feel left out?' I don't feel left out. I read the papers; I talk to people; I keep up. What are you missing except going to work every day?"

"On the one hand there was this pressure that made me feel that I ought to be working – all these other women were working – and I felt strongly that I was a non-person for not working. On the other hand, I would get so angry with advertisements portraying mothers as nitwits who dance around the kitchen with packets of peas and nappy liners and things. In the end, what both pressures made me realise was that what I really wanted was to be me – as far as I was concerned, going out to work was out of the question. I just couldn't leave the child with anyone else because I loved her too much."

So, in encouraging women to reassess their primary goals in hard practical terms, the women's movement has paradoxically highlighted for some the supremely rewarding aspects of motherhood *per se*. The point that the second young mother above is making is that most housekeeping jobs like cooking, cleaning, washing and ironing are repetitive and boring. Only the 'nitwits' in the advertisements would find otherwise. But the care of babies and the rearing of children is in a different category of work altogether because it involves an intimate relationship with a developing human being. For this reason, nappy changing is different from washing up.

One can make a good job of cleaning a house without ever experiencing any warmth for the place. On the other hand, an essential component of mothering is a feeling of love towards the baby and a sense of joy and satisfaction at being involved in his growth and development, as well as disappointment and frustration at the inevitable times of difficulty and failure. Such involvement makes the career of 'mothering' *at least* as worthwhile as being a teacher, social worker or car mechanic, and a good deal more valuable than most jobs.

Faced with all these conflicting pressures, it is not surprising that a new mother should feel at sea (particularly as each school of thought has so many persuasive elements). What *Babyshock* does first is to recognise that although there are common themes involved in the experience of parenthood, each family's experience and needs are *unique*. From the moment you announce that you are pregnant, you will be on the receiving end of advice from friends, family (some of which you may have forgotten existed) and the media. Their advice, probably distilled from one or more of the above theories, will have a common theme – 'how *best* to do this, that or the other'. In fact, whether one is concerned with child-care or parent-care there are very few absolute rights and wrongs. Good advice to one family could be bad for the family next door. There is only one imperative 'do' and that is to make up your *own* mind. This book tries to provide information on which you can base decisions which you feel are best for you.

BABYSHOCK

We make no bones about the hard work that motherhood involves in the initial months. In general, the more you put in at that stage, the more you will benefit from the whole experience. Furthermore, research during the past ten years has shown that the more secure your baby feels in the first few months, the sooner he will start to become independent. But above all, it must be stressed that the quality of care that a mother is able to provide depends upon the encouragement that she is given to satisfy her own needs as an individual. A woman who is lonely and isolated, and who feels unfairly treated and wasted is hardly likely to enjoy or to make a success of bringing up children.

The problem with many fashionable theories of child-care is that what they recommended for the baby was exceedingly tough on the mother. Trudy King's rigid approach to feeding schedules is a classic example of this. Underlying everything in this book is the question: "How can we do our best for our children without losing sight of the sense and direction of our own lives?"

This book tries to give information which you can use to help reach your own decisions. For example, if you are concerned with the question: "Should I be a working or full-time mother?", no expert can possibly answer 'Yes' or 'No', except to state the obvious if your financial situation means you must work. We examine the likely effects your absence may or may not have on your baby and try to help you evaluate what is essential to his successful upbringing. *Babyshock* encourages *you* to decide whether the child's natural mother or a surrogate alternative may best tackle the demanding business of parenthood. The answer will depend on the attitudes and personalities of both yourself and your man, if you have one. It will depend on your economic situation, the amount of support you have from your family and neighbours, the availability and quality of local services and not least on the personality of your baby.

Of the thirteen consultants who contributed, six have written the main part of the book – three women and three men. Three of these are medical doctors, two are journalists and one a psychologist. Not only do all the contributors have children of their own but, during the course of the book's preparation, no fewer than five of us conceived or gave birth to a new baby. As such, our involvement is as much practical as theoretical, and the comment "the baby is distracting me from my writing" was as common as the complaint, "I can't get enough time with the baby because of the book deadline".

Confidence depends upon being informed and, throughout we have tried to inform rather than instruct; to consider possible alternatives rather than to

pontificate. We have tried to avoid riding our own particular band-wagons, as we are well aware that today's cult can soon become yesterday's mistake. The medical men have been asked to teach rather than to prescribe, to explain rather than to dictate. We hope not to have offended too many readers by referring only to male children and female mothers. For practical purposes too, relevant addresses and telephone numbers are included near the end of the book and referred to in the text – e.g. **Ref 1:2.**

First, we look at the stages of planning and preparation. A woman who maintains her self-confidence during pregnancy, and at the same time prepares herself for childbirth and the following months of pressure and fatigue, is clearly in a prime position to savour the moments of joy. Next, we examine the inherent problems of the birth itself and try to give you the confidence to make your own decisions in the face of family, friends and hospital staff. The ability to cope with childbirth and its immediate aftermath is important because it determines a mother's capacity to adapt to the role of mother.

In the main part of the book which is concerned with motherhood itself, we look at how best to manage the physical and emotional problems which characterise the early months; why the successful development of your child and your need to continue functioning as a complete, individual person, are not necessarily incompatible – satisfying your needs should be encouraged for your child's sake. Finally, we consider the adjustment implicit in coming out from behind the apron of full-time motherhood – if that has been your role – when the youngest is aged five.

Additionally, a team of interviewers collected numerous interviews with mothers from a wide spread of backgrounds. They showed that mothers were thinking along the same lines as the consultants, and by displaying their very real needs, encouraged us in our writing of the book. Many of the points made have been quoted in the text. Our thanks too to the BBC Man Alive team who so readily helped us in our research.

The book might well have been dedicated to the new mother who asked, "Is there life after birth?" We hope to show that however often you may doubt it, indeed there is!

1
Planning and preparation

"Planning my children made a big difference to my feelings towards them, both before and after the birth."

"I made a decision, but it was a thoroughly irresponsible one. It was a question of involving myself more in my job or having a child – there was no way that I could weigh up such a decision responsibly because I had no real idea of what having a child would involve. In the event, after the initial shock and adjustment, I couldn't have been happier."

Planning and preparation

How will a baby change my life?

With an increasing respect for parents as people, comes a more realistic picture of what motherhood involves. The romanticised image projected for so long by the media is being firmly discarded and the full implications in terms of rewards *and* constraints on freedom and independence are being considered.

It is unlikely that the 'warts and all' picture of motherhood will deter those who truly want to care for children. It is certain that it is the first step towards helping parents to understand the nature of this transitional point in their lives and turn it into a rewarding experience for the whole family.

When a new baby enters your life, the effect will be total. However complicated your life may seem on busy working days at present, you will one day look back on them as carefree. It is

the permanency of motherhood which immediately comes home to you. You will move from a situation in which you are able to devote yourself exclusively to your job, your partner as lover, and your own interests, to one of absolute selfless commitment to another human being. To begin with, the baby is wholly dependent upon you, and he will remain a lifelong concern.

You will become involved in a network of people whose existence you may barely have acknowledged before – neighbours, nursery teachers, health visitors, community welfare personnel, babysitters, paediatricians, children's librarians, and above all other parents with children of the same age. You can practically say goodbye to childless friends, especially when you turn down yet another invitation because you cannot locate a babysitter. Goodbye also to relaxed evenings at home, late Sunday mornings with the papers in bed, spontaneous excursions… You are simply not free to visit whoever you want whenever you want. On extended visits, it will be like an army manoeuvre – carry cots, prams, and other paraphernalia. It may surprise you to learn that there actually is an organisation called the British Organisation of Non-parents, made up of people who have elected to remain child-free (as they put it).

These are only some of the ways in which your life will alter, and which are discussed throughout the book. How you cope with them determines how you will adjust to parenthood, whether you will enjoy the experience, and how successful a parent you are to your child. 23

BABYSHOCK

In the light of this more realistic picture of motherhood, it may be helpful to look at some answers to the question.

Why have a baby at all?

"It was conformity. You got married in order to have children. My mother had had me when she was 21. I was 23 and already felt over the hill."

"There's always this fear that, until you do get pregnant, you're not able to."

The desire to conceive is a basic and powerful instinct. If asked why they decided to have a baby, some parents will answer with apparently well-thought-out reasons. Very often these reasons are false because the actual emotions that have inspired them are difficult to define or put into words.
The fact is that there is a high proportion of unplanned pregnancies. Subconsciously, a couple may want a child, but not be up to taking a positive decision to do so possibly because there are too many other conflicting desires or demands. Very often, in these circumstances, a woman may play a game similar to Russian roulette. She may decide that her contraceptive is risky and give it a rest for a while. Perhaps, she thinks, she will get away with it. Lightly, she weighs the risk of contraceptive against the risk of having a baby, and makes a sort of decision in that way.

"I didn't plan my pregnancy but it was my fault. I didn't take as much contraception as I might. We wanted children some time soon anyway but I had no idea that conception would be that easy."

"I decided to have a baby because I'd got to that stage in life when I didn't know what I wanted. I was fed up with my job, my marriage was rocky and I thought a baby would give me a focus in life. The whole thing was a disaster. I discovered that I had no maternal instinct.

When I discovered that I was pregnant I was terrified and wondered if I had done the right thing. My ex-husband is very ambitious. Children just didn't feature in his plans at all."

If a conscious decision is made, it is unusual for it not to have been influenced by pressures of one sort or another.
There may be pressure from the child's prospective father – perhaps even a chauvinistic wish to keep the woman at home and not compete as an equal working partner.
Frequently there is pressure from either of a couple's parents who want to have grandchildren.
Friends with toddlers may make open or veiled insinuations of selfishness to a childless couple.
Doctors may provoke anxiety by exaggerating the dangers of waiting too long.
Most disastrously of all, the baby may be seen as a solution to an unhappy relationship.
Other reasons frequently include:
A wish to leave something of yourself behind after you are dead.
A positive wish to benefit from caring for another human being.
A wish to be creative in the most elemental sense.
Whatever the underlying motivation, bear in mind that it is you and the child who will experience the consequences, not your parents or in-laws, neighbours, friends, or doctor, and not always the child's father. While planned parenthood does not necessarily entail happy and successful parenthood – he may be a blessing in disguise – there is more likely to be a satisfactory outcome if you face some of the consequences right away.

"Planning my children made a big difference to my feelings towards them, both before and after the birth. You see the first two were planned and everything went smoothly – they were

lovely – no problems. *My third was un-expected. When we knew I was expecting again we were very upset. We didn't honestly look forward to it. I mean, it was a big age gap and I didn't want to start all over again. People used to say rotten things like 'fancy starting all over again' and 'you are stupid' and I used to pretend he was planned and everything was lovely when I knew inside they were right. But I wouldn't let on. All through my pregnancy with him I was frantic, thinking, 'Oh dear, we'll have to move this and that around – things just won't be the same.' I would never have though it was the same me feeling that way; I had so looked forward to the other two.'*

"Because I had a career and a job which I knew I couldn't continue after the child was born I had a love/hate attitude to being pregnant. I didn't admit to being pregnant and tried not to give into my fatigue or give up the ballet and yoga I had done for years. I worked until a month before the birth. Luckily I was very healthy throughout my pregnancy. The trouble was that I just couldn't get enthusiastic about equipping the baby for the world and had it not been for some very good friends the child would have arrived to a couple of babygrows and a wooden box for a bed. This attitude made me

even more resentful because when the baby did arrive it meant that I had to do even more for it. I was so frustrated because I hadn't organised myself for her and I wanted to be organised so that the baby could at least look cared for."

Here are some of the best and worst things which some mothers recall about motherhood:

What's best:
"I think that motherhood prepares you to cope with life. It's far harder than any sort of work, but in the long run it's worth it and you have points in the day when you just love your child so much you can't explain! She says something to you and you could just eat her up she's so wonderful."

What's best:
"Motherhood is the focus of all my attentions. It's the raison d'etre."

What's best:
"What's nice about having children is that you grow up all over again. When you show them flowers and things, you see them all over again yourself."

What's best:
"Having a child made me more of a person, more mature. Also, the humour you see developing in your child, and the affections she feels."

What's best:
"Later, it's the companionship they give you."

What's best:
"On the plus side, I think children bring out qualities in a partnership which might other-wise remain hidden."

What's worst:
"Having children destroys all romance be tween you. I suppose because one has little time or energy left for each other."

BABYSHOCK

What's best:
"The second child made us all aware that we were a unit and have to work together more instead of demanding. We give more to each other now."

What's worst:
"It's the constant noise – how she just rabbits at me and follows me around the house. I never get to be on my own, not even in the lavatory. There is, simply, no privacy."

What's best:
"All that love and trust. Yes, I think the way children turn to you with absolute trust – that's the best thing about having a child."

What's worst:
"Being tied down. The monotony of daily routine, especially now that the older one attends school."

What's best:
"The best thing is that I get on much better with my parents. I really understand what they went through for their kids."

What's worst:
"He and I had very different upbringings. This is what causes friction. Although, overall it has improved my relationship with my husband, we do still have a lot of disagreements about this."

When is the best time to have a baby?

The best time to have a child is not when you can afford to or while you are still under thirty or when your mother spells out what you are missing. The best time is when you really, genuinely, over-whelmingly feel that you want a baby. It is possible to quantify the problems of child-bearing and relate them to a mother's age. For women over thirty-five the risk of a baby being stillborn or dying soon after birth is more than doubled and for teenage mothers nearly doubled. The 'safest' ages are between twenty and twenty-five but there are only minor differences in safety to mother and baby at any time between twenty and thirty-five. Many women believe that the older they are the more likely their baby is to be abnormal. In fact, it is only true for two major problems. Firstly, Downs Syndrome (Mongolism), a basic abnormality in the make-up of the child which results in both physical abnormality and mental handicap. This is a one in a thousand chance for a mother under thirty-five, one in three hundred for women aged thirty-five to thirty-nine, one in a hundred for those aged forty to forty-four and one in thirty for those over forty-five. The other age related defect is cleft lip and palate which occurs in about one in 1,500 babies of women under thirty-five and about one in eight hundred of older women.

So really the risks of being an older mother are small. Of a thousand babies delivered from mothers over thirty-five, about 935 will be alive and normal. For those mothers between twenty and thirty-five about 955 will be alive and normal.

What is the best age difference between children?

In terms of their surviving pregnancy and the first few weeks, the best interval between babies is two to three years. In terms of the difficulties presented by brothers and sisters, there are no hard facts, only opinions. One could say that during the first two years a baby's eagerness for stimulation is such that it may seem unfair to deprive him by your preoccupation with a new baby. Perhaps, then, one should wait until the older child is two. But from about two until three most children are busy practising their newly-learned skills and using their freshly-discovered personality to assert control over their surroundings –

including their parents. This is the time of 'negativism', of tantrums, of apparently wilful disobedience. The appearance of a new baby during this time sometimes provokes extremely difficult behaviour by the older brother or sister. In that case, maybe three years is a good gap. But having, say three children at three yearly intervals means eleven years of being tied to the house. The desire to preserve your own sanity or financial pressure may make this course unattractive.

There is no best age difference. What is right for one family is wrong for another. What really matters is whether or not the child was wanted in the first place.

BABYSHOCK

Should I have more than one child?

The first and most important consideration is how *you* feel about it. The popular view is that 'only' children will be lonely and also spoilt and egocentric, and that it is unfair on them not to allow them brothers and sisters. There is in fact very little evidence to support this view. It may have been a useful myth when infant mortality was high and large families were the rule but there is far more evidence regarding the disadvantage of being a child in a large family of more than four or five children. Children in large families are twice as likely to develop aggressive or destructive behaviour, and are statistically more likely to become delinquent as they get older. They also tend to be less bright and do less well at school. It is very difficult to give each child the care and attention he needs in a very large family. Parents tend to be too busy keeping up with the chores and paying the bills – money is likely to be short. There is more noise and confusion and less parental control, an atmosphere less conducive to successful development.

So if you do not positively desire another child, there is no reason to feel you should have one just out of a sense of duty. If you enjoy children, and have an adequate income and space then two or three children will feel more like a complete family. It may seem materialistic to stress the importance of money and space, but they should not be underestimated in your calculations. If you have two or more children on an average income, most of it will go on feeding, clothing and housing the family. Chronic anxiety about money can make marriage and family life a misery, and if you have any tendency to extravagance, it may become a nightmare.

Can the one-child family produce special problems?

In general 'only' children are as well balanced as children in larger families, but they do have a very different kind of early experience. Most of their interaction is with adults rather than with other children, and they may in consequence seem "old for their age'. When they start school they may be a little too constrained and polite, and not very happy with the rough and tumble of the playground. Most parents of only children are well aware of their need for opportunities to play with other children, and make a special point of encouraging their friendships. As they get older, other children can be invited to stay for a few days, or taken as companions on holidays. There is no need for 'only' children to be lonely children, though they sometimes are.

Difficulties are likely to arise if the family is very isolated, or there are other problems within the family. 'Only' children with quarrelling parents have no one else to turn to for support and can feel responsible if rows and recriminations break out. If parents are over-anxious or over-controlling, the child is the sole focus of their mixed up emotions and he may sometimes wish there was someone else to be fussed over, or nagged at, so he could have an occasional rest from it all. As a parent you may also sometimes wish you did not have all your eggs in one basket. When he later wants to ride a bicycle, or go on a climbing holiday, you have to battle with your fears of his coming to grief, while also wanting him to become independent and do all the things other children of his age do. This may be a special problem if you really wanted more children but were not able to have them. Perhaps the best solution here is to find a job involving children, so you can express your maternal feelings without overwhelming your 'only' child. **Ref 4:9** Another problem for parents is a tendency to continue doing everything for the 'only' child when he is in fact old enough to do them for himself. In a larger family, it is necessary to share out the household tasks, but with one it is not and you may drift along, unaware of how much you are incapacitating him by not giving him the opportunity to help. It is a good idea to keep an eye on what other children of the same age do at home, in the way of self-help and chores and gradually introduce them yourself.

Some 'only' children of over-devoted parents leave home unable to make a cup of coffee or clean their shoes, much less cook or clean a room, and it is no service to them in the long run.

What are the likely effects of the second child on child one? How can you best deal with such problems?

"After the second child was born, my first did show jealousy by demanding to go to the toilet all the time when I was feeding him. Now the second will give the baby a slight kick if I am changing him on the floor. Apart from that there is no nastiness. Mostly they are very happy together."

First-born children have a slightly higher risk of emotional problems than later-born children and one of the causes may be the experience of being suddenly de-throned when the second child comes along. Parents play and talk more to the first-born, so he gets used to a high level of adult attention and interest, and then quite suddenly has to adapt to sharing it with the new arrival. However carefully you prepare him, he is going to find it hard going at first, and it will help him if you let him know that you understand how tough it is. Most older children react to the birth by trying hard to regain the attention they have lost. They hang around you more, interrupt more, want more help with things and so on. If they still feel deprived they are likely to start being more provoking and demanding and may be positively aggravating, on the basis that even a shout or a slap is better than being taken no notice of at all. They may turn more to their father for comfort and companionship, and if he is at home enough it may make all the difference to how the eldest copes with the new baby.

It is always easier to cope with difficulties when you have some idea what to expect. The same applies to your first child when a second is expected. Tell him about the baby in good time, before it starts to show too clearly. He may be able to feel it moving as the pregnancy goes on. Talk to him about how it will be, where the baby will sleep and so on, and show him small babies when you have the chance. It is often very disappointing to expect a new playmate, and then find it's such a useless bundle and no good for playing with at all. Explain the father's part as far as you can, taking into account the child's age and ability to understand.

Once the baby arrives, feeding times are likely to be the most difficult. The oldest may wish he could be a baby again, with a baby's privileges, and if still quite 29 young may want a bottle or a dummy to suck himself while the baby feeds. If you can arrange your day so that some of the feeds take place when the first is having a nap, or has settled down in the evening, it will help. Another way to help him recover his equilibrium is to allow him to assist you with the baby in some way, so he feels he has a useful role to play. First-born children tend to do better in school and in later careers than later-born children, and in part this may be a result of the push to development provided by taking a 'grown up' role in relation to the baby in the family.

After a while he will probably get used to the new arrival; the baby will become more interesting as a playfellow and the first-born will forget how much sorrow and anger he felt initially. Where things go wrong, it is often because his unhappiness was not recognised and was taken for badness.

Danny was three when his small brother was born. He was already an over-sensitive serious child, and he reacted badly to the separation from his mother. The baby turned out to be delicate and was in and out of hospital for the next year or more. Danny was pushed from pillar to post and became very unhappy and resentful. When seen in a hospital clinic aged six, he stood apart from his parents, never spoke to them or went ·near them, and was reported to be the same at home. He felt himself to be a bad child, who was therefore not loved like the younger one. The parents were at their wits end and found him almost impossible to cope with.

Another possible cause of difficulty arises from the opposite situation. Parents who themselves tend to feel very jealous expect the child to be the same, and assume he will never be able to come to terms with this rivalry. The moral seems to be that the jealous emotions should be accepted as real and painful, but with an implicit expectation that they will be manageable in time with help from the parents.

Pros and cons of the one-child family

Having a second child within a year or two of the first, is, to start with, much more of a commitment in terms of time and energy than was the first. But for most couples, to make a decision on the basis of cold, clinical 'pros and cons' is to ignore the important truth that family life can be a lot of fun.

"The second child made us all aware that we were a unit and had to work together more instead of demanding. We give more to each other now."

Pros and cons of the one-child family from the child's point of view.

One child (and first child until de-throned) **Cons:**	*Two or more children* **Pros:**
Can be very lonely if no friends live near.	Always have companions for play.
Highly identified with adults – 'a goodie'.	More likely to be casual and easy-going as an adult.
May have difficulty in mixing with other children.	More readily adapt to other children.
Can be stressful if parents disturbed.	Emotional support available in the event of parental problems.
May be over-indulged and babied.	Less likely to be spoilt.
	Older children learn to be concerned and responsible for younger.

On the other hand, in terms of development, the 'only' child has theoretical advantages over children in very large families.

'Only' children	*Children in 'multiple-child' family*
More adult time and attention, in quiet orderly environment.	Has to share adult attention.
Earlier intellectual development, especially for language.	Maybe retarded in speech etc. if a later child in a large family.
Never has to cope with birth of younger siblings.	Elder children may feel 'pushed aside' when younger ones born.
More money and material resources available for playthings, education etc.	Money may be tight...

BABYSHOCK

Will I have twins?

Your chances of having twins are one in one thousand. Fraternal twins run in families, and if there are such twins in your family your chances of twins are more than one in a hundred.

On hearing that she is pregnant, no woman seriously believes or is able to anticipate that she is to give birth to twins. All initial thoughts and preparations will reflect the birth of a single baby. Then, one day perhaps you begin to notice that your tummy has grown rather larger than you expected. Maybe your maternity clothes are needed sooner than other pregnant friends'. Then, when the babies begin to move around, you will notice *much* increased activity and, quite wrongly, be worried that something is wrong.

It is quite likely that your GP will be unable to detect twins early on. Some mothers arrive in the delivery room before anyone has realised. Your doctor will be able to assure you that the babies are alive by listening to the heartbeat, but without an X-ray (which can be dangerous to the foetus) or the safe ultrasound technique, confirmation that you are indeed having twins may have to wait until the sixth month or even later. Once told, your feelings may range from joy (at getting two for the price of one) to anger and dismay at the enormous upheaval to your life. Most pregnant mothers of twins have very mixed feelings.

How will I cope?

Preparation for the birth of twin babies can be summed up in one sentence. Talk with other mothers of twins. Ask friends, family, or GP if they know any other women with young twins. Make contact with your health visitor through your doctor and find out whether there are any branches of the newly formed Twins Club in your area. Only such mothers can really tell you how to prepare.

Watch the way they deal with their babies. Help them out if you can. Get involved. Listen to what they tell you about the way they deal with problems as they crop up. Do they breast-feed one at a time or is it best to suckle them both at the same time? How do they cope with *two* crying infants?

You will notice that most women with twins rely upon the babies' father, drawing him much more into the mothering process than mothers of single children. Support is essential, so make sure that you organise this straight away. Get the babies' father talking to other fathers of twins. Sit down and discuss with him how you think you can best organise your new life to everyone's satisfaction. Discuss practicalities – the period immediately after the birth; who will be available to help out; where they will sleep; what special equipment they will need. Share the experience from the start and glean as much information from people with firsthand experience.

As your pregnancy continues, things are bound to become uncomfortable. After all, your two babies are taking up room meant for only one. Don't be alarmed if you are short of breath, it's getting crowded in there. Get as much extra rest as you can. The additional weight will very probably put a strain on your back, so make sure that every facility is available for *your* comfort. Quite often pregnant mothers of twins need extended bed-rest towards the end of pregnancy. Don't fight it; see it as a period of peaceful waiting. You will very probably find neighbours and relatives excitedly offering help. Take positive advantage of every available assistance. It is, for many mothers, exciting to be having twins, but it is also important that you come to terms with the realities of an 'instant family' and take every opportunity to ease yourself into it.

There are several differences between the birth of twins and the birth of a single baby. First, it is very common not to carry them for the full nine-month period. Their weight and size together stimulates early delivery. For this reason, twins are almost always delivered in hospital. Very commonly too, mothers of twins are admitted to hospital early and kept there until labour starts. This provides you with an opportunity to build up your resources. It is the father's responsibility to organise things so that you don't spend your time there worrying about whether your other children are being neglected (or whatever else you are likely to worry about). Second, twins are often born small and may even be classified as premature. Do not be surprised if they spend their first few days of life in an incubator. It is the warmest possible home for them and permits hospital staff to observe them at any time.

Being in an incubator is not a sign that all is not well with them (see page 107).

After the birth you will very probably find yourself with a particularly large expanse of loose skin. In fact many of the physical after-effects of birth will be at least as bothersome as for mothers of single children, and very possibly, because the twins have pushed your internal organs around to such an extent, things will take more time to settle down. One woman became extremely concerned about a bump she found on her chest. It was found to be the tip of her sternum (breastbone) that had literally been bent up to accommodate her babies. It took twelve months before everything had resumed its usual place. Follow all the post-natal advice in this book, but most important, insist upon a *two-week* convalescent period. During the first week you will be in hospital, and as soon as you feel able, begin the stomach exercises recommended to you. But the second week, spent at home, should see you very gradually working up to full-time caring for your infants. Take your time. Do not expect too much of yourself.

One cautionary note if you have identical twins of the same sex – leave their hospital name tags on them for a week or two.

Finally, the development of twins is often very different from the development of single children. Twins *are* different. They may seem slightly backward at first, but through their constant interaction and your care they will soon catch up to have the potential to develop their talents and abilities possibly even better than single babies.

2
Pregnancy

"I loved being pregnant, having her close to me, there inside me. I used to talk to her all the time, call her by her name long before she was born."

"After the initial thrill and excitement at discovering I was pregnant, I felt quite fearful of what was happening, the changes that were taking effect on my body. I remember feeling as though I was now sharing my body with an unknown identity and that it was taken over as I grew larger."

Pregnancy

"I enjoyed it. It was the only time I had any sort of figure. Normally I'm so skinny. It was the only time I could put on any weight."

Not that your highs will be limited to the physical facts of pregnancy-although in the second three months you can expect to bloom quite literally. Frequently women lose the feeling of nausea and tiredness associated with the first three months and feel more self-confident then.

"I loved being pregnant, having her close to me, there inside. I used to talk to her all the time. In fact, after the birth, I couldn't get used to not having her there inside me."

But difficulties do arise sometimes.

"After the initial thrill and excitement at discovering I was pregnant, I felt quite fearful of what was happening. I remember feeling as though I was sharing my body with an unknown identity and that it was taking over as I grew larger."

"For the first few months, although occasionally sick, I was very well. Only in the last months did I find it uncomfortable to the extent of really getting depressed. Unfortunately I suffered from piles in the last two weeks and this really didn't help. Also, the child moving at night caused sleepless nights and heartburn whenever I lay flat. Generally though, comparing myself to my friends, I don't think I did too badly. I rarely had morning sickness and nausea to cope with."

How do I cope with the physical symptoms of pregnancy?

Heartburn
In the early stages a glass of milk may help as may a magnesia mixture. Avoid stooping or lying propped up in bed so as to prevent the extra acid which collects towards the latter stages of pregnancy being regurgitated.

Morning sickness
Take frequent small meals or if meals are unavoidably irregular and far between, carry biscuits. Avoid acidic or highly spiced foods.

Extra weight
Mothers in the Victorian era were encouraged to indulge themselves beyond the bounds of hunger, stuffing their bodies with almost any food within reach. Because of this they suffered from toxaemia, found it difficult to rid themselves of excess weight after the delivery, and frequently suffered from hypertension. In the last three months of pregnancy, some women develop an increase in weight accompanied by a sudden rise in blood pressure, oedema – the swelling of ankles, feet and hands – increasing headaches and some dizziness. These are symptomatic of a condition called pre-eclamptic toxaemia. Immediately these symptoms are present see your doctor. Usually, the solution is complete rest, possibly in hospital.

Nowadays it is recommended that a woman at twenty weeks should have gained no more than 0.5 Kg (1lb) a week. The total gain should not exceed 12.5 Kg (28lbs). It is not unusual for women to gain as much as four stone during pregnancy, but they find it hard to lose the last two stones after birth.

BABYSHOCK

In 1966 the DHSS issued a recommended daily intake of nutrients for non-pregnant and pregnant women.

	Non-pregnant	Pregnant
Energy (calories)	2,200	2,400
Protein (g)	55	60
Calcium (mg)	500	1,200
Iron (mg)	12	15
Vitamin B		
Thiamine (mg)	0.9	1
Riboflavin (mg)	1.3	1.6
Nicotinamide (mg)	15	18
Vitamin C (ug)	30	60
Vitamin D (ug)	2.5	10

Sources

Calories

Carbohydrates – cereal, fruit, vegetables, bread, rice, sugar, alcohol.
Fats – butter, cream, avocados, nuts, vegetable oils.
Protein – milk, cheese, meat, fish, eggs, soya beans.

Minerals

Calcium – green vegetables, milk, egg yolk, sardines.
Iron – liver, egg yolk, raisins, lean meat, yeast, wheat germ.

Vitamins

Vitamin B (Thiamine) – meat, fish, eggs, cereals.
Vitamin B (Riboflavin) – milk, cheese and thiamine products.
Vitamin B (Nicotinamide) – as thiamin and riboflavin plus peanut butter.
Vitamin C – citrus fruits, fruit juices, tomatoes, potatoes, leafy greens.
Vitamin D – sardines, tuna fish, sunshine, fish-liver oil (or in tablet form).

In general, the strict diet which such professional charts suggest do not need to be rigidly adhered to. For many women, it is a chore to do so. There is a certain amount of intuition involved –

fat women, for example, would be advised to take less carbohydrates and increase their protein intake. Bear in mind the following guidelines:

Eat what you want, when you want, and stop when you have had sufficient.

Eat a wide range of fresh unprocessed foods each week (meat, fish, dairy products, whole grains, fruit and vegetables).

Soya bean is an excellent protein source for vegetarians.

Avoid excessive amounts of carbohydrates (sugar, cakes, biscuits, white bread) and other manufactured foods.

The following food supplements may be needed:
Half a litre of milk daily for calcium and protein.
Iron is prescribed if the haemoglobin (the red pigment of red blood cells) falls below a certain level and in any case for all mothers in the last three months. This is routinely given by antenatal clinics. But avoid taking extra iron in the initial stages of pregnancy, unless

it is professionally recommended. Generally, it is unnecessary early on because the end of menstruation saves on iron and supplementation may increase bowel problems such as vomiting, nausea, constipation or diarrhoea.

With a good mixed diet, vitamin supplements are unnecessary.

Constipation

This can be a problem for pregnant women. Some iron tablets may cause it, but generally it is the result of hormones reducing the power of the intestines to expel the bowel contents. Obey every call, make an effort to open your bowels once a day, and increase the roughage and fluid content of your diet (e.g. whole-grain bread, bran, fresh unskinned fruit and vegetables, cereals).

Insomnia

"Sleeping was a nightmare, continually waking with cramps, pins and needles, and of course umpteen visits to the loo. Towards the end of pregnancy, I just felt so tired."

You may get so little uninterrupted sleep for reasons similar to the mother above, or because you are naturally more anxious towards the end of pregnancy. You may be so tired that you begin to wonder whether this is nature's way way of preparing you for the sleepless nights after the baby is born.

Cramps should be treated with vigorous hand massage.

Relaxation exercises as suggested in the exercise section (page 60) might be helpful if you find it difficult to calm yourself enough to sleep.

But most important, if you are anxious about anything talk it over with your partner, doctor, or health visitor. Traditionally, health visitors come to see you after the baby is born, but it is often a good idea to make contact beforehand.

It is preferable to avoid all medications

during pregnancy, and certainly only use them under medical supervision. Sedatives administered in small doses are actually quite safe, but it is important that your doctor sets the levels and prescribes them himself.

Very often insomnia is the result of general discomfort in bed. Your tummy may prevent you from adopting your usual position. Make sure that you have a firm bed - there is nothing worse than a bed that sags in the middle. You may find an extra pillow or two helps, but if you suffer from heartburn this can make it worse. Experiment with pillow supports below your tummy if you usually sleep on your side.

Backache

This is very common in pregnancy, and can be prevented by paying particular attention to posture, taking rest on a flat surface pressing your back downwards so that the whole length of the spine is in contact with the surface, and massage.

Shortness of breath

Again, this is most common towards the end of pregnancy and may be helped by lying in bed propped up with pillows. It is generally the result of the expanding uterus which forces your diaphragm upwards into the chest. Mention it to your doctor, but it is unlikely to be 39 symptomatic of serious problems.

Pain

Pelvic discomfort and abdominal pain is also fairly common. Frightening as they very often are, they are generally due to baby movements, constipation, or some other cause which is nothing to do with your pregnant state. If you experience sudden severe pain, call your doctor.

Vaginal discharge

Most women have a slight mucous discharge which may get heavier with pregnancy. A thicker and heavier discharge may be experienced accompanied possibly by itching, which might indicate thrush. Thrush is a fairly common infection with pregnancy and not easily cured until after the delivery. The discharge may become yellow and odorous suggesting a trichomonas infection which can be treated with tablets or pessaries. Neither of these infections is serious or harmful to the baby. If you notice vaginal bleeding at any stage during pregnancy, you should consult your doctor at once. Just prior to the onset of labour it is perfectly natural for a woman to have a 'show'.

Varicose veins

These may develop at any stage during pregnancy and are often the result of excessive weight gain. A proper diet and exercise is recommended, although varicose veins may sometimes be hereditary. If you are predisposed to varicose veins, then you will almost certainly suffer from them while pregnant. Relief may come from avoiding tight underwear and sitting down with your feet up on a stool.

Although support stockings or tights cannot prevent varicose veins, they may help to prevent further deterioration. Varicose veins can be removed surgically after the delivery.

Stretch marks

Some women are more susceptible to stretch marks than others, but of the two main reasons for their appearance - hormone levels and excessive weight gain - the latter can be dealt with. Many women imagine that oils and creams will help, but in actual fact stretch marks have nothing to do with the kind of skin you have.

Overcoming or preventing some of these common physical problems will certainly increase your enjoyment of those nine months. It is nevertheless a fact that the three stages of pregnancy will be traversed by *all* pregnant women. They are referred to in medical journals as trimesters - three monthly periods.

The first trimester

During the first trimester it is normal to experience nausea and tiredness, particularly around the sixth week. How marked this general fatigue is, varies greatly from woman to woman - some actually feel better than before becoming pregnant, despite the fact that the same bodily changes happen to all women. This highlights the point that psychological factors play a very real part in how you will feel throughout pregnancy (see page 45). Your moods are invariably affected by your attitudes to the upcoming birth, and may be the reason for fairly common feelings of irritability and depression. Early morning sickness may not be accompanied by vomiting, but if it is, you could require hospital treatment for re-hydration. This is called hyperemisis gravidarum (see below).

The second trimester

During the second trimester, you will bloom. In place of the nausea, tiredness, and vomiting, comes a radiant complexion, partly due to the natural increased pigmentation of your face.

Very probably you will feel more confident about your appearance, the tummy bulge will be more obvious of course but there is no confusion that you are pregnant and not simply over-weight. Feeling more attractive and self-confident, you will radiate more positive self-esteem which will bounce back at you from people you meet.

The third trimester
The third trimester is invariably the point at which you feel things have gone on just too long. It is common to feel heavy, fat and ungainly. The increased weight of the load you are carrying may cause backache as you lean backwards to balance your body. Insomnia is prevalent too during this period – it is difficult to feel comfortable in any position. Constant visits to the lavatory due to pressure of the baby on your bladder further adds to a feeling of general discomfort. How you weather this final trimester depends so much on how you have tackled pregnancy from the beginning. If you have taken advantage of all the information available from ante-natal instruction, if the baby's father has been involved and continues his support now, very natural feelings of anxiety and fatigue will more probably be diminished. It is common to suddenly feel energetic just before the arrival of your baby, and this too reflects your positive attitude towards the onset of motherhood.

What can go wrong in pregnancy?
Many women worry unnecessarily that ordinary symptoms of pregnancy are signs that something is radically wrong. This is particularly true when abdominal pain is mistakenly seen as a sign of miscarriage. Below is a check list of possible serious problems to prevent anxiety about common minor physical problems, and also to let you know when you *must* consult your doctor.

Excessive vomiting (hyperemesis gravidarum)
Modern drugs will usually stop the nausea and vomiting of pregnancy. In a few cases vomiting becomes continuous and leads to dehydration, and a short spell in hospital may be beneficial.

Miscarriage
Any bleeding in the early stages of pregnancy is worrying. Slight bleeding as the only symptom may suggest a threatened miscarriage which may be avoided with bedrest and pregnancy may continue.
If the bleeding becomes heavier and is accompanied by pain or a bearing-down feeling you may be losing your baby and should go to hospital.

Excessive tiredness due to anaemia
If you do not take your prescribed iron tablets and vitamins regularly you might become anaemic.

Loss of movements of the baby
After a fall or sometimes for no apparent reason, you may notice that your baby is not moving as much as he used to. Nowadays, monitors can detect the baby's heartbeat when human ears cannot; and it may be helpful and reassuring to have a test.

Increasing weight and headaches
This is one of the reasons why women should attend ante-natal clinics where weight is checked, blood pressure recorded, and urine tested for excess protein; if there is an above average increase you may be developing toxaemia which could be dangerous.

Usually the condition settles quickly with bedrest.

BABYSHOCK

Abnormal position of the Baby

Some mothers become aware around the seventh month that the baby is kicking in the groin but sooner or later he will turn round and kick under the ribs. If for any reason the baby continues kicking in the groin, it may suggest a 'breech presentation'. The doctor may suggest turning the baby.

Bleeding in the last three months of pregnancy

This is a serious sign and may suggest a low-lying afterbirth blocking the baby's exit, or a detaching afterbirth. both of which are considered an emergency. Sometimes there is a simple explanation for this – such as a small erosion on the neck of the womb.

Premature labour

Occasionally contractions begin and even the waters may break resulting in premature birth. Bed rest with the aid of drugs may arrest or delay this process.

Prolonged pregnancy

Around the expected birth date you may become anxious that *nothing* is happening. There is a good reason for not allowing the pregnancy to go beyond forty-two weeks – the placenta loses its efficiency and can no longer nourish the baby. Provided everyone is certain about conception date, your doctor may well advise inducing labour.

Cigarettes – smoke, and your baby smokes with you

Smoking can damage your health and your baby's. No mother could say that she is unaware of this fact, although some may argue that so-and-so's child did not suffer as a result. Forget the excuses, there is absolutely no doubt that smoking when pregnant gives your baby a worse start in life. What every article and book which mentions the subject fails to realise is just how difficult it is to give up smoking at a time of such monumental change and re-adjustment. A cigarette can seem an easy and effective prop in times of stress. For this reason, and because giving up smoking *at least* during pregnancy is absolutely vital, a thoroughly practical Action Plan has been devised and incorporated into the following section.

What are the effects of smoking when pregnant?

If a mother smokes, her baby receives some of the products such as nicotine and carbon monoxide.

These reduce the amount of oxygen available to the baby.

The baby's growth is retarded and he develops fewer cells in his brain. This is mainly due to the reduction in the availability of oxygen at the most active stage of his development. Some other unknown products of tobacco smoke contribute to this effect.

The retardation of growth reduces the baby's birthweight by an average of 170 grams (6 ozs).

As a result of growth retardation more small babies are born to smoking mothers. These smaller babies are more vulnerable, and this accounts for the higher rate of stillbirths and deaths in early infancy in the case of mothers who smoke during pregnancy.

The loss of brain cells due to smoking in pregnancy has a permanent effect. At the age of eleven these children are three to five months behind the children of non-smokers in reading and mathematical ability and are also less well-adjusted socially during their early years at school.

The damage due to mothers smoking affects *all* babies though it kills only one in a hundred. Similarly, it affects the brains of all babies, though this is only detectable in some.

The damage due to smoking occurs only if smoking persists after the fourth month of pregnancy. If mothers stop smoking before the fourth month their is no evidence that their babies will be damaged.

As few as five cigarettes a day affect the baby, but the damage is greater at ten per day. Further increases in consumption have little effect. It is therefore not much use if mothers simply cut down from twenty to ten cigarettes per day.

What should the pregnant mother do to stop?

Since the harmful effects of smoking on the baby occur during the last six months of pregnancy, it is especially important for a mother to stop smoking over this crucial period.

There is no way other people can do this for her, by treatment, hypnosis, or drugs. The effect on the child of parents who smoke after he is born is relatively small, so that if the mother must she can smoke again after the pregnancy.

Cutting down is no use unless it is to below ten cigarettes a day and this only reduces, but does not eliminate, the damage to her baby. Similarly, switching to a low tar, low nicotine brand of cigarette may reduce but not eliminate the damage. A mother who smokes but does not inhale need not be concerned. However, most people who think they do not inhale are shown to be wrong when their blood is tested.

Many women do stop smoking when they are pregnant. About forty per cent are smokers at the start of pregnancy.

About one in four of these give up smoking during the first few months, leaving about thirty per cent of doubters and hardliners who smoke throughout pregnancy. It is not known whether the ones who stop do so because they are aware of the harm it does to their baby or whether they are deterred by the nausea and sickness of early pregnancy. Whatever the reason we are more concerned with the thirty per cent who go on smoking. About a third of these are aware of the risks but are too hooked to stop easily. Two-thirds (twenty per cent of all pregnant women) go on smoking without realising the damage it does to their child. These are the ones we hope will respond to reading this section. If they do, it will certainly prevent damage to their babies; for many it will save their baby's life.

Guide-lines for stopping smoking

As mentioned above, cutting down and smoking less is not the answer. In the long run it is also more difficult than giving up altogether. The most important thing is to come to a *firm decision* that you *are* going to stop, not that you will merely try to stop. If you decide to stop you will succeed. However dependent or addicted you may be, the habit can be broken if you remain determined. The difficulty and craving you may have experienced before will be only temporary. It will not go on, and if you remain determined and do not smoke it will eventually become easy.

So do not keep putting off your decision.

Decide one way or the other and, when you have decided that you are going to stop, start thinking about your plan of action. There is no single remedy for stopping. What works for some people may not work for you. But there are certain basic points which should be part of any plan.

Action plan

Prepare yourself for two to four weeks of effort in which giving up smoking has priority over all other activities. You will not be able to overcome your smoking problem if you are dealing with other difficult problems.

Choose a time when you are not under too much pressure from other matters. You may have to set other things aside to make giving up smoking your main goal.

Decide on your own D-day for stopping and prepare yourself for it mentally as it approaches. Think about your smoking, for example, and as you smoke a cigarette picture the nicotine and carbon monoxide that you take in with each puff finding its way into the blood and brain of the baby inside you. Each cigarette that you smoke will be knocking out some of its developing brain cells unless you stop before it is four months old.

Plan to stop smoking completely on D-day, or as quickly as possible. Gradual reduction is not the best method and is often an unconscious way of putting off the time of stopping.

Get rid of all the cigarettes around you on the night before D-day, but do not start cutting down before D-day. You will be wasting precious effort and you will need every bit of it on D-day and after. So smoke normally up to the time you have decided to stop.

On D-day and after, for at least two weeks, keep away from smokers as much as possible. Avoid tempting situations; especially avoid drinking alcohol with smokers. You may need to avoid lingering and relaxing over cups of tea or coffee if you are tempted.

If you find it difficult, remember that it will eventually become easy.

Don't abandon your effort if you have lapses or are not immediately successful.

Make sure that you put aside the money saved to buy something specific that you would not otherwise have bought. Perhaps buy something big on hire purchase. But spend the money on something specific that you can see and appreciate during the first few difficult weeks, or use it to go and enjoy yourself in ways you might not otherwise have done.

Even when you have succeeded and are finding it easy, you should keep up your determination until your baby is safely delivered to avoid carelessly slipping back to smoking. Above all, do not let yourself think you can smoke just one or two cigarettes on a special occasion.

Coping with the emotional changes that pregnancy brings

The bodily changes that occur in pregnancy are inextricably bound up with changes in the way you feel about yourself and your new role.

If you are overweight, you will probably feel down, yet may be unable to take the seemingly simple decision to pay attention to your diet because you feel anxious about the delivery or uneasy about how you are going to adapt to motherhood. Of course it is important to learn all about the changes that are happening to your body. But sometimes trying to solve physical problems, such as overweight, tiredness, or insomnia, without tackling the underlying emotional changes which becoming a mother involves, may be to avoid the real issues. Usually, most attention is paid to physical problems and the emotional side of pregnancy tends to be neglected at classes and in books. Yet pregnancy is one of the most critical stages in a woman's life, and in managing changing moods and attitudes, you will not only feel better, but will prepare yourself in the best possible way for motherhood itself.

How will pregnancy affect my mood and attitudes?

In order to find out more about how women react during this period, a team of researchers in a London Teaching Hospital recently studied a sample of one hundred and forty-seven married women who were pregnant for the first time. This study took place both during their attendance at an antenatal clinic and then on through labour into the post-natal period.

A significant factor was that whereas only one of these women had become depressed in the three months *before* pregnancy, no fewer than fifteen became depressed or anxious enough to need help in the first three months after they became pregnant. The number dropped during the middle three months, which is traditionally recognised as the 'golden age' of pregnancy, and the women stayed well until after delivery, when again there was an increased incidence of depression and anxiety (see page 117). The researchers tried to see if they could find any clues to suggest why some women did not. There was no easy answer, though certain groups of women appeared to be more vulnerable – those who had unhappy marriages; those who had previously had an abortion; and those who had previously suffered from 'nerves'. It is also of interest that those women who were upset before the birth were not necessarily the same as those who became depressed post-natally.

The importance of this study to you, if you are pregnant for the first time, is to be aware that pregnancy may make you more sensitive and more liable to be upset. This is relatively common, and is 45

likely to get better as the pregnancy progresses, particularly if you are able to talk about the way you feel. Unfortunately, as the researchers point out, "in general little attention is paid to the emotional needs of expectant mothers". Doctors and nurses are too busy weighing you and taking your blood pressure to notice if you are on the edge of tears.

It may help you share your feelings if we explode a modern myth which has arisen from a misunderstanding of the ideas of certain experts, and which is now widely maintained in women's magazines and popular romantic novels. In these, the 'good' pregnant woman is portrayed as being radiantly happy all the time without suffering any regrets, doubts or bitterness, and simply experiencing complete, natural fulfillment. This is as unreal as a fairy story. If women tell the truth when talking about their pregnancies, they will tell you that periods of happiness and excitement may be followed by periods of feeling fed up and apprehensive.

What causes upset feelings in pregnancy?

People are easily satisfied with simple explanations even if they are not true. For generations all sorts of emotional and physical problems suffered by women have been put down to 'hormones'. While for a few women, hormones may be the cause, for the majority they are not. In the first three months of pregnancy hormone levels will be much more stable than they are during a normal monthly cycle, and it is difficult to see how they alone could cause swings of mood and outbursts of emotion.

"My first pregnancy was planned, but for all the wrong reasons. We decided to go ahead and start a baby because my boss at work had left and I was really fed up about that and also my dad and my husband's grandad were dying and

he wanted them to see their grandchild before they died. These are peculiar reasons for having a baby and I didn't think of the baby as a person at all. Then when I was about 5 months pregnant I decided that my marriage was really a mistake and this affected the way I felt about it. I stopped taking my iron tablets. I put them high up in the cupboard and said, 'There you shan't have them.' I really wanted to lose the baby. I got guilty about the way I felt and went to the doctor and told him a little bit and he said, 'Don't worry, it's your hormones.'"

Instead of regarding increased emotional sensitivity as evidence that something might be wrong, try and take the opposite view. Maybe your heightened awareness is a natural reflection of the great change that is taking place in your life. You are not just going to bear a baby, you are going to become a mother. Maybe the weepiness is a mixture of joy in anticipation of the new baby and sadness for the loss of a lifestyle that will be gone forever. Most women recognise that the thought, "I can't wait to see the baby," is about as common as, "I must have been crazy to let myself get pregnant"; just as the thought, "What a wonderful thing it is to be pregnant," is followed by, "All I'm good for is producing babies". If you have always been a nervous person; if you have been through a previous upsetting experience connected with pregnancy, such as an abortion; or if you are not getting on well with your man, these normal reactions to pregnancy may become intensified to the point where it looks to your doctor as if you are suffering from anxiety and depression.

How can the baby's father help me with the changes that pregnancy brings?

The more information your partner has about pregnancy and the way you feel about it, the better. He needs to know about changes both in your emotions and your body. For example, if your man is surprised and angry when you don't want to go to the pub, he should be informed that in the first place pregnancy turns some women off the taste, even the smell of alcohol, and in addition, that the least argument can reduce a pregnant woman to tears. With this information he can and should adjust his behaviour.

Sometimes you may be over-wrought and find that everything you say and do has the opposite effect from what you really want. You do want your man to be around, but at the same time he infuriates you and everything you find yourself saying seems to be aimed at driving him away. If he tries to sympathise and hints that you only feel this way because you are pregnant, you think that he is being patronising and artificial and you might say, "How the hell do you know what it's like!" If he fusses over you, you feel he is treating you as though you were ill and helpless and you may resent that. On the other hand, if he doesn't help any more than usual you say, "I'm just the servant in this house." He drives you crazy when he is with you, and you miss him dreadfully when he is away.

Some problems in life have no easy answers and this is one of them. It may help to remember that many women go through this experience, and that it will not last forever. Try and avoid storing up incidents which were particularly irritating; and when you feel loving make the most of it.

It is no accident that many couples who have lived together amicably, productively and in love for several years, start to split up after the birth of their first baby. Pregnancy has a way of seeking out weaknesses in a relationship, there a number of reasons for this, one of the most important being the widely held myth that "nothing will change after we have the baby". While it is difficult for women to continue to believe this after the baby has arrived, many men continue their lives as though nothing had happened. At best the couple drift apart, at worst they split up.

It is only if both partners face up to the fact that there are going to be changes that they can discuss how much they should alter their lives. Negotiation sounds a hard word to use in the context of something as unbusinesslike as a marriage, but this is what is needed. If the changes in life-style are not negotiated openly, then they will take place by subterfuge.

Take the question of emotional support. You are going to need a great deal, especially if this is your first pregnancy, and in its most obvious form this means having more of your man's attention. Equally, if you are giving up work, your partner may see this as a time when he needs to work harder and longer to boost your joint income. Clearly a balance has to be reached.

Another important issue, which you may want to talk over, is the amount of personal freedom each of you intends having after the birth. By this is meant the degree to which you will be able to do things primarily to please yourself. The tendency is for the new baby to take over all his mother's personal space, at least for the first three months, but the father will lose far less of his freedom. Such discrepancy usually seems unfair to mothers, but quite reasonable to most fathers. This is fertile ground for a continuous running battle, which is the one thing that is not going to help your emotional needs in pregnancy and after the delivery. It is impossible to lay down any rules as to what is fair. Every couple must try and find their own solution. The question is, "What is best for us?" It should not be, "How did our parents organise themselves?" or, "How do our neighbours organise their time?", but, "How close can we get to 47 pleasing each of us." Obviously the adjustments to be made by a self-employed business man, whose wife has no close friends or relatives, are going to be totally different to those which will suit a bus driver whose wife may have her own family living just around the corner. It may help for you to be fairly precise in this discussion, and some couples find that making lists clarifies the 'giving and taking' which needs to be done. Each of you might find it useful to list: the things I value most in my life now; the things I expect to have to give up after the birth of the baby. Do this exercise on your own and when you have finished swap lists and read your partner's before going on to discuss changes.

The importance of sexuality is that not only is it a great pleasure but it is also an index of how well you are getting on with your partner in general. Lying in one another's arms may be the only time in the day when the two of you are really alone together. It is a chance not only for physically thrills, but also for intimacy, sharing joys and worries, even discussing day-to-day achievements and problems. This is especially important when you have a young baby, and when you have been feeling fraught, unattractive and 'on your own'.

How will pregnancy affect my sex life?

Pregnancy affects people in different ways as far as sexuality is concerned, and a woman may not have the same experiences in different pregnancies. Thus, some women find that their sex drive will increase while others lose interest. Some find orgasms easier to achieve, while others lose the ability to reach a climax for the duration of the pregnancy. Vaginal lubrication may increase to an almost embarrassing degree, or decrease to the point where it

is a good idea to use an artificial lubricating jelly.

Furthermore, a woman can expect to feel different at the various stages of her pregnancy. In general, the middle three months is the time when you are likely to feel at your best in every respect. During the first three months, especially if this is your first pregnancy, you may wonder what on earth is happening to you and your body. Just as your appetite for food may be altered, so may your appetite for sex. Many women experience intense emotional tenderness in this period. They feel a need to be close to their partners, to be held, cuddled and comforted. While some will feel this intermingled with increased sensuality and sexual desire, others discover a real need for physical closeness, rather than sex.

Some changes in your body may be obvious to you, but less so to your partner. Early in pregnancy the sensitivity of your breasts may increase to the point where even gentle touch is painful. Likewise your bladder may become more sensitive. You will experience not only a need to pass water more frequently, but you may also feel unusually uncomfortable when you make love. Early morning sickness is certainly no aphrodisiac, and the man who likes sex with his morning tea may need to be reminded of this. Later in pregnancy, the sheer size of your tummy makes sex uncomfortable or difficult, and deep penetration of the penis into the vagina may cause pain. Your emotions as well as your body may become over-sensitive, especially in the first three months. Boisterous remarks which you would normally answer back or ignore, start to reduce you to tears or anger. If your man tactlessly but affectionately calls you a 'fat old cow', you may feel sulky and be 'turned off' for days.

Is it harmful to have sex during pregnancy?

It is quite common for both men and women to have considerable doubts about sex during pregnancy, especially once a mother's belly starts to swell and the baby's movements are first noticed. Such doubts may stem from religious convictions, from psychological conflicts, or be based on myths or old wives' tales. If your religion teaches that sex during pregnancy is wrong, then you must follow this advice. There is certainly no evidence that total abstinence for nine months does any physical harm, though on the other hand there is absolutely no evidence that it produces happier parents or healthier babies.

Psychological conflicts stem from a number of common themes. Let's look, for example, at what might be called the case of the Princess and the Prostitute. Even within marriage sex may often be felt to be ever-so-slightly risquée and naughty and, as a result, great fun. But, once you both realise you are going to become parents, attitudes can rapidly change. 'Naughty girls' become mothers, and 'randy boys' become fathers. Sex, on the face of it, appears inconsistent with these new roles.

Though real life is never quite the way psychologists describe, this over-simplified example makes the point that pregnancy is a time of change. Not just in terms of bodies, but also in changes of responsibilities, attitudes and emotions.

Myths about sex and pregnancy

You may be worried about sex in pregnancy because of stories you have heard. Gynaecological experts agree with the following:

There is no evidence that sexual intercourse, with or without female orgasm, can cause a miscarriage in a healthy woman, with a healthy baby inside her. Remember that spontaneous miscarriages occur in twenty per cent of all pregnancies, and usually this is nature's way of getting rid of a foetus which is not properly formed. Most couples make love once a week at least, so if you are unlucky enough to have such a miscarriage you will have probably made love at some time during the previous seven days. To connect the two events, and blame yourself, is as silly as blaming the television programme you watched the evening before.

There is no evidence that either sexual intercourse or semen can in any way damage the unborn baby in the womb.

Are there any times when we should avoid sex during pregnancy?

When you don't feel like it.

If you have previously had a series of miscarriages, or a history of premature labour and your doctor advises you that 49 sex is unwise.

If you do start to bleed following intercourse you should contact your doctor and follow his advice.

What can I do if things are not going right?

This question should be "what can *we* do?" Masturbation apart, sex always involves two people. One of the major contributions made by Masters and Johnson, famous for their research into sexuality and for their methods of treatment for sexual problems, is the recognition that when sexual difficulties arise, couples need to be seen and treated together. If you are unhappy about your sex life, talk to your husband – tell him how you feel, emotionally and physically. Equally, if he is unhappy it is up to him to talk to you. It may be relatively simple, it is certainly perfectly normal. If your breasts hurt when he fondles them tell him to go easy, and tell him why. Lying there in silence, gritting your teeth, will only lead to increasing resentment and an unnecessary emotional distance between you. If you don't want his penis inside you, tell him so; let him into your own thoughts and feelings. Sex is surrounded by irrational ideas, anxiety and inhibitions, all of which may make discussion difficult. But remember:

Change in sexuality is a normal part of pregnancy. You have no need to think there is something wrong with you, or that you are less of a woman because of a variation in your sexual feelings.

Pregnancy and childbirth are going to lead to big changes in your marital relationship. If you work together, the relationship can deepen and mature. On the other hand, ignoring changes and problems – however small – and hoping they will go away, is a common recipe for future unhappiness.

Pregnancy can be seen as an opportunity to extend your sexual repertoire. Reading books can be helpful in finding solutions, but so can trial and error. For example, the intriguingly titled Missionary Position (that is the male superior position), is usually impracticable and uncomfortable in the latter stages of pregnancy. So try other positions and find which ones suit you best. Remember that those positions which allow deep penetration can more easily hurt you, so as in all exploration proceed slowly and with care. If you haven't done so before, and you like the idea, this might be a good time to try oral sex or mutual masturbation. You might even try lying together in the same bed, and masturbating on your own. Alternatively, you might agree to ban sex for a while, and just enjoy lying naked in one another's arms, perhaps taking it in turns to massage one another. Awareness of the changes in your body, and particularly lying with his hand on your belly, feeling the new baby move inside you, can be a powerful experience for your partner. It will also help him get involved in the process of pregnancy and childbirth.

During pregnancy your self-confidence can take a dive. Confidence in yourself and re-adjustment to a different self-image both in how you see yourself and how others see you is helped by taking trouble to look good. The two sections which follow – dress and exercise during pregnancy – can be great morale boosters.

3
Confidence
in yourself

"As I gained weight, my sexuality and self-confidence diminished. It was so important, for me at any rate, to pay attention to my hair, feet, hands and face – anything that detracted interest in my weight. I wasn't manic about it; it was just a natural reaction to being pregnant."

How can I look good during pregnancy?

You cannot predict how large or how quickly your body will grow during pregnancy. Some women, after four months, are obviously pregnant; others take six months before there is a really noticeable change. You will know when as your clothes suddenly become tight and uncomfortable. When the day arrives, take stock of the clothes in your wardrobe. Pack away all your best clothes – they'll come as a welcome surprise to you when you regain your figure. Then select from those that remain, clothes that can be altered, such as skirts and trousers. Finally make a list of clothes you need to buy, make or borrow.

The early months of pregnancy and the weeks following delivery are the most difficult to dress for – your body tends to be rather shapeless and plump. Then is the time to do a cover-up job. Separates are usually successful – large T-shirts, jumpers, and smock tops over trousers or skirts. Draw attention to your face and legs and take extra care with your make-up; wear jewellery or scarves to accentuate the neckline; cut your hair into a flattering, easy-to-cope-with style – especially just before the delivery, carefully choose tights, or possibly socks. Dark tights and shoes can be very flattering.

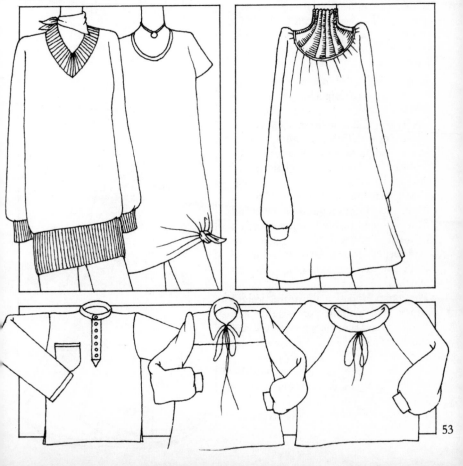

BABYSHOCK

How much will I need to spend?

Think carefully before buying clothes – always try them on or make sure that they can be exchanged. You are buying for a body you are not used to and which will change at a faster rate as pregnancy continues. Clothes that fit at six months will be unwearable at eight.

An important part of preparing for birth is talking to other mothers, and making friends now may reduce the need to spend a lot of money on clothes too. You will get useful tips and very probably the loan of clothes and equipment.

Scan the columns of local papers, local shop notice-boards, charity shops, even jumble sales can be useful. You might even place an advertisement yourself.

You should only need to buy in the last resort, although some specially chosen items will, if you can afford it, transform an otherwise second-hand pregnancy wardrobe and boost your morale.

Shop around and compare prices, as you go from shop to shop build up an idea of what you look best in – think ahead to how you will look in these clothes when you are near delivery; try things on for colour and pattern too. You will find a fair selection in high street chain stores, but look also at ethnic clothing. Traditional Indian, African and South American clothes tend to be loose and flowing, hand printed, and very often reasonably priced. Most garments are made in pure cotton, for instance cheese cloth smocks and shirts, kaftans and ponchos.

The skirts opposite illustrate designs which will remain comfortable and attractive as pregnancy progresses, and can be easily made. Note drawstring, wrapover, shirred waistbands.

The three dress designs are equally suitable, the shoulder-tie being especially versatile. The poncho is an obvious and attractive addition to any pregnancy wardrobe.

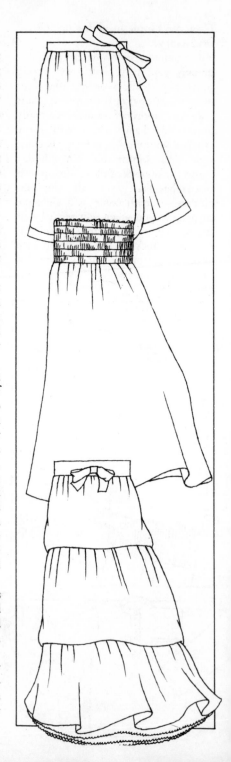

BABYSHOCK

Adapting the clothes in your wardrobe

Do not be tempted to cut up your favourite dress, skirt or trousers. Save them until after the baby arrives. Try out your skills at adapting your least favourite garment.

Trousers and skirts may be adapted quickly and easily using the following methods:

Remove zippers from skirt or trouser openings, and replace with criss-cross lacing. A wide piece of elastic can be inserted into the opening. Introducing extra 'give' in this way can also be applied to side seams and centre backs.

Remove zipper and waist band, let out darts, insert triangles of fabric at side, centre front and back seams as needed. Cut these triangles on the bias as this will allow extra stretch. Fold under

waist edge and machine. Elastic (or adjustable drawstring) can then be threaded through. Remember that the garment can be worn above or below your tummy, whichever is more comfortable. Do not underestimate the length of elastic or drawstring you will eventually need.

You might like to finish waist edges with shirring elastic which will fit your body without applying pressure. It takes a little extra effort – you may need to experiment with a sewing machine and the material to effect the best tension – but it is certainly worth it.

Dresses can be cut down to make smock tops for wearing over trousers. Always try on and pin up before cutting, and make sure that the final proportions suit a smock as well as the original dress.

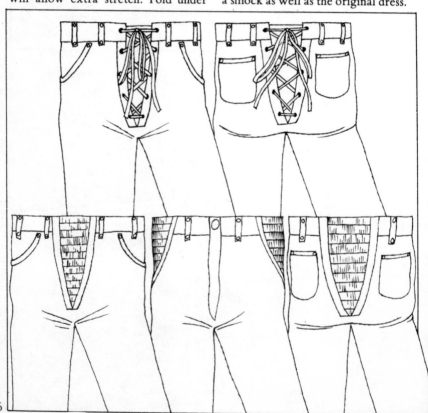

Making new clothes

Go window shopping and try on clothes for inspiration. Decide which colours and designs flatter you most. Just because you are pregnant you do not have to look unfashionable. The more concerted your efforts, the more rewarding they will be to your morale. With a few simple patterns (they do not have to be maternity patterns) you can achieve many varied looks.

Experiment with various techniques – 'on the yoke', 'machine quilting', 'embroidery', 'pin tucks and patchwork'. These are very simple but nonetheless effective on small areas.

Give hemlines emphasis. Consider using deep frills or ribbon and lace which will give a young, pretty appearance.

A simple dress gathered onto a band and tied at each shoulder is a flexible garment. It can be worn with a T-shirt or polo neck jumper underneath, or in hot weather on its own. Consider too, that pattern can be adapted to be worn hip-length over trousers or a skirt; calf-length with contrasting tights and shoes; full-length for evening wear, or lounging, depending on the fabric.

BABYSHOCK

Buying fabric

Avoid large bright designs and stripes.
Buy small feminine prints in muted or
fresh colours. Natural fibres are more
comfortable and will wash better. If
wool, cotton or silk are too expensive,
go for fibre blends – cotton polyester,
wool viscose, etc. Look for fabrics in
sales and at local markets, but always
inspect for flaws before purchase. Be
aware of fibre content when pressing,
making up and laundering.

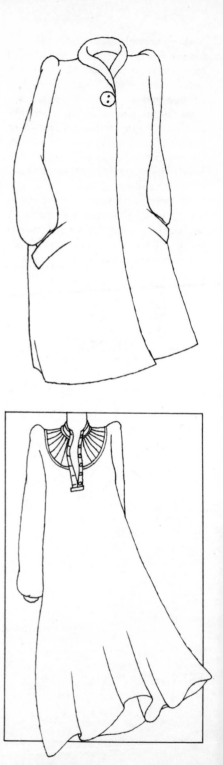

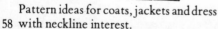

Pattern ideas for coats, jackets and dress
58 with neckline interest.

Beachwear can be a problem, but if you are unfortunate enough to be pregnant in a particularly hot summer, all is not lost. If you are sensitive to stares when you don your favourite bikini, wear the bikini bottom and make an attractive hip-length strapless sun top in complementary fabric.

Shoes

They must be comfortable, which is not synonymous with unfashionable. Remember that your feet and legs can swell – it is easy to ruin boots and shoes so that they are unwearable after the baby is born. Keep a pair of flat, really easy to wear shoes for the house. Espadriles can be invaluable when pregnant as they are comfortable and available in attractive colours.

Tights and pants

Both are more pleasant worn below the tummy, but tights can cause skin irritation and many women prefer to wear knee or ankle socks. Support tights are designed to support aching legs and are available in fashionable colours. Cotton-stretch, bikini-type pants are most comfortable and fit snugly under the tummy.

Nightwear

You can use a large man's T-shirt or ordinary shirt, so long as it is loose and preferably made from cotton. When you go into hospital take two or three long nighties – front-opening if breast-feeding – so that one can be kept for nights – it will help you separate night from day. Again small floral prints or fresh colours look great. White tends to become grubby too quickly.

Bras

Generally, breasts enlarge during pregnancy, but not always. It is vital to choose the correct size and this may involve buying various sizes. Try them on at the shop or check that you can exchange them if uncomfortable.

Coats

Hip-length jackets, shawls, capes and ponchos are attractive and inexpensive. 59

The Ante-natal exercise programme
This programme is aimed firstly at the parts of the body that are affected by pregnancy, secondly at the areas that need to be strengthened for labour and delivery, and lastly there are exercises designed to relax the body.

If you are attending ante-natal classes you will already know about the three types of breathing:

Diaphragmatic or abdominal breathing causes the top of the stomach to rise with the intake of air, the chest remaining still. This done slowly will aid relaxation.

Lateral breathing causes an expansion of the lower part of the lungs – with your hands you can feel the ribs moving sideways. This is a good lung exercise and is often taught in drama schools or when you are learning to play a wind instrument as it permits a well-controlled exhalation of air.

Apical breathing expands the top of the lungs under the collar bone. This is the panting that you use in the last stages of labour.

It is the first of these, diaphragmatic or abdominal breathing that will be used throughout these exercises. When this slow, deep breathing is combined with exercise the oxygen level in the body increases. This leads to an increase in energy which is utilised by the muscles during the exercise programme. Breathing for too long in this way may lead to dizziness (too much oxygen in the system) if not combined with the exercises. Additionally, the abdominal breathing is beneficial during ante-natal exercises because it removes tension and relaxes the whole body. Finally, if you concentrate on the stomach muscles as you do your abdominal breathing, they will naturally be toned up. Relax the top of the stomach as you take in the air and contract the muscles of the stomach as you expel the air.

Exercises sitting in a chair
Relaxation Breathing should be learnt and practised in conjunction with all the exercises. It relaxes the whole body and strengthens the stomach muscles.

Sit in a straight-backed chair, slightly forward on the seat. Place a cushion at the base of the spine. Relax your chin on your chest and place your hands lightly on your abdominal muscles.

Breathe out completely

Breathe in through your nose, expanding your stomach. Keep your chest still. Count one, two, three slowly to yourself.

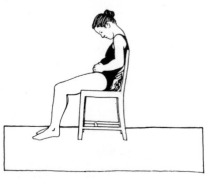

Breathe out slowly through your mouth gradually pulling the stomach muscles tighter and tighter in a controlled fashion. Do this to the count of one, two, three, four.

Repeat this exercise five more times.

This breathing can also be practised lying down.

Ankle Circles. This exercise strengthens the ankles which may ache as you become heavier and often swell due to water retention.

Remain in the same position and stretch out your legs. Keep your thighs on the chair and stretch the knees and flex the feet which should be about six inches apart. Let your hands remain on your stomach. Do not move your legs and never let your feet touch each other.

direction and four times in an anti-clockwise direction. Make all these movements slowly.

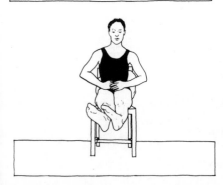

Breathe in and circle your feet in a clockwise direction until they are pointing down.

As you breath out complete the circle and bring your feet back into the flexed position.

Circumscribe this circle with your feet four times altogether in a clockwise

Breathe in and circumscribe quick, full circles three times in a clockwise direction, finishing with your feet back in the flexed position.

Breathe out and circumscribe quick, full circles three times in an anti-clockwise position finishing with your feet in the flexed position.

Make two quick clockwise and anti-clockwise circles.

The Squeeze. This exercise will strengthen the muscles of the breasts and also firm the upper arms.

Still seated on your chair, remove the cushion and sit with your spine straight. Interlock your hands in a prayer position in front of your chest, with your elbows level with your hands. Do not hunch your shoulders.

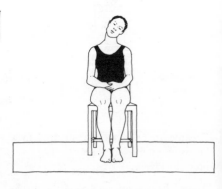

Breathe in and pull the palms apart moving your elbows out sideways. Still keep your fingers interlocked.

Breathe out and squeeze the palms together as hard as you can. Lift the elbows up slightly at the same time but keep your shoulders pressing down.

the centre with your shoulders still relaxed.

Breathe in and tilt the head to the left.

Repeat the above at least five times.

Rolling the Head. This exercise is a relaxation exercise for the neck and shoulders, an area which is often full of tension.

Seated on your chair, try to keep the spine straight and the shoulders down and relaxed.

Breathe in and tilt your head to the right. Press the shoulders down and feel the left side of your neck stretching.

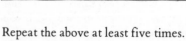

Breathe out and bring your head back to the centre.

Repeat the exercise tilting your head back, to the centre, and forwards.

Breathe out and bring your head back to

Leaving your head in the forward position with your chin on the chest, breathe in and circumscribe a half circle slowly to the right until your head is in the back position.

Exercises lying down

The Bottom Squeeze. This exercise is a relaxation exercise for the spine. It also tightens the muscles in the pelvic region (the vaginal muscles and buttocks).

Lie on your back with your knees bent but not touching. Feel your whole spine touching the floor. Place your hands on your abdominal muscles.

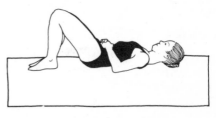

Breathe in feeling the top of the stomach rise up on your hands.

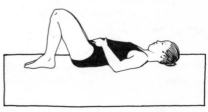

Breathe out and tip the pelvis up off the floor, pressing the small of your back into the floor and squeezing the buttock muscles tightly together.

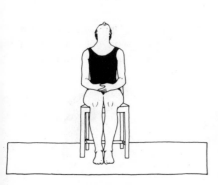

Breathe out and complete the circle round to the left, finishing in the forward position.

Make three full circles to the right and three full circles to the left in this way.

Breathe in, lowering your bottom and relaxing.

63

BABYSHOCK

Tip the pelvis in this way six times breathing slowly.

As you continue this exercise, instead of squeezing your buttock muscles as you tip the pelvis off the floor try to pull in and hold tightly the muscles of your vagina. To start with this will feel as if you are squeezing your muscles around the anal passage. Try and locate your vaginal muscles, concentrate on them as you perform the exercise.

Do the bottom squeeze a further six times.

The Inner Thigh Stretch. This exercise stretches the muscles down the inside of thighs. It is also a useful exercise for learning how to control your breathing without tension whilst lying down.
Still lying on your back, place the soles of your feet together, letting your knees fall apart. Place your hands on your abdominal muscles.

Breathe in and feel your abdominal muscles rise up on your hands.

Breathing out, still with your hands on your abdominal muscles, press your knees close to the floor.

Repeat this exercise three more times with your hands still on your abdominal muscles.

Transfer your hands to the inner side of your knees, repeat the whole exercise

four more times, using your hands so placed to exert a little extra pressure as your knees get closer to the floor.

Head to Feet Exercise. This exercise is also useful for stretching the muscles along the inner thighs. It also stretches the spine, the neck and the shoulders. Once again your abdominal muscles will be toned up if you are breathing correctly. It may become difficult, and is not advised beyond the first four months of pregnancy.
Sit upright with the soles of your feet together and allow your knees to drop outwards. Clasp your feet with your hands.

Breathe in, relaxing your abdominal muscles.

Breathe out, bending slowly forwards, your elbows going out sideways and your abdominal muscles pulling in.

Breathing in, recover the upright position.

Do this exercise ten times more, trying each time to get your head closer to your feet, your knees further apart, and your stomach muscles flattening a little more each time you breathe out.

Whole Body Relaxation. This is one of the most effective relaxation exercises and enables you to locate and release tension from every part of your body. Lie down on the floor and repeat the exercise for *Relaxation Breathing.*

When you have completed this exercise clench the muscles above your eyes (around your eyebrows) for a count of five, then release the muscles. Work right the way through your whole body until you come to your feet. Feel each muscle as you clench it up for a count of five. Relax totally as you release it. You will work through your facial muscles, the muscles in your neck, each arm one at a time, your chest, your stomach, your thighs, your vaginal muscles, your calves and finish by clenching your toes and relaxing your finger muscles. Do this exercise slowly and methodically in order to achieve the best results.

4
Preparation for the birth

The eighteen hundred mothers who contributed to Sheila Kitzinger's excellent Good Birth Guide (see Further Reading page 246) – a consumer's guide to maternity services assessing three hundred hospitals in England, Wales and Scotland – agreed en masse that the ante-natal clinics provided the grimmest view of our maternity services.

In this section, some of the problems of the services are examined alongside benefits they supply. The advice is aimed at helping pregnant women, wherever they are, to get the most out of ante-natal clinics and classes in terms of practical information, better treatment, and increased confidence about the coming birth.

Preparation for the birth

What is the difference between an ante-natal clinic and an ante-natal class?

Ante-natal care follows two parallel courses. The first is the ante-natal check at a maternity clinic where your health and progress will be supervised by professional obstetric staff with the aid of various medical screening techniques and devices. The second is a series of ante-natal classes which are aimed at helping you to help yourself by giving information and teaching relaxation techniques to apply during pregnancy and labour. Statistics show that the sooner a pregnant woman begins her ante-natal care, the lower are the chances of problems connected with her pregnancy and labour.

What exactly happens at the ante-natal clinic?

At your first visit to the ante-natal clinic, either at your hospital, or at your own GP's surgery if he is responsible for your ante-natal care, certain standard procedures will be carried out.

An obstetric history will be taken and a physical examination and routine tests will be conducted. There is a standard procedure for the taking of your obstetric history which will go down in your notes. The person taking it will want to know your whole medical and family background. They will want to know what work you and your partner do, whether there are twins in the family, how long you have been married, whether you have had any children or miscarried pregnancies before. They will want details of your menstrual cycle and of any childhood ailments or accidents. These facts will help build up a picture of you which will help in estimating possible risks in your present pregnancy. Your weight and height will be measured. This will help to estimate the size of your pelvis through which your baby will be born. Your weight gain in pregnancy will be checked against your weight at the start. At every ante-natal visit they will check a sample of your urine for the presence of protein and sugar, and on your initial visit they will take a blood sample to check the haemoglobin level. A standard test called the Wasserman reaction is also made on every pregnant woman. It tells the doctors whether you have contracted syphilis. This is a routine protective measure for your baby.

Your blood pressure will be taken at each visit.

On the first visit the doctor will also give you an internal vaginal examination to make sure everything is normal. Some women hate having this done, but if you breathe deeply and consciously relax it should not be uncomfortable. If you think he is being rough, say so. The doctor will also check the level of your uterus and look at the estimated date of delivery which is calculated from the first day of your last period by adding on two hundred and eighty days. If the size of the uterus tallies with the dates, all well and good. If not, you may be given an ultrasonic scan at a later date. This will determine the size of the baby and allow a more accurate estimate of the date of delivery.

You will be asked to attend regularly every four weeks until the last four 69 weeks when you will be asked to attend every week so that they can keep a closer check on your progress.

If the clinic seems to you to be particularly inefficiently run or the staff especially offhand, then find out the name of the consultant in charge and complain directly to him. If there are practices in your hospital which you don't like, discuss them with the staff, or enlist the help of your local Community Health Council or branch of the National Childbirth Trust in approaching the hospital. Pregnant women are perfectly healthy patients who attend hospital regularly, and their capacity for introducing change by steady pressure is well illustrated by the way in which maternity hospitals have changed over the last ten years.

Instead of attending the regular hospital ante-natal clinic you may elect to have your ante-natal care shared between your GP and the hospital. If your GP is on the obstetric list he will be happy to give you your regular monthly check at his surgery and save you the journeys and long waits involved in attending the hospital. You will have the advantage of being seen by the same person each time – something which all too rarely happens in hospital. This can be arranged when you first visit the hospital with their agreement and the agreement of your GP. You will return to the care of the hospital in the final weeks of pregnancy.

Why do some women not attend ante-natal clinics?

Part of the answer lies in the clinics themselves, even the very best-intentioned women may look on the visits as something to be endured rather than enjoyed.

First, there always seems to be a queue. Waiting for two hours, perhaps after a tiresome journey, is not unusual. And it stems partly from the idiotic but widespread practice of giving every patient an identical appointment time. In larger hospitals, the mother rarely sees the same doctor on successive visits.

"During my last pregnancy at a large London teaching hospital I saw seven different doctors at the hospital (including the consultant, once) and three at the local clinic. To each new doctor I was therefore an unknown quantity."

Meanwhile the nurses appear to be so busy keeping everything running to schedule on the doctors' behalf, that nobody seems to have the time to answer your questions or indulge in a lengthy informative chat.

This impersonal attitude makes some women feel that the hospital doesn't really care. Worse, they may feel that they are being patronised, as if a pregnant woman (who is after all the healthiest of all hospital patients) is not quite sound enough in mind to be accorded the common courtesies.

Yet the ante-natal department should be the most important unit in the entire hospital. Its aim is simply to keep things as normal as possible, and as such it can provide the simplest and most direct form of preventive medicine. Three-quarters of all babies who die shortly after birth are of low birth-weight and for every one who dies, two survive handicapped. It does not have to be that way. The at-risk baby can be identified if the mother goes early to the ante-natal clinic so that problems which lead to death, disease and handicap can be discovered.

It is a brutal fact that women desperate for their maternity grant **Ref 1:4** often come for their first registration at twenty-eight weeks, when they qualify for the money. Medically, this is three or more months too late. These mothers are potentially those at highest risk. The French realised this situation several years ago and introduced a generous maternity grant of over £300 plus. To qualify for the first instalment the mother *must* attend the ante-natal clinic by the end of the third month of her pregnancy, a month earlier than normally recommended in this country. With the help of this 'bribery' only five per cent of French women fail to receive proper ante-natal care. And the French infant mortality rate is now twenty-five per cent below ours, from having been twenty-five per cent higher than ours a decade ago.

Sweden, too, has an excellent record of attendance at ante-natal clinics, which reflects in their world record for a low peri-natal mortality rate: it is only 10.7 per thousand births. Unfortunately even with the best care in the world, complications at birth can result in death or handicap. Our national average is a sad 17.9 per thousand births. But the Spastics Society reckon that a thousand babies a year could be saved from death or handicap, if only all mothers had high-quality ante-natal care from the start.

It is true, our ante-natal clinics leave much to be desired. They could provide a crêche for a mother's other children; often, the care of older children prevents attendance. They could make the waiting area pleasanter, and indeed also the lavatories where each mother is required to go. What about having a library of pregnancy books and magazines, and supplying coffee or tea as a matter of course? Why not give proper appointments, as GPs do? It is infuriating to travel a long way to the clinic, wait up to two hours and then have a cursory examination conducted in stony silence in five minutes flat, by someone who has never seen you before and probably won't again. No wonder it all seems geared to making women feel like part of a production line, where no individuality is permitted.

How can mothers help themselves to enjoy their ante-natal care more?

You will enjoy your ante-natal visits more if you *expect* a long wait, and treat it as an opportunity to get some reading, letter-writing or knitting done in peace.

No sense in raising your blood pressure by sitting in a rage with nothing to do. Then, when you see the doctor, be friendly and interested; astonish him or her by a cheerful greeting, and peer at the name on the lapel of the white coat, to convey the fact that you have noted it is another new face; if you use their names, they jolly well ought to use yours.

Ask questions. There is no point in complaining that doctors seem superior or impersonal if you have made no effort to appear interested yourself. You ought to want to know what is happening to your body. You ought to read about it and to inquire, as your stomach is prodded and pushed, what the doctor can feel. If you are appreciative and *smile*, the doctor will probably comment encouragingly on the baby's healthy heartbeat or let you feel the bump of the head and bottom. Talk about it and you will get a response; doctors are human too.

BABYSHOCK

Interpretation of the Co-operation Card

These differ in form and layout from clinic to clinic but the basic information is much the same.

They give the date of each visit, and the estimate of the number of weeks pregnant you are, sometimes noted as 'height of fundus' – calculated first by dates and then by size. If there is a discrepancy between these two figures – twelve weeks by dates, but sixteen weeks by size for instance – you may be given an ultrasound, marked US on card, to check if there is more than one foetus.

Presentation and Position. In this column the doctor uses his own shorthand system for judging what position the baby is in. Nothing is noted on the first few visits because the baby is moving around; later it may say 'Ceph' (for cephalic) meaning that the head is down, or 'Vx' for Vertex, which means the same. Other abbreviations you may see here are LOA (left-occipito anterior),

LOP, ROA and ROP – all perfectly normal positions. Discuss them with the doctor. Breech position may be indicated by 'ecv' – external cephalic version; the doctor will undoubtedly talk about it to you. If the head is engaged (i.e. the baby has moved down so that it has entered the pelvis) this is noted as 'E'. It usually happens some weeks before labour in a first pregnancy, though not in later pregnancies.

Foetal Heart or 'FH' notes whether the baby's heartbeat can be heard – 'FHH' – is often combined with 'FMF' foetal movements felt, as soon as you have told the doctor about the first kicking movements inside.

Your blood pressure is taken (BP). There is an enormous variety of normal blood pressure figures. Your own figures may differ on every single visit; ask to have them explained if you wish. In simple terms the top number is the pressure of the first beat, the bottom number is the pressure of the second beat. Any rise in blood pressure is

ANTE-NATAL RECORD

INVESTIGATIONS	DATE	RESULTS	HISTORY	
A.B.O Blood Group *	A		Oedema	
Rhesus Blood Group *	PCS		Headache	
Antibodies *	NEG		Bowels	
WR/KAHN	NEG		Micturition	
X-Ray Chest			Discharge	
*IMPORTANT NOTE.—In the event of a transfusion this record of the blood-grouping should always be checked and cross-matching should always be carried out.			Date of quickening	

DATE	WEEKS	WEIGHT	URINE ALB. SUGAR	B.P.	HEIGHT FUNDUS	PRESENTA-TION AND POSITION	RELATION OF P.P. TO BRIM	F.H.
23.4.79	14	65	NAD	130/80	14	—		
4.6.79		4/5 →	52.5	= 20+ 90/50	65kg	(19+ – 21+)		R C
"	20	66	N	90/50	20			
22.6.79	23	67	NAD	110/80	24	—	—	
6.8.79.	25	71.5	NAD	115/60	28	Br	free	H
20.8.79	31	71.5	NAD	115/65	30+	Ceph long	high	✓
3/9/79	33	73.0	N.AD.	100/80	33	Ceph	hd	
17.9.79	35	74.0	NAD	115/8	35	Ceph	NE	✓
1-10.79	37	76.0	NAD	110/70	37	Ceph	N?	H
8.x.79	38	75.0	NAD.	115/75	36+	..	at brim	✓

watched for – this is why you must attend the clinic early, so that they are familiar with your normal blood pressure – as a rise may indicate pre-eclampsia (page 37).

The next two columns will probably be marked Oedema and Urine. If there is no swelling it will say 'Nil'. Your urine is tested each visit for the presence of sugar or protein (albumen) and the notation will, if all is well, read 'Nil' or 'NAD' (nothing abnormal discovered) or 'no sug/no alb'. These notations, together with the blood pressure record, are to identify pre-eclamptic conditions or toxaemia of pregnancy.

You are weighed at each visit to check that the weight gain is steady. Both weight loss and excessive weight gain cause concern.

The column marked 'Hb', or Haemoglobin, refers to the red colouring in the blood. If there is not enough, you may be anaemic and iron is prescribed.

In the Remarks column what you want to see most is 'V.well'. But in this column the doctor or midwife may note anything of interest – whether you need something for persistent heartburn, or even whether you are going on holiday. The chart will be signed by the doctor or midwife, and the date when they next want to see you noted. If it is two weeks' time this may be noted as 2/52 just to flummox you.

All the notes, as is clear, have the simplest possible explanation so ask if anything puzzles you.

In fact it is a good idea, and makes for good relationships with the staff, if you make a note in advance of anything you want to inquire about. It is easy to forget what you meant to ask, once you are lying flat on your back. If you want to ask about epidurals, ante-natal classes, how much you should drink, how normal is the size of the baby, whether you will need breast-shields in order to breast-feed, whether anything you have been experiencing is a cause for concern – now is the moment. For specific information you may be referred to the

FIRST EXAMINATION		Date	Sig.		EXAMINATION 35/37 week	This patient is fit for inhalation analgesia.
Height	5 6 '/4	Special observations			Date	
Teeth						
Breasts		⨯ Culposcopy			Head/Brim relationship	
Heart		NAD. Clinic			Pelvic capacity	Date
Lungs						Signature of Doctor
Varicose veins						
Pelvis					Sig.	

OEDEMA	Hb	NEXT VISIT	SIG.	NOTES. e.g. antibodies, infections, drugs, polio immunisation, classes attended etc.
nil	11·5			
+ placenta.				
nil	28			
nil				Well. GP 30 wks.
nil	4			Heartburn & Ailing wsp. Fetal 30
nil	GP 4 / 34			Well.
nil	2			Well.
nil				Well.

resident dietician, the physiotherapist or the medical social worker.

What are ante-natal classes about, and how do I find a good teacher?

There are two main sources of ante-natal education in this country. One is the hospitals. Most hospitals run ante-natal classes but the quality and quantity are entirely up to them and they vary from excellent to indifferent to non-existent. The other main source is a body called the National Childbirth Trust **Ref 1:1**. They carry out their work through two hundred local branches based on volunteer, but experienced and well-trained ante-natal teachers. Classes are held in the teacher's own home or in a hired room and they can cost anywhere from £8 to £15 for a course of eight lessons, although if payment is difficult for an individual, a nominal fee can be arranged.

Ante-natal classes are invaluable, especially during a first pregnancy. They represent an enormous advance because they help women to regain control over their own pregnancy and labour, and by giving them self-confidence and knowledge they need both to cope with the experience itself and with the professionals involved. All ante-natal classes offer basic information on pregnancy and childbirth in varying degrees of detail. Of course, a lot of this can already be found in books. The time value of the classes is in getting expectant mothers together with an expert teacher in a relaxed atmosphere which is usually entirely missing at the rushed ante-natal clinic. Here mothers can share worries, ask questions and bring their fears into the open. The mothers act as group support for each other.

The great advantage of National Childbirth Trust groups is that their support continues after the birth of the baby, which is often the time when the new mother needs help most. At class reunions they can share their experience with women who had babies at the same time as themselves, and can call on the expertise of the teacher in answering queries. Many NCT groups act as a self-help group for isolated mothers. Most groups also have a breast-feeding counsellor attached who will give some guidance before the baby is born, but who is readily available to help with any problems after birth. Post-natal support is now a growth area of the National Childbirth Trust's work.

By the end of a course of ante-natal classes the mother should know what will happen during labour. She should have learned about the various methods of pain relief in common use and what their advantages and disadvantages are. She will have learned about the monitoring devices used during labour so that the machines will not be alarming when the time comes to use them. She will have been taught every stage of the progress of labour so she is aware of what is happening to her at each stage and not frightened or taken by surprise. She should have been taught about the different interventions in labour which hospital staff might think it necessary to apply, such as induction or Caesarean section. And she will have learned the various medical reasons for this so that if a choice must be made, she will be able to discuss the matter rationally with her obstetrician.

Perhaps the most valuable help of all, comes from learning the techniques of relaxation that will help a woman, if not to a painless delivery, at least to keep in control during the tremendous physical process of labour and enable her to participate in what is happening to her. These breathing and relaxation techniques also come in useful after the birth and will help both to recover the figure and to make the most of rest periods. All ante-natal classes should have a special father's night, not just to give the father a little basic instruction in the business of pregnancy and labour, but to enable the labour to be real teamwork. If the father knows what the wife has been taught he can help her through the more difficult moments and participate actively in his child's birth, rather than being a nervous, passive onlooker. This is not only of enormous help to the wife but can be a revelatory experience for the father and it certainly helps to make a very powerful bond with the child he helps into the world.

Hospital classes may be equally as good as NCT classes and there is no reason why you shouldn't attend both sets of classes if you are really keen.

"They showed you what everything was for in the delivery room – what the bed was like, what the machines were for, what they did. That was very good. It wasn't so much of shock. I think everyone has this picture-book idea of what it's going to be like."

The advantage of hospital classes is that you will become familiar with that particular hospital and its ways and with the staff before you actually go into the labour ward. What is vitally important is that you attend ante-natal classes of some kind. It can make all the difference to your self-confidence and to your personal experience of childbirth.

"I found them very amusing and really enjoyed them. I find the idea of a whole load of pregnant women in one room quite extraordinary. But it's very helpful. There may be three or four women out of a class of twenty that you like and can get to know and share your experience with. You're in such a strange position at that time."

Where else can I get more information about childbirth and parenthood?

The most obvious source of information is your local bookshop or library. New books on the related subjects of pregnancy, babies and child-care are published frequently. Some have been tried and tested by time, others last a year and then vanish, but the supply is never-ending. For a very comprehensive list of books and sources of information, contact the National Childbirth Trust **Ref 1:1** for their leaflet *Education for Parenthood – Starting with Birth: a list of Useful Books and Sources of Information*. This recommends some seventy books on childbirth and related subjects, and they also produce a list of films and visual aids that groups may wish to hire. It also suggests further sources of information such as the Family Planning Association, the Health Education Council and the National Association of Maternity and Child Welfare. See also page 246 for a specially recommended list, **Ref 1:2**.

Parents who wish to go into the business of child-care and development in a more systematic way might consider taking one or all of the Open University Short Courses in Child Development. There are two already in the syllabus and a further course – 'Childhood 5–10' – is planned. You need no qualifications to take the course, although they say it helps to have a child of the appropriate age available. One is called The First Years of Life and covers the development of the baby from conception through to two years old. The second is called *The Pre-School Child* and covers the busy years from two to five. For further details write to the Associate Student Central Office **Ref 1:3**.

5
Money, my rights, and the cost of the baby

Pregnancy makes you into a new kind of consumer – a prize target, ripe for exploitation, and vulnerable to all sorts of marketing pressures.

Money, my rights, and the cost of the baby

What state benefits can I claim when I am pregnant or when I have children?

There are two main kinds of benefit which pregnant women can claim from the Department of Health and Social Security. One is the maternity grant and is available to almost everybody. The other is the maternity allowance and is only payable on the woman's own National Insurance contributions. The details of both these payments are laid out in Leaflet NI 17A, which you can find in your local Social Security office. The maternity grant is a flat payment paid direct to the mother and it is payable even after miscarriage provided the pregnancy lasted at least twenty-eight weeks. Mothers of twins, triplets or quads receive the grant for each child who lives more than twelve hours unless all the babies die, in which case only one payment is made. Maternity grant is paid on the full National Insurance contributions of either husband or wife but only on the woman's if she is unmarried. It must be claimed less than three months after he is born. Maternity allowance is a weekly payment made for eighteen weeks starting at the eleventh week before the baby is due, provided you claim before the baby arrives. If you claim it after the baby is born it is payable only for the week of confinement and for six weeks after that. Maternity allowance is based on the woman's National Insurance contributions only, which must be Class 1 or Class 2. They are based on a tax year roughly twelve months before the year in which you claim. It is wise to check with your local National Insurance office in plenty of time to see if you qualify. If your payments in that year were insufficient, you can make them up, but only within a certain time limit, otherwise you lose benefit, so check early. You can still claim maternity allowance even if you are getting maternity pay from your employer –

though not if you are actually working – women who claim the maternity allowance are also entitled to the maternity grant.

Apart from the actual cash, pregnant women are entitled to free dental treatment up to their child's first birthday, so pregnancy is a good time to go for a thorough check-up. They are also entitled to free prescriptions, again, up until the child is one year old.

Once the baby is born they are entitled to claim Child Benefit paid directly to the mother and payable on each and every child in the family. Everyone is entitled to claim and receive Child Benefit and your local Social Security office will explain it to you and give you the claim form and relevant leaflet CH1 which explains it in detail. **Ref 1:4** for payment timetable.

Will my employer give me paid time off to have my baby and look after my children? Do I get my job back after maternity leave? Is my husband entitled to any paternity leave?

If you have been in your job for two years or more and have been working for sixteen or more hours per week when you become pregnant, under the terms of the *Employment Protection Act*, your employer is obliged to allow you to return to your old job or an equivalent job within twenty-nine weeks of the baby's birth. If your employer will not take you back you are entitled to appeal to an industrial tribunal. Your employer is obliged to pay you a proportion of your regular salary for the first six weeks of your maternity leave, whether you return to work or not. The full details of your statutory rights as an employee seeking maternity leave and re-instatement are set out in leaflet Number 4: New Rights for the Expectant Mother, available from the Department of Employment.

This lays out the statutory arrangements between employer and employee but individual employers may have their own arrangements which you should discuss with them. This applies to paternity leave too. Paternity leave is not a statutory right in Britain, but certain firms – notably in the publishing industry – do have paternity leave agreements which allow their male employees anything from two days to two weeks off. Other countries are more generous than Britain over both maternity and paternity leave. In West Germany, mothers qualify for fourteen weeks of fully paid pregnancy leave and then four months of paid paternity leave. In East Germany, the government allows twenty-six weeks of fully paid pregnancy leave and a year's sabbatical at three-quarters of the mother's full salary for every child after the first. In France either parent is entitled to up to two years' unpaid leave with the guarantee of the job back at the end.

However pregnancy changes your life, it is certain to make you into a new kind of consumer – a prize target, ripe for exploitation, and vulnerable to all sorts of marketing pressures. As a consumer, you can make choices. This section is intended to guide you in that role.

What should I buy before the baby arrives?

The first rule is that you will need far less equipment than you think. The genuine essentials that you ought to have ready when you bring the baby home are fewer than three dozen items: ignore the fact that in the latest edition, Dr. Spock's list of infant care equipment runs to nine pages, one of the first items being 'Child's nose syringe'.

The second rule is that the greater the quantity you have of the real essentials, the easier your life will be. For instance, there is more heart's ease in having two dozen nappies than in having only one dozen. You are likely to get through eight in a day and you may not want to do the laundry instantly, overnight.

Women often think it is tempting fate to buy everything they will need before they actually have the baby. Then again, it's hard to shut your eyes to the bewitching, bewildering displays of pretty baby things in all the shops. Some others are taken completely by surprise – you may suddenly find you have a baby but no nappies. In fact this may not matter a bit. Any husband, friend or granny can go shopping with your list while you are in hospital.

What about second-hand clothes and equipment?

Every ante-natal clinic has a notice-board, and most advertise what local mothers have to offer second-hand. A bouncing cradle seat for £1.50, an almost new papoose carrier for £4.00, lots of French baby clothes up to eighteen months for £5.00, a car safety seat for £2.00, a safety harness for 25p, a travelling cot for £4.00, and so on.

It is a cliché that a baby's needs vary with the seasons and that they grow out of everything at an alarming rate. There is no stigma attached to buying second-hand equipment and clothes – indeed, you may be scorned if you do not take advantage of the second-hand cornucopia!

Where do I look for second-hand clothes and equipment?

You don't have to join in the scramble at Saturday afternoon jumble sales. Apart from your clinic noticeboard, the health visitors there are a useful source of information. Specialist second-hand children's clothes shops are becoming widespread; sometimes operating from the front rooms of private homes. Local mothers supply the stock from their own outgrown children's clothes and toys, and are paid in cash for them. The shop organiser then gets every garment cleaned and pressed and wrapped or hung on a rail as in a proper shop – most things look as good as new after this treatment – and she takes a small percentage of her resale price. This way mothers can buy the most exclusively-labelled dresses and coats of high quality for a fraction of their original price. Nurseries and playgroups, Mother and Toddler Clubs, Parents' Clubs, baby-sitter networks are all useful sources of second-hand clothes and equipment too. You just have to keep an eye open - don't forget the window-cards in the local newsagents' – but if stuck, inquire at the Citizens Advice Bureau, consumer aid centre or community centre in your neighbourhood.

When buying second-hand equipment remember to check stability and safety just as if the item were brand new. In the case of bath or crib stands, are they steady? Has any part been repainted with possibly toxic paint? In the case of prams, do the brakes work efficiently? Any loose nuts or bolts? Do the tyres need replacing?

In general it is true that equipment used by a newborn and immobile baby is of greater use second-hand than anything used by a lively toddler.

Where can I get reliable consumer advice on baby products?

Which?, the Consumer's Association's 81

BABYSHOCK

Magazine, has periodically tested things like prams, nappies, baby seats, children's safety belts and plastic pants, but in a lively market some of their information is out of date. They also publish two books containing much information for the mother-as-consumer: *Pregnancy Month By Month* and *The Newborn Baby*. Write for details to the Consumers' Association **Ref 1:5**.

What baby clothes will I need?
Four all-in-one stretch garments
You can't have too many of these, and they can be worn day and night. You can, on the other hand, have far too many woolly matinee jackets in pastel shades, knitted by well-wishers. Pure wool is not a practical babywear material. If people must knit for you, let them knit bonnets in winter; mittens and bootees are only occasionally necessary – most of the time they just get kicked off and lost.

Six vests
Get either the tying kind or wide-necked envelope-topped ones.

Sun-bonnets in summer, *cotton dresses with matching rompers,* and *long white nightgowns* in flameproof material are all optional extras but both traditional and flattering – so don't hesitate to ask for them as gifts.

The same applies to *bibs,* which are useful and make ideal gifts. People are astonishingly generous about first babies. If you can, always specify some no-first-size garments, and also stress the need for clothes that are easy to wash.

One bath-towel
Keep it exclusively for the baby's use.

Nappy paraphernalia and washing facilities
Towelling nappies
No point in economising here. You will need them day-in, day-out for up to three years and may re-use them for subsequent children, so they had better be durable. The consensus seems to be that the more expensive towelling nappies are, the better quality. The expense is worth it. T-shaped nappies may be less bulky and easier to put on, but not practical for very long.

Disposable nappies – do you need them?
Points in favour include:
No washing or steeping or drying.
Much neater and less bulky. Very necessary on journeys to save you carrying soiled towelling ones in plastic bags.
Ideal for the newborn, before you get into the steep-wash-dry routine at home. Hospitals issue them usually supplied by manufacturers who hope you will get hooked.
Points against include:
Too expensive to contemplate in the long run and inconvenient when you run out of them.
Towelling nappied babies are less likely to suffer from nappy rash.
They sometimes fail to contain a tiny infant's loose bowel movements.

Plastic pants
These are essential unless you are determined to use only disposable nappies. You might care to start with side-tying ones, for their versatility in size. After a few months you could graduate to neat popper-fastening ones,

82

and then to large elastic-topped ones. But always buy in half-dozens, as they need washing along with nappies and some tend to become hard and uncomfortable.

One-way disposable nappy liners
These are usually considered more useful than muslin squares and cloth liners. One-way disposables save the nappy from getting badly soiled and the baby from getting nappy rash. If you decide to use them, it is worth buying in bulk.

Plastic-cushioned nappy pins

Baby powder
It feels good and smells nice.

Zinc and castor oil cream
It prevents soreness

Baby soap

Tissues, kitchen rolls and cotton wool
Buy in large quantities for cleaning up various messes. 'Baby bottom wipes' which come in sealed packets like cologne-soaked tissues, are a luxurious extra but may have their uses.

Plastic nappy pail with lid
This is essential, and will hold up to one day's supply of nappies steeped in *Nappy Cleanser*.

Changing mat with stand
This is not essential (a nice bed will do as well) but a *changing mat* (or rubber sheet or old towel) is useful to put under the baby in case of accidents.

Baby bath
This is not necessary and its use is short-lived; a washbasin may be as convenient, or a washing-up bowl on the floor, until the baby can be put in the ordinary bath.

Washing-machine and spin-dryer
Although you could manage without, your life will be considerably easier with this labour-saving machine.

Feeding-bottles
Even if you intend to breast-feed for the first few months, you may need to use a bottle in an emergency so you might as well be prepared. You can buy bottles in complete sterilising units. In America sterilising is becoming obsolete, but most mothers would prefer to do it in the first delicate few months. A *sterilising unit* consists of a tank in which to submerge the clean bottles until they are needed again, plus sterilising fluid or tablets.

Sleeping and carrying equipment
A Crib
Not essential, but when baby manuals advise you to forget about wicker cradles trimmed with broderie anglaise, they ignore the susceptibility of the first-time mother. The solution is, don't buy one, borrow one. You will use it for roughly six months.

A Carrycot
Alternatively get a carrycot-and-transporter, doubling up in daytime as the pram. Again, don't buy if you can borrow. Some say even a drawer or a cardboard box will do for a newborn. After six months or so you will need a high-sided *cot* – and some people use a fullsize cot from birth.

Mattress, rubber sheet
Also two soft towelling or flanelette *undersheets* and two or three soft cellular *blankets* or shawls are all the bed-linen you will need, whatever the bed.

Pram (or carrycot-and-transporter)
There are plenty of second-hand or borrowable ones around.

A cat net to cover the carrycot or pram while out in the garden or on a balcony, even if you have no cat yourself.

If you have a car you will need *carrycot restraint straps* for the back seat, and later you will need a *child safety seat* (nine 83

BABYSHOCK

months to four years); later still a *child harness* (four to ten years).

Baby sling
Very much in vogue since somebody said that babies of Third-World mothers cry less than westernised babies because they are carried everywhere close to the breast, to the heartbeat and the warmth.

"I was devoted to my sling in the very early days, but found it didn't stop the baby crying and it certainly didn't remain useful for the two and a half years advertised."

However, slings are improving all the time and they are deservedly popular as they leave both your hands free. Look at all the altrnatives carefully before buying a new sling. They vary considerably in both price and functional design.

6
Decisions
to be made
now

Being informed through ante-natal
instruction is important not least
because it enables a mother to make
her own decisions. Faced with contradictory but nonetheless convincing
advice from doctors, friends and
relatives, making your own decisions is a habit to be cultivated as early
as possible.

Decisions to be made now

In sections 6 & 7, you are encouraged to make up your own mind about issues which will have a direct affect on your birth experience and the immediate post-natal period. Some, like the eternal breast or bottle-feeding controversy, home or hospital delivery, the various methods of childbirth, attract immutable though often contradictory views from medical experts. That is why it is important that you have the essential information now, before labour begins, to allow you to make up your mind.

Home or hospital, where should I have my baby?

On your first visit to your GP, once your pregnancy is confirmed, he will make arrangements to book you into the nearest maternity unit. This is the time to discuss the pros and cons of a home versus a hospital confinement. But the choice is hardly a free one. 95.9% of women in Britain have their babies in an NHS hospital maternity unit and although you are theoretically free to give birth to your baby at home with the help of your GP and your district midwife, it is quite likely that you will meet some opposition.

In America, home deliveries are virtually unheard of, but some European countries notably Holland, have a higher proportion of home deliveries than the UK and report a lower peri-natal mortality rate. Despite the high rate of home deliveries in Holland – around forty per cent – most mothers do still have their babies in hospital. The excellent mortality figures in Holland are due to a very efficient home back-up obstetric service and to rigorous selection of any at-risk cases

for hospital delivery. Their home delivery figures should not, therefore, be taken at face value as simple proof that all home deliveries are as safe or safer than hospital deliveries.

Delivery at home

There are real advantages to having your baby at home. There is a higher degree of control and you are likely to suffer minimum disruption to your own and your family's routine. If you have other children, there will be no problems resulting from enforced separation, and the birth will become a family event.

Many women find the routine of hospital life both disorientating and unrestful. At home, there is no need to obey the inevitable hospital rules – within the limits that your newborn (not the hospital) imposes, you can choose when to wake, sleep and eat. Nor will you be disturbed by other babies in the ward.

If you opt for a home delivery, it is absolutely essential to have a close and reliable helper. Once this is laid on, you will return to normal life more quickly than if you have a hospital delivery. The presence of close friends and family and the familiarity of the surroundings will all help towards a satisfactory emotional experience.

Although safety for mother and child is one of the main advantages of a hospital confinement, the re-organisation of the NHS in 1974 has brought great advantages to the district midwife who will attend you if you opt for a home confinement. Hospital cover is available in the form of an obstetric 'flying

squad', which consists of a hospital registrar, a hospital midwife, and an ambulance service which can be called upon by the GP. This squad usually arrives fully equipped with blood and other emergency aids.

Delivery in hospital

There are also advantages to having a baby in hospital. Many women feel safer in hospital, and birth is safer now largely because of improved hospital obstetric services. Your health, and that of your baby, can be monitored throughout labour. If intervention is necessary for mother or child during labour, it can immediately be dealt with by highly trained staff. You do not want an emergency ride in an ambulance at a crucial stage of delivery. If you live in a rural district, or an area short of good health services such as specialised obstetric facilities or well-equipped hospital units, consider your choice with the greatest of care.

In hospital, you will have the option of an epidural (see page 92 under **Methods of birth**); at home simpler, less 'drastic' forms of pain relief, such as gas or pethidine, only are available.

In hospital you will be able to share your experience with others in the same situation. This can be a great help particularly with certain basic practical problems such as folding nappies. Although thorough ante-natal preparation should solve these kind of problems, the camaraderie can be supportive for all sorts of reasons.

Why might I be refused a home delivery?

Your doctor will try to dissuade you from a home delivery in certain, well-specified circumstances. He will base his case on statistics which show that when certain factors are present, pregnancy and childbirth carry a higher element of risk.

First labours are very unpredictable. You could be pushing your baby out effortlessly in a few hours or you could have a long and difficult labour which is stressful for you and the baby. Doctors are trained to look on the gloomy side and will be happier if you are safely in hospital with necessary help to hand. This is especially the case if you are over the age of thirty and having your first baby.

If you are a single, unsupported mother, your doctor will bear in mind that the peri-natal mortality rate for babies of single mothers is twice that for married women.

If you are under five feet two inches he will know that you have a small pelvis which could make labour more difficult for you.

Even if he agrees to go ahead and arrange for a home delivery, you will save yourself disappointment if you realise that there may be medical reasons against it which will only become apparent nearer the date of delivery.

Breech birth – if your baby is positioned feet first in the womb and not head down, then you will be advised to go into hospital.

If you go into labour more than three weeks prematurely they will want the baby in hospital so that it can have the immediate attention of a paediatrician and special care if necessary.

If you have placenta praevia – this means that the placenta is lying between the baby and the birth canal.

If you begin to suffer from toxaemia in late pregnancy – raised blood pressure, water retention, and protein in the urine.

And, of course, your doctor is unlikely to consider home delivery if you have any previous history of obstetric difficulties.

The consideration you must bear in mind is what will be safest for you and your baby. The National Childbirth Trust **Ref 1:1** produce a very useful leaflet called *The choice of birth at home for those thinking of having a home confinement.* This sets out the procedure if you decide to have a home delivery and includes the names of various officials and organisations to contact if you meet opposition, such as The Society to Support Home Confinements, The Association for Improvements in Maternity Services, **Ref 1:7** , and your local Community Health Council whose phone number will be in the directory.

How can I arrange a home confinement?

If you manage to find a GP obstetrician willing to deliver your baby at home he will refer you to a midwife. She will then visit your home to assess facilities – Is there ample space? Is the bed too high or too low? What heating facilities are there? The midwife will then advise you about what you will need for the delivery – old sheets, a clean bucket, disinfectant, etc. She will then deliver a 'confinement pack' containing instruments necessary to undertake a normal delivery: sterile packs, instruments for cutting the cord, performing an episiotomy, etc.

Can I choose my hospital, and if so, how?

There are two different kinds of maternity unit in NHS hospitals. One is the consultant unit which is run by a team of doctors, midwives and nurses under the overall direction of a consultant obstetrician and gynaecologist. If they are in teaching hospitals they will also have academic duties and you may be called upon to be teaching material for a group of medical students. It is quite likely that you will never see the consultant although his attitudes and policy will set the tone of the unit. Consultant units are usually attached to paediatric units which can provide intensive care for newborn babies who need it. It can be reassuring to know that your hospital has one of these Special Care Baby Units at hand.

BABYSHOCK

The other main kind of maternity unit is the General Practitioner unit in which your baby will be delivered by your own GP. These have some of the facilities of a consultant unit, such as round-the-clock nursing staff, special equipment and so on, and if they are attached to large hospitals they have quick access to more high-powered facilities in case of emergencies. Many mothers like them because of their greater friendliness and informality and because they ensure their patients continuity of care. However, if you fall into any of the high risk categories mentioned previously, your doctor may prefer to book you into a consultant unit.

How do you exercise personal choice? If you live in a rural area your choice may be limited. Distance may be a primary consideration in your choice of hospital. It is very tedious making long journeys for your check-ups, and it can be worrying to think that you have a long journey to make when you are in labour.

Apart from cases like this, although the tendency is for mothers to attend the hospital in whose catchment area they live, you can ask to be sent elsewhere. Discuss the matter with your GP and other mothers in your area. You will learn from them what the general atmosphere of a particular hospital is like, whether the food is good, the staff friendly, visitors welcome, routine flexible. But take into account that giving birth is a very emotional business and women tend to argue very strongly for or against a particular hospital depending on their personal experience. You will get a more accurate idea by checking its approach to certain key questions.

What questions should I ask?
Will the hospital allow a companion of your choice to attend the birth?
Does the hospital conduct its own antenatal classes? Are fathers encouraged to attend?
What pain relief methods are available? When you have decided what method of birth you would prefer, discover what methods of birth the hospital prefers to administer. Very many hospitals provide a facility for epidural anaesthesia. But you may discover from other mothers that if they can dissuade you, they will. Alternatively, if you have decided upon a Leboyer delivery, find out whether they will perform it for you.
Does the hospital have a special care baby unit on the premises?
What are their rules about contact, between baby and mother following

delivery? Some hospitals keep babies in a nursery at night or if you want also during the day. Others insist on your keeping him by you twenty-four hours a day. The latter can be exhausting for you, but you may feel a desire to be close to your baby all the time. Make up your mind and discover individual hospital practice.

You do not have to be a private patient to enjoy privacy. Ask if the unit has amenity beds – private rooms for NHS patients – under what conditions one is available, and what it costs. Currently an amenity bed costs £3 a day.

What choice are you given about discharge dates?

What are the hospital visiting times?

Are there any other rules and regulations you should know about?

There is no point in moaning later, so if you have any queries at all, ask now. For further information about your rights in hospital, and as a maternity patient in particular, contact the Patient's Association **Ref 1:8** , who produce a booklet called, *Can I Insist?*

What is the father's role in childbirth?

"I couldn't have conceived what it would have been like without him there. You think he's on your side. You trust and recognise his voice and when he repeats the instructions you go with him.'

Traditional roles for fathers at the time of childbirth have varied enormously between cultures and from one period of history to the next. In some societies the man is so involved psychologically that he actually experiences the physical pain of labour – a phenomenon called couvade. A generation ago in England it was widely believed that fathers should be kept out of the delivery room, and all that was left for him to do was to pace up and down outside, or alternatively to retire to the nearest pub and get drunk. Nowadays most experts will argue that it is important from both mothers' and fathers' points of view for fathers to be present. When nodding in agreement with this, it is important to be aware that medicine is as prone to changes of fashion as other aspects of life, and while

most changes in medical practice are based on scientific advances, others are largely the result of changes in taste and life-style. As far as childbirth is concerned, there is evidence that if both parents agree, and if the birth is straightforward, the father can help both physically and emotionally. Not only is the need for pain-killers likely to be less, but sharing the experience of childbirth is likely to be an important landmark in your relationship. However, if you do not feel like having your husband around, and if he does not want to see the birth, it does not mean there is anything wrong with either of you. Neither does it indicate that you are going to be any less adequate as parents.

"My husband wasn't present at the birth of either of our children. With the first one I remember thinking, thank God he's not here. With the second I wanted him there, remembering the loneliness in my first labour. But the point is that he just felt he couldn't stomach the whole business when it came to it. In fact he stayed until about ten minutes before the birth of our second child and was then sent home."

Which method of childbirth is best?

"There was this great feeling of isolation. I seemed to be left for extraordinarily long periods of time completely alone on a long high narrow hospital bed. I was also drugged up to the eyeballs so although I was conscious of pain I was not really able to control it."

This is, once again, an area in which fashion dictates popularity. There is no reason why any of the methods included here should lead to post-natal problems (see page 118). Some mothers have complained that they are treated as mindless vehicles of reproduction by hospital staff, but there is no reason to be so treated provided you inform yourself of the options and make sure, in

advance, that the hospital you have chosen is prepared to undertake your choice (see page 90).

Natural childbirth

This proceeds from the first stage of labour – from the time when contractions are regular to the time when the neck of the womb is fully dilated – through the second stage – which is the period of time when you push – to the third stage – which begins after the delivery and ends after the afterbirth delivery – *without pain-killing drugs*.

In his book, *Birth Without Violence*, Professor Leboyer describes how the natural process of childbirth may be enriched. His recommendations are designed to minimise the violence of a baby's first few moments of life. For some women, his method will be attractive. For others, their own pain is as important an issue – particularly at the birth of their first babies – and there is no reason to feel pushed into a decision to give birth in this way.

Childbirth with pain-killing assistance

"What upset me was that it was so mechanical – wires coming out of me, attached to me, machines bleeping. It was so seedy. There was this huge bell-like thing on my tummy and it hurt when I pushed, so I ripped it off and they were very cross with me."

There is no telling how this mother would have reacted to natural childbirth in this instance. Clearly she was not well-acquainted with the equipment frequently used in hospital deliveries possibly because of inadequate ante-natal information. If so, it underlines the need to find out for yourself prior to childbirth about the labour ward and select an ante-natal class which provides access to such a ward as a part of its service.

Childbirth may still be a rude awakening. The experience of pain is impossible to describe adequately and in any case varies from woman to woman and birth to birth. At the first delivery, a woman's tissues are rigid, and often it is the most painful delivery. Many mothers spoke of a feeling of achievement when they underwent natural childbirth. They felt they had given their babies the best possible start in life and were justifiably proud that they had weathered the storm without medication. Other women were made to feel guilty, either by the attitude of their ante-natal teacher or hospital policy, because they wanted as serene a delivery as possible and as far as they were concerned that meant an epidural (see below). That is no way to begin motherhood. You must allow yourself freedom of choice in the matter. Take advantage of all ante-natal information, be aware of the changing fashions of medical science, and make your own mind up with your own comfort clearly in mind. *There is no evidence that drug-assisted deliveries pose more than normal risks for mother and child.*

Caesarian section

This is professionally regarded as the safest method of delivery if any complications arise, such as foetal distress, breech birth, or a head which does not engage. The operation involves anaesthetising the mother and performing a longitudinal, or more commonly these days for cosmetic reasons a 'bikini-line' cut.

In America, caesars are getting somewhat out of hand. They are performed far more frequently than could be justified by delivery complications. It has been suggested that the trend is not so much due to making childbirth as physically easy as possible for mothers, as to the fact that doctors in America can charge more for a caesar and also run less risk of malpractice suits.

Artificially induced birth

This method of delivery should only be used where the safety of mother or baby is at risk. Very often it is used for mothers who are late in giving birth. A syntocinon drip may be set up to accelerate contractions and an epidural anaesthetic is generally given to overcome the strength of contraction pain. Because an epidural anaesthetic desensitises the body from the waist down, it may be that you are unable to push the baby out during the second stage. Frequently, however, the anaesthetic wears off sufficiently to allow you to push the baby out without experiencing very much pain. If not, the doctor may use forceps to hasten the end of labour.

What is the best labour position?

This is a point which should definitely be discussed at your ante-natal class. If you are having your baby at home it will probably be more possible to experiment and see which position suits you best. Usually, in hospital, the preferences of the person who is delivering your baby will be voiced, and since he or she will want to feel confident that there is sufficient access to complete the second stage of labour, their points of view should not be overlooked.

Reclining at forty-five degrees with your knees drawn up or put in stirrups is the most popular method because bearing down is aided by gravity and the baby's head is clearly visible at the point of birth.

Squatting can also help at the bearing down stage and may well be accepted by the person delivering your baby as a feasible position.

Lying flat on your back with your knees drawn up or put in stirrups is generally preferred by doctors performing a 93

forceps delivery. It allows the doctor
maximum control.

Lying on your side may suit you and was
generally preferred by the Victorians
who felt it the most modest birth
position. It also suits the lone midwife
who can put your top leg over her neck
and use both hands to control the birth.

7
Feeding

"To begin with, feeding is virtually all they do; that's why it's so explosive an issue. Breast-feeding is tying – you're the only one who can do it; it was also very painful at first. But now, I feel a real sense of achievement and satisfaction when he's weighed at the clinic that I have done it for him."

"I couldn't have breast-fed. I know it sounds daft now but in order to cope I had to keep some distance between us. It was almost as if she was a leech, draining me of everything."

Feeding

Breast-feeding versus bottle-feeding, what are the pros and cons?

The decision about breast- or bottle-feeding should be made before the baby is born. You will then be less likely to be pushed into the wrong decision for you during your stay in hospital.

About two-thirds of mothers in Britain bottle-feed their babies, whilst the majority of medical experts strongly advise that breast-feeding is best. Can these mothers be wrong? Are the experts merely following another medical fashion?

The reason there is such a difference between what the experts say and what most people do is that by and large experts are either male doctors or childless female doctors and nurses, who are experts in nutritional science but have little concept of what it is actually like to have a baby suckling at the breast.

Healthy, well-adjusted children can be reared either by breast or bottle, and the deciding factor should only be whether or not *you* want to breast-feed. A mother who is pressured into breast-feeding for the sake of her baby – to the point where she would feel guilty if she didn't – is on the way to sacrificing her own life and feelings for the baby.

To help you decide, here is a list of arguments in favour of both sorts of feeding.

Arguments in favour of breast-feeding

The milk is produced at the correct strength, contains all the nourishment, salts and vitamins that a baby requires, and is served at a perfect temperature.

The inconvenient paraphernalia of washing and sterilising bottles, together with the mixing and warming of artificial milk becomes unnecessary. If the baby is hungry in the middle of the night you just pick her up and put her to your breast.

The supply of breast milk is matched to demand. If the baby feeds, more milk is produced; if he does not, the supply diminishes.

The consistency of the milk varies subtly during the course of the feed to satisfy both the baby's thirst and hunger. It looks quite thin compared to cow's milk, but babies' stomachs are more sensitive than calves. The milk at the start of a feed is relatively diluted and low in fat and calories which ensures that thirst is rapidly satisfied. As feeding continues, the milk becomes more concentrated, fattier and higher in calories. This change makes the baby's appetite fade and he ceases to suck. When put to the other breast he will resume feeding on the 'foremilk' just as an adult, replete after a main course, finds a sudden return of appetite when faced with a light pudding. This mechanism controls the amount of food taken by a breast-fed baby, and they are much more likely to remain at a normal weight. On the other hand, bottle-fed babies, whether they are thirsty or hungry, always get milk of a similar consistency, and, as a result, may take extra calories when all they need is fluid. A number of reports confirm that bottle-fed babies are more likely to become excessively fat.

None of the marketed milks contains the anti-bacterial and infection-protecting chemicals which help prevent infective illness in breast-fed babies. There are three main ways in which breast-feeding is likely to protect your baby against illness. In the first place, human breast milk contains certain antibodies, which give partial immunisation against colds, influenza and some of the common childhood infections, such as mumps and measles. Second, the breast milk is not only sterile – germ free – but also of exactly the right acidity for the baby's stomach. This means a breast-fed baby is less likely to suffer from diarrhoea and vomiting. Finally, breast milk is free of anything to which the baby might be allergic.

Breast-feeding is sometimes – though not by any means always – a pleasurable experience. Some mothers find it a satisfying experience. It may foster the development of a loving attachment between you and your baby, though, of course, breast-feeding is not essential to a loving attachment.

Arguments in favour of bottle-feeding

The supply is independent of mood and the state of your physical health. Breast-feeding can be difficult if you become miserable or anxious or if you become over-tired or physically ill.

Bottle-feeding is easy and comfortable. Once the milk is prepared bottle-feeding is usually very straightforward. You will have no problems with breast abscesses or engorgement; split teats, unlike cracked nipples, can be painlessly replaced. You will not have to endure wearing underclothes made soggy with milk, or have to put up with the indignity of a sudden release of milk when you hear your baby gurgling or when you become sexually excited.

"Everyone always recommends breast-feeding but they forget to remind you that you are the only person who can do it. If anyone has got to get out of bed at night, it's you. I am not saying that this is an argument for bottle-feeding. In fact I would probably breast-feed again, but at least I am equipped for it now. I know what it involved."

It does not have to be you that feeds the baby every time. Your partner can take a turn, so can the baby's elder brother and sister, or the baby-sitter. This is particularly important for a mother who plans to return to work soon after the birth of the baby, but even if this is not the case it helps to lessen the feeling of being 'chained to the baby'. Breast-feeding enthusiasts claim that you can express breast milk and store it in a bottle, and while this is certainly a possibility it is not as easy in practice as it sounds.

Some mothers are embarrassed to expose their breasts, even though logically they know there is nothing indecent or immoral about breast-feeding. Such mothers retire to the privacy of their bedrooms or bathrooms to breast-feed, but this limits freedom of movement.

Sometimes, underlying the feeling that breast-feeding is immodest, lies a conviction that it is in some way degrading to women, reducing them to the status of cow-like milk producers.

The origins of such beliefs are likely to be complex and deep rooted, and may well cause you to opt for bottle-feeding.

The supply is easily monitored. Mothers with bottle-fed babies can easily measure how much milk is taken each day. This is a doubtful advantage since a baby's behaviour and weight are better guides to whether or not he is being fed correctly. A satisfied baby who is gaining weight reasonably without getting fat is feeding adequately; a fat or a thin, miserable baby who is having exactly what the book says is probably being wrongly fed.

How easy is it to breast-feed?

The first baby may take time, patience and the help of other experienced mothers to establish a regular, reliable supply of breast milk. Breast-feeding in the early stages may be uncomfortable, or even painful. You may take at least six weeks before you and your baby master it. Experience has shown that, given help and encouragement, about ninety-five per cent of women can breast-feed perfectly satisfactorily.

If I want to breast-feed, where can I get advice?

Try and talk to other mothers with experience of breast-feeding.

Ask your midwife or health visitor for advice with particular problems.

Some Associations, such as the Natural Childbirth Trust and the La Leche League **Ref 1:6** provide breast-feeding counsellors who will visit.

How will breast-feeding affect getting my body back into shape?

If you are breast-feeding, you are in need of a very nourishing diet. This does not mean that you have to give up all hope of regaining your figure, but it does mean that you should continue the dietary plan discussed on page 38 and pay particular attention to taking plenty of fluids which will improve the flow of milk. If bottle-feeding, the return to your normal diet should be almost immediate. Supplementation of iron and vitamins is quite unnecessary unless you are anaemic or have lost an unusual amount of blood at the birth.

99

Will breast-feeding alter the shape of my breasts?

Surveys have shown that breast-feeding does not by itself lead to breasts becoming pendulous or developing stretch marks. If you are anxious not to spoil your breasts it is important to avoid gaining too much weight, which may lead to stretch marks on your stomach as well as your breasts (see page 40), and to wear suitable bras during pregnancy.

Which is cheaper, breast or bottle?

On the face of it, you might guess that breast-feeding will be cheaper, after all, you won't have to buy all that milk powder, plus the special equipment. However, breast-feeding makes you hungry and you will need to eat more. Probably, there will be little difference between the amount of money spent on milk powder or on extra food for you.

How soon can I get him onto solids?

From a strictly nutritional point of view, both human and cow milk provide sufficient nourishment for babies up to the age of one year, or even eighteen months provided that vitamins and iron are added. Not uncommon in some countries, this diet does have inherent disadvantages.

From your point of view, his diet and eating habits do not conform to those of other members of your family, and extra work is involved. Secondly, the longer you take to wean your child, the more difficult it is likely to be. Finally, relatives and acquaintances may criticise you for taking what for them seems so long to get him onto solids. The last of these 'disadvantages' is entirely spurious. From the developmental point of view, most decisions regarding feeding are irrelevant. But once a child can reach for, firmly hold, and transfer to his mouth a rusk or biscuit, it seems reasonable to let him do so. You will probably notice this ability around his fifth or sixth month. It is only in the encouragement of such movements in your child that feeding solids to him is important – once he can wield a spoon and gain pleasure from smearing food on his tray, why deprive him? – but these actions can of course be encouraged in other ways.

One word of warning about early introduction to solids. There is a small danger in giving some children cereal at a very early age. A minority of children are allergic to a component of wheat – namely gluten – and as a result suffer coeliac disease, accompanied by weight loss, diarrhoea and misery. If this disease is contracted by a one or two-month-old baby, it is very difficult to diagnose and thus could be dangerous.

In general, therefore, solids are best left until six months. Babies who persistently vomit and some very large babies are exceptions. Cow milk can take over at this age since the baby is now capable of withstanding infection. Meticulous attention to sterility is no longer necessary. It would be ineffective anyway since by this age he behaves like a human vacuum cleaner and there is no possibility of you making him behave otherwise.

Many ideas about solid foods are myths. Typical notions include the fallacies that solids are more satisfying and that they induce sleep. There is no basis in fact for either. Nor is there any particular merit in the order in which solids should be introduced, although they are best sieved until he has a reasonable number of teeth. Suitable foods include potatoes, carrot, fruit, eggs, cereals, bread, butter, meat, fish, and cheese. Babies do well as vegetarians. A few have come to harm following an unmodified vegan or macrobiotic diet. If you want your baby to follow one of these, you must obtain sympathetic medical advice.

Solids are best offered before milk in a baby's meal – initially as little as a teaspoon, increasing daily to the baby's requirement. One new food is introduced at a time. Don't be surprised if he refuses something, it may well be a character trait and is most unlikely to be a fault of yours. Try other foods, or withdraw with dignity and try again after a few weeks.

Some babies reject milk when solids are introduced. No harm will result; fluids can be given as water or fruit juices, or milk can be disguised in cereal or custard.

A cup can be used from about six months, a plate and spoon is probably best left until about eight or none months. Early results may be chaotic, but he will succeed with them sooner if they are introduced at this stage.

Be prepared for your baby to develop food fads. It is certainly tedious to grill fish fingers every day for six weeks, but it is neither harmful nor particularly unreasonable of him.

Convenience foods – they save time and effort, but are they alright?
The manufacturers of baby foods have done their homework well. It may be a source of frustration that your baby prefers a tinned to a home-made meal, but they are nutritious and there is no reason to feel bad about not preparing your own food.

Before you make a selection, consult the list of ingredients. Many tinned 'dinners' have added lactose, milk powder, or cereal which may result in excessive weight gain. Taste them too. Some are far too salty. In general, start healthy dietary habits early. A minimum of sugar and manufactured foods and a maximum of vegetables and fresh fruit is the ideal.

By definition the greatest advantage of these foods is their convenience. Provided you make a wise selection, the only disadvantages appear to be cost – you are paying for packaging, advertising and additives as well as the actual lamb, carrots, apricots or rice – and the fact that they tend to be bland – spacemen get a nutritionally adequate diet, but no one would want to live on what they eat full-time.

The nub of the whole discussion about solids seems to come down to how soon a baby can be encouraged to eat with the rest of the family. In fact, you may be surprised what he will tackle given the chance. Start by offering him a manageable version of your own diet – he will happily chew on fingers of bread, cheese, carrots, cucumbers, and raw fruit, and may often show a preference for stronger flavours than you give him credit. There's no need to cook him special little meals all the time; put a small portion of your meat and two veg. through the blender.

8
The birth

The birth

How do I know when labour has started?

There is no set pattern, although any one of the following is good enough reason to call the hospital, or if it is to be a home confinement, the midwife.

Contractions begin to get stronger, starting from the back, like period pains and radiating downwards. Very often, during the week prior to the beginning of labour, women feel such contractions coming at an irregular pace. When they become strong and regular (every five to ten minutes for a first-time mother, every fifteen minutes for a woman having her second or subsequent baby) it is time to make that call.

If there is a 'show' – a loss of reddy mucusy discharge – it does not necessarily mean labour is imminent, but be prepared for labour to begin that day.

Breaking of the waters. A sudden loss of watery fluid from the ruptured sac heralds labour. Sometimes this does not happen until the contractions are strong and regular enough for you to be admitted anyway.

What happens by way of preparation for the birth?

Such questions should by this time have been settled at ante-natal classes. Fortunately, nowadays, uncomfortable formalities like pubic hair shaving and enemas are not regarded as essential. You may, if it hasn't already happened naturally, have your waters broken and an internal to establish how far labour has progressed. It is a good idea to have had a bath or shower earlier, if time permitted, and to have emptied your bowels.

What will a hospital offer by way of pain relief?

Ante-natal classes will teach you the psychoprophylactic method of pain relief. It really is important for you, and whoever accompanies you to the labour ward, to understand what this breathing and relaxation technique is about. It helps very many women to cope with the pain of childbirth, acting as it does by re-directing your concentration and maximising your control of pain itself.

If he joins in, it is also a practical way for your companion to be more than an observer. Other helpful hints (again the ante-natal class is a rich source of such advice) include a thermos full of ice chips, a cold compress (wet flannel), and a companion who has practised massaging your lower back.

Strong analgaesics, like pethidine, are very often administered. Pethidine does tend to make you sleepy and may slow down the contractions. For this reason it is generally given at the end of the first stage of labour.

Epidural anaesthetic has already been discussed. The anaesthetic is topped up throughout labour. If the mother is unable to push during the second stage of labour, a forceps delivery is usually performed.

Pudendal block. This is an injection in both buttocks, and is usually used for a forceps delivery.

General anesthetic is rarely administered in Britain unless complications arise during the birth. It is more prevalent on the Continent.

BABYSHOCK

What sort of things can go wrong?

New mothers worry about their new-born's health. Generally, after "Is it a boy or girl?" comes the question "Is he alright?", and you may be disconcerted to receive no reply. The explanation is simple. If your baby has been taken to the resuscitation trolley, the paediatrician dealing with him may have a stethascope in his ears and not hear a word. In any event it is vital that he should not be distracted from what is often a technically intricate job. Resuscitation can only take five to ten minutes. The obstetrician or midwife present will be delivering the placenta and not watching the baby. Once these operations have been accomplished; you will be told what has happened.

Just as most labours are straight-forward, so most babies are born fit and well. 60% leave hospital with no problems whatsoever and the majority of problems that do arise are of little importance and solve themselves. Typical minor problems which tend to cause unnecessary anxiety include:

Jaundice
This sounds frightening, but occurs in nearly one third of all babies. It frequently clears without treatment, though sometimes a jaundiced baby is nursed under fluorescent light to speed up the process of recovery.

Bruising or blood-shot eyes
This is quite common and resolves itself in a few days.

Rashes
Babies do not have perfect skin, but no treatment is necessary.

Sticky eyes
Again, quite common, and usually treated by bathing with salt water.

Minor grazes and blisters following a forceps or breech delivery

These may look alarming, but have no long-term effects.

What if my baby is premature?

7% of all babies are born early, i.e. before thirty-seven weeks. When the term 'premature' was introduced, it was meant to refer to babies weighing less than five-and-a-half pounds. Most premature babies do weigh less than this amount, but a few – for example those born to diabetic mothers – weigh more. Additionally, some non-premature babies weigh less than five-and-a-half pounds and behave normally.

Premature babies are incapable or inefficient at basic functions like feeding, keeping warm, breathing normally, maintaining correct levels of blood chemicals, and resisting infection. Those who are ill or at risk of becoming ill are usually admitted to a special care baby unit (sometimes called neo-natal unit or intensive care unit). Not all hospitals, and very few maternity units, nursing homes or GP units have special care baby units on the premises. It can be doubly distressing to have a sick baby and then have him transferred to a distant hospital. Prematurity is specially significant to a new mother if it involves separation from her baby at a time when they very much want to be together. But it need not provoke long-term problems in every case. See page 115.

In taking a decision to admit a premature baby to a special care unit, good paediatricians balance the risk of immediate physical danger against the possibility of psychological distress. Although admissions are decreasing, the number of admissions vary enormously from hospital to hospital. In some it is as low as 8% of all babies, in others as high as 30%. It is fair to say that admission – just like admission of a normal child to hospital – is not necessarily a sign of serious illness. Indeed it may reflect local custom and practice, or even be the result of excessive parental anxiety.

Why are some babies nursed in incubators?

All small babies and sick larger ones are nursed in incubators. An incubator provides a warm home and permits observation at any time. It is not a form of treatment.

What causes stillbirth?

For about one in one hundred women, pregnancy ends in stillbirth. The causes are many, but in the majority of cases are obscure or unknown. Common causes include an abnormally formed or sited placenta, toxaemia, certain infections such as German measles, severe inborn foetal abnormalities, occasionally an abnormally short or looped umbilical cord, and certain drugs and poisons (including nicotine and alcohol).

Death may be a tragedy at any time, but for a mother it can seem the death of a part of herself. Her baby has been literally a part of her existence for nine months, and the closeness of the tragedy typically raises feelings of guilt and self-blame.

However unfounded such feelings are, stillbirth *is* a traumatic experience. Generally, parents will want to work out their loss together, away from other babies and new mothers in the quietness of their home. But do not strive to come to terms with it at once. You are bound to feel numb for a time. No promise of another child seems quite the answer. Sympathetic listening from people close to you, reassurance that you are not responsible for the tragedy, and physical and emotional closeness with the man you love is the best road to recovery. Be prepared to steel yourself against unthinking reactions of some people, as well as the necessary formalities.

"It was a terrible blow, particularly because it wasn't long after we had got married. My husband wasn't with me at the time but was terribly understanding afterwards. It was an easy delivery and the doctor who came in to tell me about it was very nice. It was the lack of tact in one of the nurses that really hurt. In a matter of hours after they told me, this woman came in and said, 'Sign this.' I asked her what it was and she said, 'Just the form for the post mortem.' She was that cold about it . . . I just had to get out of the hospital. All those babies around me crying, reminding me all the time."
Ref 5:1

Why might my baby be abnormal?

When things go wrong it is a natural human reaction to try and find a cause – something or someone to blame. If there is no obvious cause, we tend either to invent one or resort to a superstitious belief. The worse the problem, the more important it is to name a cause.

Examples of typical false reasons for an abnormal baby are:
Suffering a minor fall during pregnancy.

Being frightened by an animal or object.

Not eating enough.

Eating too much.

Eating certain foods (e.g. strawberries are said to lead to birth marks).

Failing to eat certain odd foods for which you may have had a craving.

Having sexual intercourse during pregnancy – semen is not poisonous, nor the end of a penis physically harmful to a developing foetus.

Reaching up too much, as when hanging out the washing, or painting a ceiling.

Actual causes

Chromosome and genetic disorders
Chromosome disorders – for example Downs syndrome (mongolism) – or 107

genetic disorders – such as cystic fibrosis, a lung and gut disease, are in-built in one or other parents. Nothing they have done – apart from conceiving a child together – can be said to have contributed to the child's problem. In these cases the malevolent influence generally produces its effect early, usually in the first few weeks of pregnancy and rarely after three months.

Rubella (German measles)

Rubella is the commonest infection known to cause foetal abnormality. Vaccination is now offered to school-girls but there are many pregnant women who have had neither disease nor vaccine. Ante-natal clinics will check for immunity when your blood is taken at the first session. If you are not immune, vaccine will be offered after the pregnancy is over. The vaccine consists of live virus so cannot be regarded as safe to give during pregnancy. If you are planning to become pregnant and have no idea whether you are immune to the infection, ask your doctor to perform a test now.

Drugs

Surprisingly few drugs are definitely known to damage the foetus in a manner like Thalidomide (long withdrawn from the market). As a general rule, any drug is best avoided in the first twelve weeks of pregnancy when the organs of the foetus are being formed. But if you are being prescribed medication, it would probably be more dangerous to stop and become ill than to take the medication as prescribed. If you are in any doubt, medical advice is essential. Most drugs must be safe since a study in Edinburgh in 1975 showed that 97% of all pregnant women take a prescribed drug, and 65% take an 'over the counter' drug. A few women may unwittingly be taking the contraceptive pill during the early weeks of pregnancy. This is not harmful.

Alcohol is a known foetal poison producing a pattern of severe abnormalities – both mental and physical if taken in excess over a considerable period. A glass of Guinness or white wine each day is harmless, a daily bottle of gin is not. See page 42 for the effects of smoking on your unborn baby.

9
Coming home

"When I came home I was on a tremendous high . . . Then I went from that to an awful, curious, blank void . . . I really felt on my own . . . couldn't communicate to anyone."

Coming home

Whatever your experience has been in hospital, coming home can be disorientating, particularly so if it is your first child who is accompanying you.

In the maternity ward, a routine was organised for you. All essential equipment (disposable too, not washable) was provided; all meals (however reminiscent of school), morning coffee, afternoon tea and nightcap arrived promptly, and nobody expected you to lift a finger to wash up; your bed was freshly made each day; professional advice was on hand; and if you were lucky you were inundated with cards, flowers and gifts.

Now, on returning home, you are on your own with none of this support. It is an excellent plan to arrange for someone, your mother or a friend whom you know you can rely upon to cope without adding to the confusion, to be there to help you for at least a week.

"One needs somebody who can think for themselves, and that can keep the house together without disturbing you. Holland and Germany provide hausfraus – one has to pay, but it's worth it."

The home help service, which provides domestic help through the social services department of your local authority, is theoretically available to anyone with what the authority considers sufficient medical or social need. Approach your GP in advance to see whether you are eligible – a medical certificate is needed in order to apply for the service. Charges vary from authority to authority and some do not charge at all. Check with your local social service department.

How will I feel physically?
Physical discomfort varies from birth to birth. Although you may experience little discomfort and recover quickly, it is as well to be prepared for the worst.

"When I returned from hospital," wrote one mother, *"I felt mentally and physically exhausted. Emotionally susceptible to the slightest upset. Gradually, as the stitches and soreness went, I was able to sit for a length of time without pain. I think it took upwards of six months before I really felt normal again. Mostly tiredness was the problem – with the broken nights and continual calls for my attention."*

Towards the end of your pregnancy you may have looked forward more than anything else to regaining your figure after the birth. But you may find that the socially-acceptable pregnancy bulge has, far from disappearing altogether, turned into a sea of unwanted slack muscle and flesh. And there are other more pressing discomforts to face. There could be a cramp-like discomfort in your lower abdomen – a pain similar to a contraction 111 pain which should disappear fairly soon. If it persists, see your doctor and/or take an analgesic pill.

In Victorian times there used to be a forty-day lying-in period – new mothers were segregated and labelled 'unclean' because of the slight loss of blood from the vagina known as lochia which follows delivery. This normal discharge soon clears up, and turns from brown to yellow as it does.

Then there is the soreness. In hospital you will have been encouraged to take salty baths to ease this discomfort and dissolve your stitches (if you had an episiotomy – a slight cut in the skin tissues below the vagina).

When you are back at home, take a luxurious bath, often. Soak in it. Detail someone to allow you at least half an hour to indulge yourself.

Finally, your breasts. If you are breast-feeding, your breasts will probably feel rather uncomfortable on the second and third days as the milk begins to flow. Treat cracked nipples with protective sprays, creams, even breast shields if they help. If you feel pain and tenderness in your breasts or notice redness and warmth, you may have a breast abscess or, more likely, it may be due to engorgement. If so, discuss the problem with your NCT breast counsellor, mid-wife, health visitor or doctor. There is probably no need to stop breast-feeding, but it is important to get advice and treatment.

When will my body return to its usual shape?

That depends on you. In hospital, the physiotherapist will have prescribed a course of exercises, similar to those below and designed to tone up your muscles. Do them regularly at least once a day, if you want them to have a real effect. Within a week or two, turn to the exercise programme on page 132. You may be surprised what it will do for both body and mind.

First day onwards

1. Breathing
   Lying on your back with knees bent and feet resting on floor, deep breathing.

2. Leg Exercises
   Lying on your back with legs straight:

   (a) ankle bending and stretching slowly.
   (b) roll feet in circle.
   (c) tense knee and seat muscles, hold and relax.
   (d) bend and stretch each knee alternately.

3. Abdominal Exercises
   Lying on your back with knees bent and feet resting on floor, draw in abdominal muscles, tighten seat muscles and press small of back against bed, hold and relax.

Second day onwards

4. Pelvic floor exercises
   Lying on your back with legs straight and slightly apart, tighten back passage as if trying to prevent bowel action and passing water; hold and relax.
   As a guide to doing this exercise, practise stopping mid-stream when passing water.

Third day onwards

5. Abdominal Exercise
   Lying with your legs straight, shorten legs alternately by tightening at the waist and drawing leg along floor; keep knee straight and abdominal muscles drawn in during exercise.

6. Lying on your back with knees bent and feet resting on floor draw in abdominal muscles, raise head and reach with one hand towards opposite side of hips; relax slowly to lying position. Repeat to opposite side.

Fifth day onwards

7. Lying with knees bent and feet resting on floor, place hands on abdomen; keep elbows off the bed. Draw in abdominal muscles and raise head and shoulders off bed. Hold and relax.

8. Lying on back, raise right leg approx. three inches from floor with knee straight; hold and slowly lower. Repeat with left leg.

9. Lying on back, both knees bent, roll knees to either side keeping shoulders on floor.

Lifting

Use your legs. To lift bend your knees, then draw in abdominal muscles and lift by straightening your legs.

All exercises should be done slowly and deliberately. At home do them on the floor with one small pillow for your head.

EMOTIONAL UPSET

How will I feel in myself?

There is no telling how you will feel, but the amount of sheer physical work involved in labour is enough to produce a state of emotional tension, which may bubble over either in elation or tears, or both. Add to this the effects of tough 'on-and-off' pain and various drugs . . . the bodily readjustment occasioned by the sudden loss of a lump that has been steadily growing for nine months, and which (including the weight of the baby, after-birth and waters) amounted to about twelve pounds . . . and the emotional impact of missing that warm, moving being inside you – *"At first, I couldn't get used to not having her there inside me. It was a feeling of loss, a sort of emptiness."* . . . Finally, allow for the rapid changes of body hormones which are known to occur after birth.

However you feel, if this is your first child, by now it will be clear that an essential irreversable change has occurred.

On the credit side, you should also realise that the change is just one part, albeit a most dramatic part, of a whole process of personal growth which can produce a more mature, self-sufficient and positive individual.

In hindsight it seems incredible that the medical profession has treated new mothers as though they were un-intelligent, naive children, frequently dismissive of a mother's sense of anxiety and uncertainty. How could they at once thrust the responsibility of your child's development firmly upon you on the one hand, and dismiss your own feelings with a remark like, "It's the hormones," on the other.

In examining the much publicised baby blues, post-natal depression, and ways in which you might make yourself less vulnerable to them, useful principles of self-help and 'mother-care' emerge to help you cope with the new maternal role and transform it into a positive transitional point in your life.

What are the baby blues?

Usually on the second or third day following the birth new mothers experi-ence an emotional reaction. Similar reactions have been described follow-ing surgical operations, so it is not a unique phenomenon. Although follow-ing an operation you can look forward to a period of convalescence, following childbirth, life is likely to be anything but restful.

"I don't cry. I mean I'm not a woman who cries at all. I'm not the person who would be in tears at the happy ending of a film or anything like that. But it just wells up and it just happens and I can almost sit beside myself and see it happen, thinking, 'Oh, how odd. It's not me at all.'"

The important thing is to acknowledge 113

the possibility of a reaction of this sort and not see it as any kind of personal failure. Just because your childbirth experience is not the same as your mother's (or that of an over-confident neighbour), just because it does not proceed exactly along the lines described in baby books or in ante-natal classes, it is in no sense a sign of fallibility. In interviewing new mothers it has been shown that each has a different story to tell, albeit with many similar themes.

Baby blues are characterised by swift changes of mood, possibly crying bouts, and often feelings of helplessness. They are also usually mild and short-lived, lasting only for a few days. One woman described how she burst into tears when her husband arrived in the maternity ward and simply said, "Hello." Another felt desperately lonely and irritated when her husband took his two older children out in the afternoon, three days after a home delivery.

It is as natural to think, "How can I possibly love this squawling messy creature?" as it is the next minute to feel great sweeping surges of maternal care. And as you oscillate between such emotions you may generate guilt and anxiety at your negative thoughts. But why *should* you fall suddenly in love 114 with your newborn?

How soon will I love him?

For some mothers, the moment when they see and touch their baby for the first time after delivery is an intense and joyful experience, a fit climax to the long period of waiting during pregnancy and to the effort and struggle of labour. Some midwives and doctors, especially those influenced by the French obstetrician Leboyer, like to place the naked baby on the mother's tummy while they complete the delivery. After the cord is cut, they may give the baby to the mother to hold whereupon some babies immediately suckle at the breast. You may find this an important first step in establishing a bond with your baby. Indeed you may look back at this moment as one of the peak experiences of your life.

Other women take time to feel any positive emotion towards their infants. They may be disappointed, even guilty that the expected feelings of warmth and tenderness simply do not appear. One recent research study shows that the majority of women take several weeks, sometimes months, before they feel deeply attached to their children. On reflection, it is hardly surprising. Motherhood myths have ignored the plain fact that human feelings, of any depth, develop over a period of time – some marriages may indeed begin with 'love at first sight', others display a slow development of affection and love. How love between mother and child grows has absolutely nothing to do with the character of the eventual bond and should not be the cause of disappointment or guilt.

"After he was born I felt strange and couldn't take to him at first. He cried a lot. To compensate for feeling guilty and not wanting him, I tried to do everything for him. When I came home after two days in hospital I didn't feel like doing anything at all. I was that tired. But I just had to do it all. I had to keep my routine going and keep things going for the rest

of the family just because I felt nothing for the baby. Things went from bad to worse. I couldn't understand it since everything had gone so smoothly with my first two. Looking back on it now, I was just pushing it all too hard. I was convinced there was something lacking in me and that I could never be a proper mother to him.''

As your child grows and his ability to respond to you develops, as it surely will, a positive relationship should soon replace any despondency you may have felt if you did not fall in love with your child right from the start. In the end, it is a capacity for love and devotion rather than sudden, intense feelings – which may disappear as fast as they came – that is the best foundation for both family and married life.

It has become fashionable to claim that close physical contact with your child immediately following birth is *essential* to the future bond. Some research evidence indeed shows that early, close, physical contact does help the later relationship between mother and child. In one American study it was found that mothers in hospital who were permitted to have their naked babies in bed with them for several hours a day were more responsive to them at follow-up examinations.

But our questionnaires, like other recent research showed conflicting results when mothers were asked whether they felt that holding their babies immediately following the delivery was important. Some said that they were so exhausted by labour that all they really wanted to do was sleep! And in no case was there a significant loss of love between mother and child as a result of this lack of immediate contact. Although enforced separation following birth complications can lead to bonding difficulties, as in the first quote, the second mother illustrates that this is not necessarily so.

"My second child was small, only six pounds. He couldn't suck and he had to go into special care. He ended up being in special care for about three weeks. I never really took to him for about a year, maybe because he wouldn't be breast-fed or maybe because I just didn't have that physical contact with him straight away. When we got home I just used to feed him, change him and put him down. I was afraid my husband would notice my attitude, so I always busied myself with the washing up and things like that. I felt so guilty, but I couldn't do anything about it."

"They gave me this scan up at the hospital and said I would have to have a Caesar. I was terrified. When I went in to have him, my husband took me in and I was shaking like a leaf. But all that stuff I'd read about not feeling affection if you have a Caesar is a load of rubbish. I even saw a doctor on television saying the same thing – I could tell him a few things. They didn't give him to me after the delivery because I was all dopey after the operation. But not holding him made no difference at all as to how I felt about him."

In placing undue stress on immediate attachment, or bonding as it is called, some progressive hospitals take it upon themselves to decide for mothers that their babies should be in cots beside their beds twenty-four hours a day. The noise, day and night, of squawling children can make a mockery of the hospital recuperation period from the mother's point of view. There will be plenty of occasions for sleepless nights once you are at home. Perhaps the answer is that while close physical contact and proximity to your baby after the birth can be helpful, it is not essential for the development of a loving relationship, a happy mother and a contented child.

How severe are the baby blues likely to be?

About nine out of ten women pass through the post-natal period with no more than mild upset of the sort described. However, recent surveys in Britain and Scandinavia have shown that some mothers experience a depressive state, similar in kind to the baby blues but more severe, which may last longer – up to three months or more. This reaction, which is called *post-natal depression*, results in symptoms similar to depressive states unconnected with childbirth.

What are the symptoms of post-natal depression?

Despondency

Tearfulness may be persistent and prolonged, and reflects an inner sense of despondency, gloom and pessimism.

"Inside me there was a big black hollow. I just couldn't talk about it."

Sense of inadequacy

An unrealistically strong sense of inadequacy is often present with such feelings as, *"It's impossible, I just can't cope."* Frequently this is experienced together with an intense sense of guilt.

Irrational fears

You may have irrational fears about the safety of your child or about your own health. Probably every mother has woken in the night and wondered if her

newborn baby is all right. She will listen anxiously for the baby's breathing and possibly go so far as to wake the child to check that all is well. It is natural to be concerned about your health and that of your child, but excessive over-concern is frequently symptomatic that all is not well within yourself.

The first clue that your doctor may have that you are experiencing post-natal depression is when you persistently complain that your very healthy baby *"doesn't seem to feed properly"* or that you are *"incapable of feeding him right"*.

"Mothers don't come and say, 'I'm ever so depressed doctor.' They come and tell you such things as, 'I'm ever so worried about my child and he doesn't seem to be feeding; he's cross and angry all the time; he wakes every two hours right through the night and wants something to eat.' And then if you know how to ask the right questions, the mother will break down or cry or admit to deep feelings of misery, guilt. 'How could I feel like this, doctor, with a new baby? Everybody said I'd be happy, but I'm not.' And they also, all of them, describe the feeling of aloneness, that only they have it and they can't tell anybody about it."

Irrational fears about your own health might include concern that you are developing a physical complication following the delivery, or some other illness – normal vaginal blood loss, for example, may be seen by you as indicating a haemorrhage or an infection of the womb. Such fears seem perfectly justified to the new mother since post-natal depression is often accompanied by physical symptoms such as palpitations, racing pulse, dizziness and headaches, which she may interpret as signs that all is not right in her body. In fact they are well-known symptoms of anxiety and depression.

Occasionally, irrational fears are directed towards other members of the family. For instance, in one case a mother was convinced that her husband had had an accident every time he went out of the house for more than five minutes.

Tension and anxiety

Increased tension and anxiety may well cause you to become unusually irritable and lose control at the least provocation Whoever happens to be around – your husband or boyfriend, a well-meaning visitor, your health visitor – anybody may get it in the neck, as indeed may the newborn baby. Because this irritability appears to come from nowhere – *"It just wells up inside me"* – and frequently fades as quickly as it arises, you may be left feeling ashamed or resentful, which only makes matters worse.

Physical symptoms

Sometimes it is the physical symptoms which present themselves to the virtual exclusion of underlying emotional symptoms. Fatigue, of course, is the paramount factor in making new mothers more vulnerable to post-natal depression. This is due to lack of sleep, the energy employed during labour and the demands made by the baby which all combine to sap your reserves. But when tiredness turns into total exhaustion – *"I was completely drained of all energy"; "I was so tired that I couldn't sleep"* – it may be evidence of post-natal depression. Mothers spoke of feeling physically ill, aching all over as though they had food poisoning. Their appetite diminished and weight was lost at an alarming weight. *"I began to shake; I got what I supposed to be hot flushes because I had read about them; I even found it difficult to walk."* Looking pale and physically ill, your friends or neighbours might tell you that you look anaemic and ought to see a doctor and get a tonic. Perhaps you go to the post-natal clinic, have blood tests, even a full physical examination, and are told that they cannot find anything

wrong with you. If you are already upset, this may well make you feel still more isolated, knowing that all is not well yet being unable to make anyone believe you.

It is the failure to recognise the symptoms of post-natal depression and take positive action to rid yourself of it that can cause things to spiral. As time passes, sympathy and concern from those around is replaced with irritation and advice to pull yourself together. This is bound to make matters even worse. The strains already imposed on a woman's relationship with her partner may at this stage be further heightened by a lack of sexual interest and responsiveness (loss of libido). Again this leads to more anxiety. Trapped in a cycle of apparently inexplicable emotions, feeling increasingly isolated from people she loves and trusts, facing an overwhelming present and an uncertain future, things may reach the point where a woman starts to wonder if she is going mad. In a survey carried out in a London Teaching Hospital in 1968, out of thirty-three women who had developed post-natal depression only five received any treatment. This can be due as much to the new mother's inability to recognise the symptoms as an unaware medical profession:

"I never considered that I needed medical help; in fact I didn't ever consider it at all. If I have to go to a doctor and tell him I'm depressed, it shows a weakness in me. That's a hang-up of mine. I find it very difficult to accept weakness. That was another thing I felt resentful about – feeling so weak at that time."

Can we isolate a cause and solve the problem of post-natal depression?

It would be comforting to think that there is one major cause of post-natal depression, but unfortunately it is now almost certain that there is not. Just as a number of straws add together finally to 117 'break the camel's back', so a variety of circumstances combine to produce depression.

Because of the emotional changes already described, all women are vulnerable after childbirth. Just one relatively small stress may be sufficient to set off a vicious cycle of emotional turmoil.

From a medical point of view, it would be simple if post-natal depression was due to a single infective agent in the way that measles is caused by a virus. Experts on this often appear in the media championing opposing viewpoints – each one arguing in favour of his own particular view. It is all very misleading since it is likely that the cause which each expert is championing may be correct, but only in part.

Rather than look for any single cause, it is far more constructive to ask the question:

What makes a woman vulnerable to post-natal depression?

In any one case we would expect some of the following to be involved:

Previous personality
There is some evidence to suggest that if you have a particular type of personality then you are more likely to develop problems. Women who are perfectionists, preoccupied with making a good impression, are vulnerable. So are women who rely a lot on other people, or who are always ready to give in to others in order to keep the peace.

Age of mother and number of children
Scandinavian, British and American statistics show that there is *slightly* more risk as the age of the mother increases, and puerperal emotional disorders are *slightly* more common following the birth of the first baby.

Hormones
There is no doubt that during the days immediately after childbirth there are massive hormone changes in the mother's body. There is also evidence that in other situations, such as the normal menstrual cycle and the menopause, changes in hormone levels can affect mood. Hormones involved include not only progesterone and oestrogen, but also others such as prolactin, which is involved in the production of milk, and corticosteroids, which are involved in the body's reaction to stress.

At first there seems to be good reason to implicate hormones as *the* cause of depression. However, women who do not suffer from depression have the same hormonal changes. In addition, attempts to treat depression with hormones have not proved successful.

Circumstances of delivery
If things go badly afterwards, it is easy to blame the circumstances of delivery as solely responsible.

"With the first two I felt terrific elation after the birth – they were 'natural' births. I felt as though I had achieved something. It was very exciting. But with the third I had an epidural and from the start I felt trapped. You're tied down with contraptions – the drip, the heart monitoring machine . . . I just remember thinking I was going to die. The epidural was very successful – no pain – and I maintained a slight pushing sensation so no forceps were used. But I felt panicky tied up to all those things. I felt no sense of achievement afterwards. I felt let down, cheated."

The pros and cons of the various methods of birth are dealt with elsewhere (page 92). This woman's deep fear that she was going to die continued with her during a particularly severe, case of post-natal depression. But in her case it is unlikely that the choice of birth was the main cause of her irrational fear. Palpitations and other physical sensations that she called 'panics' which accompanied her profound feelings of anxiety were shown to be due to other factors.

At present there is no evidence that long labours, the use of drugs, labours complicated by induction, or Caesarian sections have *on their own* been responsible for prolonged emotional upset. In certain cases the circumstances of delivery could be additional factors worthy of consideration.

Difficult babies

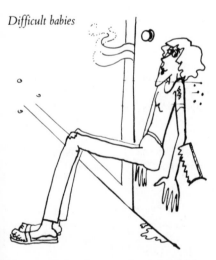

If any of the factors above could be singled out and blamed for causing post-natal depression, clear-cut solutions would be near at hand. Such solutions could never explain the mother adopting a baby and suffering from post-natal depression. One such woman was a nursery school teacher before she adopted and she was carefully screened for her new role. Clearly neither

hormonal upset nor birth complications could be blamed for the anxiety and misery which she later experienced. Her health visitor explains:

"This couple adopted a child after a long period of infertility. They had undergone extensive investigations at an infertility clinic, but no reason for infertility was found. Their adopted son was placed with them when he was seven weeks old. The GP asked me to visit the family in June since the woman had been going to the surgery almost daily complaining that the baby was not settling or sleeping well. The mother constantly complained that she was tired and had bodily aches and pains particularly in her back. She also felt she must be anaemic.

"My first few visits were met with some hostility and on these occasions I confined myself strictly to discussing the management of the baby. One day, after visiting her on a weekly basis for about two months, she telephoned me in a very distressed state . . . At this point I felt that she ought to be referred for more skilled help, discussed this with the GP and he offered the woman a psychiatric appointment. This she refused. I continue to visit on a weekly basis, and she will telephone about three times a week. When I gave her my diagnosis of post-natal depression, this seemed somehow to help her."

Here, in her own words, are some of this mother's feelings:

"It was so very different to the way I expected, and remember that I was used to small children. I had been a nursery school teacher . . . He seemed to cry non-stop. It was, and still is to a lesser extent, the most awful high-pitched wail. It sounds really desperate . . . I felt very mixed up. I had desperately wanted a baby more than anything else, but found myself thinking some wicked and evil things when he wouldn't respond to me. I began to wonder whether I was one of those people who could never give love. Then I read somewhere that babies have an instinct for smelling who their real mothers are. My GP says this isn't true. I 119

hope he's right . . . I have cut myself off from many people. I just couldn't face being social. I felt so bad physically, was constantly exhausted, looked a wreck, and the house was such a mess that I couldn't have had anyone in . . . My husband is in a very demanding job, and I don't give him the support I used to. He can't bear failure, and I'm worried that he may think I'm a failure as a mother . . ."

This woman exemplifies how the extremely demanding business of bringing up a young baby can on its own reduce his mother to a state of anxiety and misery. She had had many years of experience in caring for young children and, further, had been schooled by her health visitor in the craft of baby care. None of this had eventually prevented her from suffering many symptoms common to sufferers of post-natal depression. Finally, like so many natural mothers, she blamed herself for her failure as a mother and set herself firmly in the vicious circle of post-natal depression.

As far as the 'instinct for smelling' is concerned, the mother *was* correct. Initially, her adopted baby very probably missed his natural mother and this could have been one reason why he was so difficult.

Psychological factors

Childbirth inevitably leads to change and this is especially obvious in the case of a woman who had a successful career before becoming a mother. She has been thoroughly wrapped up in her work, enjoyed the immediate rewards of success, and welcomed the challenge and stimulation probably provided by a male-dominated professional or commercial scene. Suddenly this is swept away and the new mother finds herself in a largely female world where attention is focused on babies and the home. Things no longer run as smoothly as she had come to expect in

120

her career. Motherhood is, for the first months, an altruistic occupation without the quick results or regular 'pats on the back' more typical of careers outside the home.

"I just hated the role of motherhood. I missed the contact with men. I missed talking about things that had nothing to do with babies. I missed blokes finding me attractive. I felt I had dropped to the depths. Partly it's the way society treats you – your social life tends to revolve around your husband, and people don't talk to you at parties because you don't 'do' anything. It just seemed the whole world was against mothers – even the local supermarket had check-outs too small to take a pram . . . I felt I was a reproductive person now, no longer a sexual person. I had dropped out of the real world."

Change, even if it is for the best, is rarely easy to adapt to, and the social upheaval which the new role brings should not be underestimated:

"After the birth of your first child you have to mix with other mothers. There's no choice. Other people don't understand what it's like, why you can't get there on time, why you're half an hour late because the baby's done a shit. . . And when you get there, they're all looking wonderfully smart and their hair is great and they're thin. You've got to have other mothers as friends."

"One of the friends that I lost after having my child – she never came near me after I had had my first – I met her once in the street and asked her why. She said, 'Oh, kids are all right for half-an-hour, but I couldn't stand more than that.' I can do without a friend like that."

"I lost a lot of friends. Suddenly you don't have much in common with those who don't have children. I can understand it though. You get obsessive about your children (I mean one's mind goes for a few years!) and become boring to people without kids. If you happen to have your children earlier than your contemporaries you can get very isolated."

There is often an infuriating presumption that pregnant women, women with young babies, and especially full-time mothers, are somehow wanting in grey matter. This may sound preposterous to anyone who has not experienced it for herself. Very often it begins with clinic or hospital staff while a woman is pregnant:

"The hospital staff have this infuriating habit of talking down to pregnant women. They treat you as an imbecile really. They never talk about the baby, but about 'baby', which makes you feel about four or five and back at school – particularly as the nurses will assume those slightly raised rather twee tones normally kept for little old women in bath chairs or newborn babes. Either that or they answer your questions so as to infer that you really shouldn't bother yourself with that, it's far too medical for you to understand."

It is much worse when a similar attitude is adopted by fairly close acquaintances. An intelligent woman, in demand socially before the birth of her child may suddenly be ostracised at the very time when she needs to feel accepted as more than a reproductive animal.

"I remember going to a drinks party at my mother-in-law's house about three weeks after Katherine's birth. I suppose there were six or seven people there, fairly close friends of the family. In fact there was a professor and his wife with whom I'd had a very long and interesting conversation at a similar party a few days before Katherine was born. Well, I couldn't credit the change, the difference between this party and the one before I had become a mother. The shift in attitude to me was incredible and I felt it as soon as I walked in the room. One or two of the women wanted to talk about the baby; the professor looked clearly ill at ease when I tried to pick up the threads of conversation from our previous meeting; basically I was out of it as far as the rational intelligent world was concerned."

There are two points worth mentioning here. Firstly, after the birth of a child a mother is at her most vulnerable psychologically, more susceptible to patronising or distant attitudes. Her shaky self-confidence will need reassurance from friends and family that she is still the person she was before the birth of the baby. Be aware of a natural tendency to over-react to the kind of situation described above.

The second point is that close friends, even immediate family do all too often take the emotional strain of childbirth for granted. When a mother needs to depend upon them for support, they will expect her to revert to a supportive role as mother, very often giving more attention to the baby than to her:

"They (husband and other children) should be more sympathetically inclined to your feelings, emotions, tiredness. They should understand the strain and responsibility that women have for their children. I wouldn't mind that he doesn't help, but he could say that you're doing a good job without being patronising. In fact he was just another person to look after when I returned from hospital. I remember feeling devoured by absolutely everyone and not one half hour a day was yours to do what you wanted. I resented him. I really did."

121

BABYSHOCK

Marital stress

Lack of support from the child's father has been clearly implicated as a factor increasing a mother's vulnerability. Unsympathetic partners, who try to continue their lives as though nothing had happened, are particularly damaging in the modern nuclear family, where support from other relatives may be minimal.

"The real problem is that my husband doesn't give enough of his time. His job is such that we never know when he is coming home. Last night he didn't see her because he came home about nine-ish. The night before he didn't see her – he came home at two-thirty in the morning. I have to accept that he has to work to deadlines and a client might come along at three o'clock and say, 'I want a job by tomorrow,' which means that he is up to all hours. But even so, the interest is not really there. He never accepted the change in my life as a result of having the child. He comes home and expects the house to be in order. He makes no allowances.

"He wants us to go out at weekends and leave her with my mother. But I think that it is important to go out at weekends as a family. That, after all, is the only time he really sees her.

"When he comes home he might completely ignore her. He says, 'I don't like babies.' I remember we used to have the pram in here and I used to put her in a cocoon thing in the pram. If she was crying and I was cooking the food, I'd say, 'Look, just shake the pram and talk to her.' Later I'd still hear her crying and I'd come out and find him still reading his damn paper, standing by the pram and bashing the pram handle with his hip! He just wasn't prepared not to read the paper. He didn't make any concessions at all.

"On top of everything else he still wants to have the same spending powers. Really, he wants us to look as if we don't have a child. I am supposed to cope with the child and cope with him as if we didn't have any children. It's just impossible really."

Sexual relations

Quite often, normal sexual relations are disrupted after childbirth and this may become a source of discontent and self-effacement.

"Sex became a problem after my first child was born. Before that every night was good. I think I was afraid of having another baby. I'm not very interested at the moment – I feign sleep or pretend I'm reading my book. It's getting better though now because I'm not afraid any longer of having more babies."

"After our first child I was just not interested in sex. I had no energy and was very depressed. Then it cleared but I can feel it coming back again. I've always been able to control my emotions by taking a walk or tidying the garden, but this depression is always with me. Perhaps it will take time. It's partly the lack of communication with my husband. I do all the giving and get nothing back in return."

"Yes, I think resuming sex was a very important consideration for me – it's such an important part of marriage. In fact I think my husband found it even more important than I did. You do tend to get terribly wrapped up in the new baby and also very tired for those first few months, and your relationship with your husband can suffer."

"It's fear more than anything else. You think everything is going to fall out! Something's going to go wrong. As we were doing it after

she was born – as my legs flopped apart – I heard this voice saying, 'All right flop your legs apart,' and I could visualise five nurses and doctors with white hats. I had this vision of a hospital bed as we were doing it! Awful! You think it's going to be an internal (you've had so many!). It was quite a relief when he didn't get out one of those what-do-you-call-its, and screw it up inside me before he got started!"

So even though the vagina has healed and the mother loves and feels close to her partner, she may not want to resume sex for several weeks. It is not easy to approach the subject with as much humour as the young mother above. The woman may feel guilty at "not being a proper wife anymore". The man may find it difficult to accept that while his partner craves closeness and cuddling, she just does not want sex.

Childhood memories
The experience of childbirth may stir up and reactivate conflicts from a mother's own childhood. She may wonder if she is going to be the same sort of mother to her new baby, as her own mother was to her. If she felt deprived and unhappy as a child, this is likely to evoke painful emotions with considerable force.

One attractive, lively woman had spent long periods in hospital as a small child suffering from TB. She was the apple of her father's eye, but he was away in the Army for most of the time, and her mother appeared to show little interest in her, much preferring her younger brother. Each of that woman's own deliveries was followed by a severe attack of post-natal depression. Subsequently she remained well until her daughter gave birth when she again became depressed in an almost identical manner. At this stage she was treated with psychotherapy, during the course of which she acknowledged the way in which birth stirred up all her painful memories of feeling rejected as a toddler.

Cultural and social factors
Post-natal depression occurs in all social groups and in a wide range of different cultures. Though class, colour and creed do not by themselves alter the risk, it seems that where support for the mother is substantial there is less chance of serious upset. Lack of support and additional stress through poor housing, other family problems and financial worries, are obviously likely to make things worse.

How to overcome post-natal depression

Just as there is no single cause, there can clearly be no single way of overcoming this problem. 'Normal' reactions to childbirth, baby blues, and post-natal depression may be best thought of as varying degrees of reaction to a stressful event, rather than thinking in terms of 'normal versus abnormal' or 'illness versus health'. You would not expect everyone witnessing an accident to react in the same way, and who is to say that the person who faints and is upset for several days is any less normal than the person who carries on as though nothing had happened.

Understanding this, it will be seen that the same general principles apply to the whole spectrum from normality to the most common forms of post-natal depression. Making mother-care a priority (one of the points in the Action Plan below) is as important for women whose reactions might be characterised as normal as it is for those whose condition might be diagnosed as depressive.

The Action Plan and subsequent questions and answers which expand the Action Plan, are likely to enrich the experience of *all* mothers.

123

The Babyshock Action Plan

Before the birth

Remember you are not alone

Emotional upset is a natural part of childbirth, and there is no need for you to feel inadequate or in any way ashamed at whatever you may feel after the birth. If you expect to feel only sweet and loving feelings for a rosy-cheeked smiling little infant, rather like the ones pictured in baby clothes' catalogues or on cereal packets, rid yourself of the illusion now.

Find out about the post-natal experience

Inform yourself. Over ten years ago a group of obstetricians showed that systematic education of expectant mothers reduced the risk of serious post-natal disturbance. The twelve months following the delivery are likely to be tougher than the nine months before. If you read books, concentrate on those which cover more than the ante-natal period.

Seek out and share your feelings about childbirth with like-minded mothers-to-be or friends who have seen it all before.

Organise post-natal support

Know where you will be able to get help when you need it. There is no point in trying to anticipate *all* the problems before they arise. What every mother needs (and especially the first-time mother) is a network of people who can be relied upon. So organise some of the following:

Enlist your partner's support around the time of the birth, at ante-natal classes (at least once), and encourage his interest and participation in everything you learn about the post-natal period of adjustment. It will be an adjustment for him as well as you.

Get to know your local health visitor.

Enlist the help of dependable friends/relatives. However independent you feel now, at least record the telephone numbers of a handful of trusted friends

and ascertain what they can be relied upon to do – for example, attending you for a short period when you arrive back home, visiting you in the maternity ward, buying any last minute items (such as your maternity bra – how will you know now the precise size you will take when the milk has come in?), looking after your other children while your partner visits you in hospital.

Make out a list of 'panic numbers'. You may never need to use it, but problems you may want help with could range from getting a babysitter at short notice to getting advice when the baby takes you to the end of your tether. **Ref 2:1**

Make informed decisions about the delivery
Within the limits of what is possible and medically desirable in your case, arrange for the delivery to take place where you feel happiest (see **Hospital or home?**). From your doctor's point of view the physical safety of you and your baby takes priority, but your own peace of mind, the presence of someone you trust, and an early re-union with your baby after the delivery are the three most important factors in minimising psychological upset.

After the birth

Share your feelings
If you feel despondent or depressed, force yourself to confide in someone sympathetic whom you trust. It doesn't matter who it is, provided the person is a good listener and is able to encourage you to talk. Particularly air those negative and guilt-making thoughts and feelings in an accepting, non-judgemental atmosphere. Later, consider the available post-natal organisations. **Ref 2:3**

Learn to delegate as much as you can
Adopt the idle woman's attitude to housework; and if you are a perfectionist and cannot be happy unless everything is just so, either break the habit or draw up a list of essential and non-essential chores and share them. Remember that a happy mother is more important to child and family than an immaculate home.

Make 'mother-care' a priority
As far as is possible, endeavour to make essential baby-care activities a matter of routine (e.g. washing nappies). But be prepared to replace less important baby-care activities with mother-care activities (e.g. your relaxing daily bath is much more important than the baby's). Above all see your own stability as the ultimate aim rather than other people's judgement of your 'expertise'.

Most important, raise heaven and earth to get some time on your own (however little) every day.

Grab some sleep whenever you can.

Minimise stress-making situations
Minimise unnecessary stress in the first few months. For example, adamantly refuse to move house; if possible arrange matters so that your husband does not change his job within three months either side of the birth; refuse to act as hostess to well-meaning friends and relatives.

Don't expect too much of yourself or your baby
Try to get out of the house at least once a day, but do not expect to be able to take up outside interests or part-time work for the first few months. In general, don't expect too much of yourself during this period. Also, be prepared to be flexible in baby-care routines – no baby runs according to a pre-set timetable.

Re-new your self-confidence
"Not to have confidence in the body is to lose confidence in yourself." Simone de Beauvoir. Have a look at our exercise programme. Even if you have doubts that exercise is for you, see what it does for you as a daily discipline in those early months.

Look through our section of sexual advice.

125

The Babyshock Cycle

One of the commonest catalysts of post-natal upset is a failure to recognise the symptoms and appreciate how they can feed on one another. For this reason, we have encapsulated in visual form the symptoms of babyshock and the factors which make women more vulnerable to such upset.

Pages 128 to 154 then expound the themes of the earlier Action Plan in practical terms.

Hormonal changes
Physical exertion of labour
Psychological stress of childbirth
Post-natal physical discomfort

Despondency
Fatigue
Unhappiness
Dissatisfaction
Irritability

Irrational fears
Feelings of guilt
Loss of self-confidence
Sense of inadequacy
Feeling of aloneness
Loss of libido

Utter confusion and perplexity

Physical symptoms of anxiety: Palpitations
Dry mouth
Racing pulse
Dizzyness
Sense of unreality

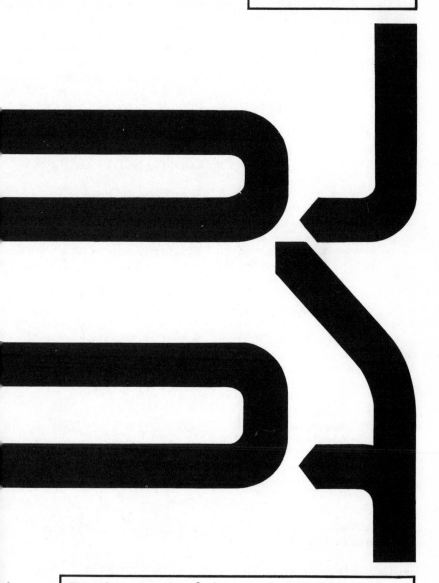

Failure to recognise the symptoms of babyshock

Excessive separation from baby following birth
Inherent personality traits
Own childhood memories
Difficult baby

Psychological factors of role change
Unsupportive reaction from those around, particularly the father

BABYSHOCK

Extreme depression

If you have the symptoms we describe and our Action Plan (page 124) is in your case inappropriate or inadequate, call your doctor. He may recommend that you see a psychiatrist, not because he thinks you are going insane – although it is possible you may fear this – but because psychiatrists have been trained to provide the treatment that will make you better. Whether the doctor treats you or the psychiatrist, the treatment will probably consist of psychotherapy or tablets, or a combination of the two.

Tablets

You may be put on a course of anti-depressants, for example Tryptizol, Tofranil, Bolvidon, Ludiomil, Prothiaden or Sinequan. These all work in a similar way and have to be taken for at least ten days before you can expect to feel any real benefit. It has been shown in a number of careful clinical trials that these tablets not only significantly improve mood, but also prevent a relapse once you are feeling your normal self again. You cannot become dependent on them and they have no long-term effects. While you are taking the tablets your mouth may become dry and you may feel drowsy. For this last reason, your doctor may suggest that the tablets be taken before going to bed. The drugs will pass into your breast milk, so if you want to continue breast-feeding, discuss this further with your doctor.

Psychotherapy

The psychotherapist is trained to help you explore your problem, to give you an understanding of the reason why you are suffering from post-natal depression, and to work out with you ways of over-coming your difficulties. Treatment may be relatively short, say one hour a week up to ten weeks, and may be carried out individually or in a group.

If I have had post-natal depression, should I consider more children?

There is absolutely no reason why you should be depressed after the birth of your next baby because you suffered over this one. But if you have had a bad time with the birth of your first child, you will obviously think twice about having another. Remember that each birth will differ enormously and one difficult experience is frequently followed by subsequent 'walk-overs'.

CONFIDENCE IN YOURSELF

What happened to my self-confidence?

It is a hard coincidence that when a woman is deprived of her freedom, earning power and status as a working person, she is simultaneously flung into the most demanding period of domesticity. Her whole being is submerged in her baby's demands, and while she was very much the centre of people's interest and concern while pregnant, now it's the baby, baby, baby . . .

In traditional societies, after the first few months of motherhood, mothers would take on a number of activities which took them outside the single-minded care of their children. Relatives and friends were close at hand and responsibilities tended to be shared within the community. Mothers were not only child-bearers and child-rearers, they were teachers, nurses, potters, weavers, farmers, and often revered temples of wisdom within their own homes. It is quite normal for mothers who enjoy their children, and even the housework, to still feel restless and dissatisfied. Provided she can make adequate arrangements for surrogate care, there is no reason why a new mother should not seek fulfilment outside the home, go back to work or even start a new career. But now in the very early period, that is hardly the question. It is difficult enough to get time on your own even to think, and it is very likely that you will feel your own identity drifting away in a sea of nappies and baby food. Because our society is not organised around families but around work, a mother can feel lonely, completely outside the 'real' world, cut off from the company of other adults. Despite the supreme importance of her new role to society and family alike, she may feel of no importance.

It is a terrible indictment of our values that young mothers feel worthless because they are not earning money. As if producing goods was more significant than producing people! Radical exponents of Women's Liberation may have done as much to devalue the role of the mother at home as centuries of male chauvinism. With the right to work and enjoy equal independence being trumpeted far louder than the right to respect for the role of full-time mother, the vulnerable first-time mother in the hectic first few months can be forgiven for feeling depressed. Interestingly, as this book goes to press, the British Liberal Party has incorporated in its manifesto the principle that full-time mothers should be paid by the State for their endeavours. Perhaps the tide is turning.

Many of the irritations involved in looking after a new baby are due to a feeling of being pulled in two directions at once, of wanting some other thing but *having* to tend to the baby. Most new mothers feel like this; most new mothers expect too much of themselves. In the end you have to acknowledge that for a while at least you need to be ninety-nine per cent a mother. And the more devoted and single-minded care a baby receives in the first few months, the more quickly he will become independent – *not* the reverse. Knowing this may help get you through, but how in practical terms can you get the most out of it?

How can I build up my self-confidence?

The maxim that if you look good, you'll feel good applies never more than during the emotionally draining period after childbirth. New mothers in hospital look positively shell-shocked. By the time you get home and confront the chaos and other demanding members of the family, you may feel worse. If you *can* make the effort to look glowing, it is a tremendous boost to your self-confidence.

Buy yourself at least two feminine and practical long nightgowns. They will   129

probably be full and floating and, if you are breast-feeding, should fasten down the front. As your weight reduces and you practise our exercises, you will soon be able to get back into your pre-pregnancy clothes.

Next you have to decide what is important about your looks. What will depress you if you let it go? If it is your hair, then take the time to wash it every day, even if you have to have your baby in the bathroom with you, snuggled say in a sea of protective towels on the floor. If it is your nails, paint them and re-paint them as often as you like. Whatever your obsession is, indulge it. If you like perfume, buy a large spray of your favourite scent. If it is getting your stomach flat again, turn to page 132 and do those exercises.

Get out of the house at least once a day. This relatively simple goal will make all the difference about the way you feel. Maybe it is just to the shops to begin with, then a walk in the park – the best way to meet others in the same situation. Perhaps neighbours within walking distance become a welcome distraction. Self-confidence is enormously boosted by seeing other mothers who have seen every stage and come through at the end. Self-confidence fades fastest when you have no contact with others. If you have moved to the area recently, turn to the section on maternal isolation (page 151). There are ways and means at your disposal.

An additional tip is the simple expedient of having a fully-stocked baby bag so you are ready to walk out at any given moment, perhaps in answer to an invitation to visit someone for the afternoon. In the bag keep two spare nappies, liners (if the nappies are not disposable), one spare babystretch, bib, bonnet, two nappy pins, an extra woolly cardigan, a rattle or toy, two plastic bags for putting soiled nappies in, and tissues. This bag will then be ready for any eventuality. You can just grab the bag, baby and papoose and be off.

Give yourself a break. Don't hesitate to accept offers from grandparents, neighbours, godparents, anyone you know well who has had some experience of babies. The more you put off this first outing as a *free* woman, the more difficult it will be and the more trapped you will feel. Soon you will begin to arrange a baby swop for the afternoon with someone in a similar situation.

Do some non-baby thing every day. This can be as simple as listening to a certain record (really listening, settling down, forgetting everything else, preferably with your feet up) or as ambitious as getting just a little work done if you are lucky enough to be able to earn money at home. Even if it is just a half hour of another kind of life, tear yourself away from that baby and that routine just once, and you can enjoy another dimension to your life besides motherhood.

When can I go out in the evening?

You'll know when you are ready to go out and leave the baby with someone else for the evening. What will probably trouble you more is a lack of confidence that anyone can care for him properly. Leaving him with relatives is the best method to drive this idea from your mind. If you are breast-feeding, either leave a bottle (the occasional bottle-feed will not drive him from the breast unless he is being inadequately nourished by the breast) or express some of your breast milk into a bottle. If relatives or trusted friends are not near at hand, satisfy yourself that the babysitter for hire is trustworthy by getting recommendations from friends who have used her before. Leave a telephone number of where you will be and start by leaving the baby for a short period, say an hour and a half, building this up with each outing.

Where can I find babysitters?

Your average babysitter is a neighbour or the child of a neighbour. Rates vary enormously from one area to another. In Britain, the hourly rate varies from the price of a bar of chocolate to the price of a gallon of petrol.

Babysitting services can be found through the Yellow Pages and these usually provide sitters with child-care experience. But a very good source is your local hospital since nurses are frequently in search of extra money. Why not put up an advertisement on the notice board of the nearest nurses' home?

Friends or post-natal groups may lead you to another alternative increasingly popular among mothers – the baby-sitting circle. These are usually formed by groups of parents in the neighbour-hood on a share basis.

Regaining confidence in your body

It is important that everyone takes part in some form of exercise. But it is never more important than after you have had a baby. There are people who believe the myth that exercise is only for sporty or energetic people and that, unless you are really exhausted after exercising, there is no point to it. This sort of exercise is for all kinds of people. *Everyone* who follows the course on a regular basis will notice a real improve-ment – the body will function better, the mind will become more alert, and you will be able to cope with all sorts of daily crises more efficiently and positively.

Establishing a routine is very important, especially so if you are to exercise at home. The best way is to set aside a time during the day to fit in comfortably amidst your daily work. Perhaps follow the exercise programme with a warm bath. With a new baby on your hands it may seem impossible to set aside the same time every day. How will you

know in advance when the baby will cease his demands long enough to allow you to settle down and concentrate, as indeed you will need to. When the baby is a few months old, settle him on a mountain of cushions beside you and see how mesmerised he becomes as he watches you. You must discipline yourself to keep strictly to your routine, otherwise you will see no results. Of course, missing exercises on occasional days when you are extra tired, unwell or really too busy, will not harm your schedule. Guard against becoming so obsessed that a day missed here and there troubles you. The most harmful thing is exercising erratically. Five minutes one day and over an hour a few days later is dangerous. You will not see any results from your exercises, worse still you are likely to strain parts of your body. A regular exercise programme followed at home every day for about twenty minutes will yield spectacular results in a matter of weeks.

An alternative to exercising at home is to enrol at a once or twice weekly class in which you have an interest. Why not get your man to babysit and go along to these classes with a friend? Not only will it help you establish a routine but will encourage you to keep fit at home. It might also do your self-confidence good as you enjoy this self-centred interest which is so complementary to motherhood. The many possibilities include swimming, keep-fit, yoga, tennis, ballet dancing and disco lessons. Your local paper or local 'What's On' magazine will give you all the necessary details.

Before you begin, take some trouble with your diet. It is almost impossible to exercise after eating a heavy meal. It may even be dangerous if you happen to suffer from stomach cramps. Also remember that it is bad to drink vast quantities of liquid during or after any particular exercise. This too may lead to stomach cramps.

The clothes that you wear must be comfortable... a leotard (not too tight) or a T-shirt and optional tights. Too often concentration and thence enjoyment disappears just because tights are too short or a leotard slips off the shoulder.

Exercise is very personal and you must guard against comparing yourself with others in a group. Some people may be more supple than others, so work within your own abilities. There are no limits to exercise and improvement is always possible by stretching and trying a little harder each time. When you know you are doing your best you will feel a real sense of achievement.

Don't begin to do all the exercises as soon as you get home after the birth of your baby. Start with the exercises that you have been given in hospital and gradually work up to the more difficult ones here. It is important to take things very slowly at first, paying special attention to the spine (being careful not to place too much strain on it, otherwise you could put your back out).

If you are tired, overweight, and depressed, you should feel revitalised as your rate of metabolism increases and you gain more energy. Although you will start to see improvements in the body quite soon, the long-term effects will take longer to show. Depending on the way you were before exercise commences, these will include an overall weight loss or gain.

Post-Natal Exercises

1. The Bottom Squeeze – relaxation breathing with pelvis tipping.

2. The Knee Squeeze – backs of thighs, bottom, stomach.

3. The Forward Stretch – spine, backs of legs.

4. Stomach Muscles (1).

5. The Cat – spine, bottom, legs.

6. The Front Thigh Stretch – front thighs.

7. Stomach Muscles (2).

8. Waist Stretch.

9. Relaxation.

These exercises are designed to tone up specific areas of the body. If you keep to the routine you will soon get back into shape now that the baby is born. Many muscles will have been stretched during pregnancy and the birth itself. Abdominal and vaginal muscles in particular need to be toned up to bring the natural elasticity back as soon as possible.

Breathing is especially important after the birth. See page 60 for a guide to diaphragmatic breathing. Remember always to relax the abdominal muscles as you take in air, then pull them in gradually and very tightly as the air is expelled.

Try to establish a rhythm in your exercises with the inhalation and exhalation of air. This will be much easier once you have memorised and understood the exercises completely.

If time is really a problem a combination of exercises 1, 2, 4, 5 and 8 is a good ten minute alternative programme.

The Bottom Squeeze

How to tone up your bottom and vaginal muscles and relax the spine

We have already discussed this exercise in full in the ante-natal section. Pay particular attention to the vaginal squeeze and your abdominal muscles and make sure that this is part of the post-natal programme practised every day.

The Knee Squeeze

How to firm up your thighs, your bottom and strengthen the stomach

Lie on the floor with your knees and ankles together and your knees in the air as shown in' the illustration. Keep your arms relaxed by the side of your body.

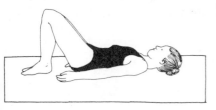

Breathe in, expanding the lower abdominal muscles.

Breathe out and squeeze the bottom and knees together, at the same time lifting the back off the floor.

Breathe in and lower the spine carefully down on the floor. Do this gradually, feeling each vertebrae of your spine touching the floor one bv one. Keep your knees pressed together all of the time.

Perform this exercise four times, but on the fourth time stay in the raised position, keeping your knees squeezed tightly together. Breathe in and stay there. Breath out, squeezing the knees together a little harder. Breathe in again and breathe out, squeezing your knees together, then breathe in and slowly lower the spine to the floor. The small of your back and bottom are the last parts of your body to touch the floor.

The Forward Stretch

How to tone up the legs and stomach and stretch the spine

Sit in an upright position with the backs of your knees pressing into the floor and your feet flexed.

Breathe in, stretching your arms upwards towards the ceiling.

Breathe out and reach forward over the legs as far as is comfortable, pulling your stomach muscles in as tightly as possible.

Lower your head towards your knees in a gradual controlled motion.

Do this exercise four times and on the fourth time let your body remain over your legs and grasp your ankles or calf muscles (depending on how far you manage to stretch over your legs).

Breathe in, holding firmly.

Breathe out, pulling yourself down towards your legs.

Repeat this 'pull' three times.

Breathe in, stretching your arms upwards towards the ceiling and lead in to exercise 4.

Stomach Rolls

How to flatten your stomach
If you find this exercise difficult at first place your feet under a heavy piece of furniture or a large cushion.

Having breathed out at the end of the

last exercise, breathe in again, stretching your arms towards the ceiling, your knees bent with your feet firmly placed on the floor.

Breathing out, roll back as slowly and gradually as you can, feeling each bone of your spine touch the floor in turn. Feel your stomach flatten as you roll back.

Breathing in, stretch your arms along the floor so that your upper arms are positioned beside your ears.

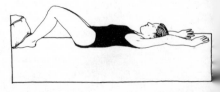

Breathing out, sit up as slowly as possible, keeping your arms by your ears, your head being the first to leave the floor and then each bone of your spine in turn.

Breathing out, drop your head between your arms, pulling your buttocks in, pulling your stomach in and rounding the spine.

Do this exercise four times altogether and over a period of time gradually increase this to eight times, placing your arms behind your head, your hands interlocked and elbows pressed back.

It is absolutely vital that this exercise is practised slowly and smoothly with no jerky movements.

Do this exercise slowly and with great control six times. Hold the last exhale position and breathe in, drawing your left knee up to your forehead and keeping your back, buttocks and head in the same position as they were.

The Cat

How to relieve back ache and tone up your bottom
Kneel on the floor with your knees directly beneath your hips and positioned about ten inches apart. Place your hands on the floor with your arms directly beneath your shoulders and about the same distance apart as your knees.

Breathing in, hollow your back and lift your head, and let your buttocks go up as high as possible.

Breathing out, extend the left leg along the floor until the knee is straight, then tighten the buttock muscles and raise your leg up in the air as high as possible. Raise the left leg in this way four times, then raise the right leg in the same way, another four times.

BABYSHOCK

The Front Thigh Stretch

How to tone up the front of your thighs, your stomach and bottom

Kneel in an upright position, your feet touching but your knees about twelve inches apart. Stretch your arms out in front of you, forming a right angle with your body.

Breathe in, letting your stomach muscles expand.

Breathing out, lean gradually backwards but maintaining a straight line with your body. Feel the fronts of your thighs stretch and pull your stomach muscles in tightly.

Do this exercise four times in all.

Stomach Muscles (2)

How to flatten your stomach, ease your hip joint and the muscles around the pelvis and the legs

136 Lie on your back with your hands flat on the floor underneath the small of your back. Bend your knees into your chest with your feet together and flexed.

Breathing in, stretch your legs up to the ceiling forming a right angle with your body.

Breathing out, slowly lower your legs towards the floor keeping your knees together, your legs straight and your stomach pressing down towards the spine, which is in turn pressing on your fingers.

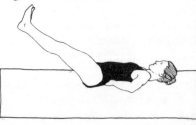

It is important not to reach the point when control is lost in the abdominal muscles. This will happen if your back arches and you let your abdominal muscles bulge. Stop before you reach this point as the purpose of the exercise is immediately lost.

Repeat this exercise four more times.

There is a variation to this exercise

which you might like to tackle as you become more confident. As you lower your legs breathing out, hold them when they are at an angle of about forty-five degrees to the floor and practice bicycling. Another alternative, at the same point in the exercise, is to scissor each leg sideways across the other – the right leg over the left and the left leg over the right.

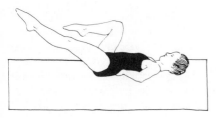

The Waist Stretch

How to regain your waist and tone up each side of your body
Stand with your feet apart, looking straight ahead.

Breathe in, stretching your arms above your head, palms uppermost and your fingers interlocked.

Breathing out, bend your body to the right side from the waist, keeping arms

and legs straight. Feel the stretch along the left side of your body.

Breathing in, return your body to the upright position.

Breathing out, repeat the exercise but this time to the left and feel the right side of your body stretching as you do so.

Breathing in, return your body to the upright position.

This time as you breathe out make a wide circle to the right, a little faster than before.

Breathing in, stretch your arms up to the ceiling.

Breathing out, repeat the wide circle but this time to the left and then repeat the whole exercise – right stretch, left stretch, right circle, left circle.

BABYSHOCK

Relaxation

How to relax your head, neck, shoulders, arms and spine

Stand up straight, breathing in a controlled fashion, perform this exercise which is designed to relax each part of your body in turn very slowly and gradually. Start by dropping your head forwards. Then feel your spine drop forwards due to the weight of your head, one vertebrae falling at a time. Keep your arms loose and your shoulders relaxed and take lots of time to do this exercise. When you reach as far as you can to the floor, just hang there and bounce gently, feeling heavy, floppy and letting all the tensions drop downwards and out through the finger

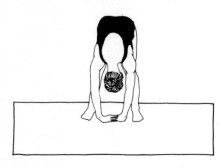

tips. Stay like this for a few minutes. Gradually start to roll back up the spine to the normal standing position. You are completely reversing the original procedure and again you should feel each vertebrae of your spine straightening out in turn, finishing by gradually lifting your head until you look straight ahead.

FATIGUE, AND PRACTICAL AND EMOTIONAL SUPPORT

After experiencing the physical rigors of childbirth, it is hardly the best moment to adapt to a demanding life which is often characterised by interrupted nights. Someone once described pregnancy and birth as a long steep hill at the top of which was a beautiful castle. The only trouble was that when you got to the top and opened the door, the washing-up hadn't been done.

Some mornings you may wake up bursting with energy, full of vigour and pleased that the long-awaited baby is indeed here at last. But be prepared at midday to feel like collapsing. It's a curious sensation because it may hit you suddenly. Wait until the baby is asleep (it doesn't matter what time of day it is), take the 'phone off the hook and climb into bed. Grabbing sleep whenever possible is a luxury allowed in old age. After the birth it is a necessity, so force yourself to forget the chores, and if you cannot sleep, turn to the relaxation exercises.

Relaxation is vital. Remember that there is an important distinction between entertainment and relaxation. Entertainment is not always relaxing, but can also provide an extremely important and revitalising change for you.

As far as household chores are concerned, you really must not attempt any heroics. You *cannot* be the perfect wife and mother with a neat home and a well-fed husband and a peaceful baby all at once.

If a neighbour offers to do your shopping, fine. If she doesn't then don't be proud, ask (although this is something best fixed up before you have the child). If your partner can cook at all – even if it's only the one dish – let him do the evening meal.

Either ignore the housework or adopt the maxim: "The quickest way to clean a room is to tidy it." Pile all books and papers into one pile (preferably hidden), plump up the cushions, look around and see what difference you have made.

Put out of sight those things which need doing but which won't matter if they are left undone (e.g. polishing the silver). Forget about hoovering, invest in a carpet sweeper if you haven't already got one, or do the carpets piecemeal with a brush. Either use duvets on your beds or give up bed-making for a few months. Do not iron shirts.

Keep two buckets for soaking nappies; be *rigid* about keeping the kitchen and bathroom basins free of nappies. It is better never to have to face the dispiriting sight of a dirty sink full of soiled nappies.

If you can possibly spare it, keep one room entirely free of baby paraphernalia. Then there will always be one spot in which you can really relax.

Keep all baby-care things in one place, preferably a place with running water (bathroom or bedroom rather than kitchen). If you own a proper changing stand and keep all the equipment on its shelf, or if you use a long flat surface of anything (say a coffee table) with a shelf beneath it, keeping to this rule will be no problem. If breast-feeding then temporarily install a comfortable chair into the baby-care room.

Be prepared to ignore all rules. Be prepared to improvise. Enlist your partner's support.

How can I enlist my partner's support when he is never here?

Things are not as bad as they were. Never before has the atmosphere been as conducive to fathers participating in childbirth and baby-care. A pregnant working woman will discover that even hard-bitten male colleagues, hitherto reticent about their domestic life, suddenly regale her with information about *their* wife's epidural and contractions, and exactly how far she was dilated by the time they got to the hospital. Such frankness, interest even, after centuries of dismissing childbirth as a woman's concern, can only be welcomed.

It is up to both of you to translate this interest into the practicalities of parenthood. Time and again new mothers complain of their partners' lack of support.

"We've had our problems in our relationship since the baby was born. I've had to get myself into this set routine and turn my life upside down, but he doesn't see it. For example, I make sure that dinner is ready when my husband comes home, so I get mad when he's late and it spoils. The mornings are relatively quiet, but then it's non-stop, seeing to the elder child, collecting him from school, getting him tea, feeding the baby, then my husband's dinner, then all the cleaning up. When he comes in he's all over the baby for a few minutes, has his dinner and that's it. I'm shattered by seven p.m. Yet he can't see why I'm tired. He says, 'You've had nothing to do all day; I've loaded so many thousand planks.' Just because I don't clock in and out."

This sheer bloody mindedness is something mothers have previously had to put up with in silence. In the past the responsibility for bringing up children was set firmly on a mother's shoulders by experts and society alike. Today, the roles of father and mother are no longer so readily defined.

BABYSHOCK

From the baby's point of view, men are capable of being just as good 'mothers' as women and must be encouraged to participate. It may be that most women prefer to care for the baby most of the time, and that most men prefer not to, but there are no grounds for justifying this on the basis that "it is better for the baby".

Your partner's role in looking after the baby should be as extensive or as limited as the two of you want. You simply have to sort this out between yourselves. Is it practical for your partner to be absent from the home for less time? Or do you feel, as one mother put it, that your husband *"participates by working to provide the money to keep our children"*. In her case (and many others) this was right for both parents and provided no cause for concern on anyone's part: *"The interesting thing is that she (the baby) is now very interested in her father and demands more of his time. It's interesting that she has saved each step, like standing on her own and bottom shuffling, to be first done in his presence."* Is your partner really opting out of his responsibilities or is he slow to adjust to your new role, thus becoming the punch bag for your natural resentment?

"For five years I was totally independent. There was no problem. Then, all of a sudden, I was not only financially but emotionally dependent upon him. When for five years you have lived with somebody and never asked anything of them, the idea of then asking, needing something from them, seems so stupid. The point is that beforehand my great thing was not having to rely upon anybody, wanting to look after myself, being totally independent. That all changed. I had to change. And I just couldn't cope with his lack of support. When I went out to work it helped me enormously; I began to meet people, I felt attractive again."

Work out quietly and carefully how, in practical terms, you can share the responsibilities and joys involved in caring for the children. You may decide to divide night feeds at first. Perhaps you could do it on alternate days, or maybe he could take charge of them at weekends. Try to work it out on the basis that at least one of you – not necessarily the same one all the time – gets enough sleep. The decisions you make have to be taken together with the happiness of the *whole* family (not just you, the father or the baby) in mind. You may decide to make for radical change. Would you do better to enlist paid help and substitute that for some 'extra' luxury, rather than fuel a running emotional battle with impractical aims and possibly dire marital consequences? It is all too easy to seize on a partner's lack of support as a whipping horse for the grind and insularity of very early motherhood. It is just as easy for a man to turn a blind eye to the fact that his new role involves readjustment to parenthood too. Which is it in your case? Try and evaluate the situation in the cool light of day. If it is counselling you need then do not be afraid to see your doctor or Marriage Guidance Counsellor. **Ref 2:4**

"Looking back on our marriage before we had her (the baby) it seems that we just existed side by side. By comparison it was a very superficial relationship. It was only after her birth that I think honestly for the first time I actually loved him. It's difficult to explain, but I feel now that we have a closer relationship than ever before."

How can I make my sex life better?
Parenthood changes the pattern and substance of your relationship with your partner. It can be the best thing about having children. However, in the early months it is perfectly natural to find sex becoming a thorny problem as well as a significant factor in your finding it difficult to come to terms with your new role.

Most women lose their libido for at least a month after childbirth, and sometimes for very much longer. Fathers may also lose interest and be unable to obtain or maintain an erection. Be prepared for this and don't take it personally. If it does happen appreciate that if you do turn it into a problem, the problem will very likely resonate between you and make you both less confident sexually for some time to come.

The following is a check list of reasons why many couples lose interest in sex following the birth of their baby.

Tiredness

This is inevitable and inescapable and no sign of inadequacy. Your partner may need to be reminded of the demands of your twenty-four hour a day job at the start. If he wants sex, then obviously it is in his interest to help you out with the chores and allow you an afternoon nap.

Feeling unattractive

Feeling good about yourself and sexual desire generally go together. If your body is flabby and overweight and your favourite clothes don't fit; if the smell of nappies, puke, and milk overpower your favourite perfume, it is hardly surprising that you lose your libido.

Becoming baby-centred

In the first few months the baby is bound to come between you and the things you enjoy. This is perfectly natural, but some effort from both you and your husband to preserve your interests in things other than the baby should be made.

For a start, most people find it difficult to become passionate when the baby is in the same room. There is no reason to believe that making love in front of the baby is going to do the baby any harm. You may have learned that Freudian psychoanalysts warned that witnessing the ' primal scene ' (i.e. hearing or seeing the sex act) leads to life-long neuroses. This prediction was based on studies of a few rich, neurotic Viennese some eighty years ago. Had the psychoanalysts studied the English working class in the nineteenth century, when families very often shared the same bed, they would probably have come to a different conclusion.

If having the baby around does distract you, however, why not find someone to have him for a couple of hours. Some people may find this solution too embarrassing to set up. An odd aspect of our prudishness is that most people would be quite happy to ask a neighbour to look after the baby while they went to the pub, but less ready to do so to be alone together to talk, cuddle or have sex. Are such things really less important than drinking?

Alternatively, why not time your love-making to the baby's nap? Night and day tend to become one during the first few months of the baby's life, and you should be prepared to snatch your enjoyment when you can.

Your partner

With the new baby as the centre of attention, many fathers feel their noses (and sometimes their penises) put out of joint. You can choose to take the view 141 that that is *their* fault and leave them to cope with it. You might be tempted to do so since you have enough to worry about with the baby's demands. On the other hand, a man who experiences emotional and sexual neglect is less likely to involve himself wholeheartedly in the new family and make the necessary readjustment from lover/partner to lover/partner/father. Unless you enjoy a 'ducks and drakes' type of relationship, shutting your man out is going to do nothing for your own self-confidence and sexuality.

When can we resume sex?

This question is often asked by the man and defies a definite answer. Every couple is different, no matter who tells you what you ought to be doing. Mutual masturbation on the day of the baby's birth may be as normal for one couple as for another not to have sex for three months following the birth. It depends on you. Many couples resume sex about six weeks after the birth of their child. Remember that whenever you decide to have sex, even if menstruation has not recommenced, you should (if you want) use some form of contraception. You may be fertile.

Your vagina is likely to remain sore, when anything is put into it, for at least ten days. If you have had an episiotomy you will probably be uncomfortable for somewhat longer.

Your breasts, whether or not you breast-feed, are also likely to remain sensitive or downright sore for a similar period. Most labour is straightforward and as far as your subsequent sex life is concerned there should be no difference following a normal natural childbirth and an uncomplicated birth involving spinal anaesthesia.

An episiotomy is done partially to make the delivery easier and also to prevent your skin tearing in an uncontrolled way. It lessens structural damage to your vagina and reduces the likelihood of discomfort during sex after birth.

The scar left by the episiotomy sometimes causes a 'catching' sensation during intercourse. This should gradually disappear as the scar fades, and can usually be avoided by asking your partner to shift his position ever so slightly.

The shape of your vagina is determined by the muscles that surround it. Although these muscles have to stretch enormously during childbirth; there is no reason for them not to return to their former shape within one to two months after the delivery. You can help them regain their tone by reducing your weight to normal. This will improve both your own and your lover's sexual enjoyment. It is also a good idea to practice some simple exercises known as Kegel Exercises.

These were originally introduced by an American gynaecologist called Arnold Kegel, who was involved in helping women who had developed urinary stress incontinence due to weak pelvic muscles. In the course of his work he accidentally discovered that many of his patients reported a greatly improved sex life. Sexual enjoyment increased and some women who had previously not experienced climax, became orgasmic. This makes sense because the muscle which controls the flow of urine also controls the size of the vagina. Though claimed as a great new discovery by sex therapists in the States, these exercises, or simple variations of them, have been taught to Geisha girls in Japan for centuries.

Practical instructions

The best way to start is when you are sitting on the lavatory about to pass water. Sit with your legs separated and your forearms resting on your thighs so that your weight is supported by your thighs. Allow yourself to pass a little urine, say about a teaspoonful, then cut off the flow of urine by contracting the muscles on the floor of your pelvis (i.e. between the tops of your thighs). After this, continue to stop and start passing urine about a teaspoonful at a time. With a little practice you will feel the muscle tug as it contracts, and, having located it, you will be able to contract and relax it at will, whether or not you are passing water. Just a few minutes practice each day, when you are watching television or waiting for a bus, will tone up this important muscle and thus tone up your vagina. To prove to yourself that you are doing the exercise correctly, put your finger in your vagina and feel the squeeze. Then practise on your partner's finger or penis.

If you are unlucky and have had a long, painful, delivery you may be put off sex for a variety of reasons. First, because, bruised and battered, you just want to be left alone particularly in that area of your body, and this outlook tends to persist if your first attempt at intercourse after the birth is uncomfortable. Second, you may decide you don't want to have any more children and this may subconsciously colour your attitude towards sex. Don't be afraid to talk about this. Probably your health visitor will be the best person to talk to, though the important thing is that it should be someone you trust and someone who is not in too much of a hurry. Remember your body has remarkable powers of recovery, and it is much more likely that a fear, such as the fear of future pregnancies, will disrupt your sexuality than any physical damage.

Sometimes you may hear that if your partner is present at the delivery, the impact on him will ruin your future sexual relationship. This is rubbish. Usually the reverse is the case since his presence increases the intimacy between the two of you. The only exception is where the man is pressured into attending much against his will, a good reason for not allowing yourselves to be fit in with a fashionable trend just for the sake of it.

Will breast-feeding affect my sex life?

There is no escaping the fact that the breast is a part of the body that stimulates sexual desire as well as an organ for feeding babies. Such anatomical confusion does not only involve women, since an equal amount of emotional and psychological muddle may be caused by the fact that the penis is used both for excreting urine and for sexual pleasure.

If you decide to breast-feed it is a good idea to ask your partner what he feels about it. Don't be surprised if he says he likes the idea and that it makes him feel good being with you while you are breast-feeding. On the other hand, don't be surprised if he says that it turns him off. Talk about it and you will soon find out whether or not breast-feeding has any bearing on your sexual relationship.

When should I seek help if things are not working out?

Again there is no rule book answer, but various milestones on the way back to a normal relationship are worth noting.

Your post-natal check
This will usually be one month after the birth. The doctor will probably offer to examine you, and if you are still sore anywhere in your pelvis it is a good idea to have an internal examination. If this proves painful it is usually due to the after-effects of the stitches (if you had an episiotomy) or alternatively the result of a small internal sore commonly known by doctors as an 'erosion'. In either case the remedy is straight- 143

forward and will not involve an operation. If nothing medical is wrong and yet you still feel sensitive, go slowly and if you are not well lubricated use artificial lubrication. Whatever you do avoid tensing up as this habit may continue long after the pain in your vagina has cleared up.

Three months later
If one or other of you has simply gone off sex, seek help when it leads to bitterness and arguments. Although sexual feelings are resilient and will normally recover in time, it may be a great help for both of you to talk through the difficulties. You may manage this on your own, but surprisingly you may find it easier to talk with someone else – a close friend or relative, or even a professional helper. Sex is no longer a taboo topic.

Is it possible to ease the immediate post-natal period by following a domestic routine?
Virtually every baby book suggests a daily routine, a pattern of precise predictability: a six a.m. feed, an extra sleep for the mother; a ten a.m. feed and bath, etc., etc. In practice very few mothers can follow or develop their own routine of this sort, because babies are just not like that.

"I kept a detailed diary after bringing my first baby home, and no one day is remotely like any other. One day it is: 'Phone calls, flowers, clockwork feeds, bliss!' The next it is: 'L. fractious again – despair.' The next: 'L. awful – entire morning washing, feeding, then L. sick.' Followed by: 'L an angel, feeds every three and a half hours.' And the next day: 'L. not angel. Never have time to get anything done.' Looking back on it now, I remember that on some days the nappy rinsing, soaking, handwashing (I had no machine), feeding, soothing and winding the baby would mean that I didn't even get downstairs till the

afternoon. On other days she would go down peacefully straight after breakfast and leave me free for the entire morning – then I'd feel cheerful and in control. Life depended totally on the baby's constantly changing moods and habits. You just have to be prepared for a totally flexible life."

There is certainly no such thing as a typical baby or a typical baby-care routine. But you can help yourself by imposing certain elements of routine on the chaos.
Learn a few tricks to make life easier:
After each nappy change prepare yourself for the next – put out a fresh folded nappy and liner in place.
Take some of the pain out of erratic feeding patterns by preparing a vacuum flask of tea, Horlicks or an iced drink to have when you are night-feeding. Keep a supply of light reading by the chair you use for feeding.
Stick to breakfasts and lunches that need minimal preparation: yoghurt, cereal, fresh fruit, cottage cheese, boiled eggs, wholemeal toast.
First thing in the morning wash the nappies you soaked yesterday and make up a fresh solution for the ones used overnight. At all costs keep up the supply.

Why does my baby cry?

The commonest reason for fatigue is the constant crying of some young babies:

"I was really taken by surprise. She used to scream every night for the first three months until three o'clock in the morning. I used to sit downstairs, smoking, or playing Patience, so that I wouldn't go up there and strangle her. It was a terrible three months. No one tells you about these things or about the effects of consistent sleep loss."

For much of this century, there has been so great an emphasis on the effect of the environment upon a baby's personality that little consideration has been given to the fact that babies are born different. At birth, various differences in babies are immediately apparent – one is their levels of arousal. Some babies are nearly always drowsy, while others remain happily alert for some time. Soon after birth, most babies can be quietened by holding or rocking, but subsequently they polarise into two groups – those who soothe easily and those who cannot remain awake and alert for long without becoming irritable and upset at the least provocation. It is not known how long these characteristics last, though in one recent study the babies who slept less in the first ten days of life were still sleeping less at fourteen months. They were also likely to be the babies who were most easily upset and cried most – so, sleep patterns and temperament seem to be related. If you have several children, you will be well aware of how different they can be.

"It's extraordinary · how both babies were totally different. The first one didn't cry at all, but the second cried from one feed to the next for the first few weeks. He would also wake every two hours right through the night."

But if it is your first baby who cries a lot and is difficult to soothe, you may easily feel you are at fault – especially if friends keep telling you how easy *their* babies are. Just feeling that you are in the wrong makes the problem harder to cope with, and what may begin as a minor problem may get out of perspective. It seems likely that some baby battering arises in this way; it is not just that some babies are more difficult and make more demands on their mothers, they can also make their mothers feel that every cry is a reproach, a demand, that they be better mothers. Very young, or unsupported mothers are particularly vulnerable to this kind of anxiety.

If your baby cries a lot and you are doing all you can to look after him, it may very possibly be a result of his sensitive temperament, rather than your mothering. You need support from those nearest to you, in particular the child's father, but also some sense *in yourself* that you are doing your best and that if you carry on doing your best it will turn out all right in the end for you and your baby.

At two weeks the average baby cries for two hours daily. As with all averages, this means that for every perfect baby who rarely cries there is another who spends a third of his waking hours 'enjoying' this activity. Crying usually means hunger, pain, discomfort, tiredness or loneliness. Most parents are ready to accept the first four of these but some find the fifth hard to credit. If your baby settles after he is fed, rocked, changed or cuddled, then everyone feels rewarded. If not, then the process can be demoralising.

How can I stop him crying?

Advice may be offered that your baby should be left to cry. This pre-supposes that the baby has no good reason for crying, that you can close your ears to his distress, and that the house is distant enough from neighbours who might telephone the authorities. Rarely do all 145 these apply. The subject has been well studied and there is no evidence so far to suggest that the baby who is picked up when he cries, deliberately cries the more in order to be picked up. Babies do not learn to manipulate their parents in this way until near the end of their first year or later. In fact, newborn babies who are soothed the instant they cry, subsequently cry less frequently and for a shorter time than those who are ignored in the early days.

In the early months, crying is the baby's only means of communication. Since hunger is the most common cause of a baby's crying he will probably settle if you feed him. He may have woken early because he was too sleepy to take sufficient at the last feed, or if breast-fed, because the mother had less milk than usual. Alternatively, he may be too cold (small babies are most comfortable at a much higher temperature than most homes are kept, i.e. somewhere in the high 80°F).

Perhaps he just wants to be held or walked about, or rocked before he can fall asleep again. When your baby was in your womb he was rocked every time you moved, so it seems to be the most effective way to calm him in the early months. Presumably, it makes him feel more at home. He is also held in a very small space in the womb and many babies prefer being wrapped around firmly or swaddled when they are put down to sleep.

Another common belief is that babies should sleep all the time, except when being fed and changed. You may feel that if yours does not sleep something is wrong. In fact, the amount of sleep is very variable between babies and some healthy babies never sleep more than twelve hours a day, while fifteen hours is about average. If your baby is wakeful he may get bored lying alone and need some company, or something inter-esting to look at, like a mobile above his

cot. Other tricks that have been successful include putting on a low-noise vacuum cleaner close to the baby – the noise is soothing – or driving him around in a carrycot in the back seat of a car.

It is particularly hard to comfort a crying baby when you are very tired or when you have a lot of other things on your mind. If you *are* tired, and there is no one else around to relieve you for a while, you can at least make yourself as comfortable as possible. If you can, sit down on your most relaxing chair; get yourself a coffee or a drink; you may find that music soothes both you and the baby so try the radio. If any other pressing jobs can wait then it's better to forget them for the moment, than feel torn between them and the baby.

Above all, do not be afraid that you're spoiling your baby by comforting him when he really needs it. The more sensitive you are to him now, the easier he will be later. Being sensitive does not mean always jumping to pick him up at the least sound. He may just have a little moan and go back to sleep, but it does mean observing what makes him better and what doesn't, and acting on it.

Some cries are more important than

others. An unwell or lethargic baby who develops a shrill or screaming cry needs urgent medical attention, as does a baby whose cry turns into a grunt or mere whimper. Repeated, sudden, totally unexpected bursts of crying lasting a few seconds or minutes alternating with quiet may imply a particular form of gut obstruction. A baby who cries unexpectedly and apparently with pain may have colic or he may have an ear infection or possibly a cold with a blocked nose (babies find it difficult to breathe through their mouths). All these need medical treatment.

In general however, the importance of crying is the effect it has on a family – frustration and exhaustion. There is no hard evidence that an anxious mother causes a frequently crying baby rather than the reverse, although paediatricians and psychiatrists frequently make both assumptions. Because an individual may cope better with her crying baby if she is rested and not at the end of her tether and because it is always easier to cope with someone else's crying baby, admission of a particularly difficult baby to hospital for a few days may cure the problem. After all a nurse is on duty for 35 hours a week and not 168! If you are desperate, seek your doctor's help. Alternatively talk to other mothers or make use of your list of 'panic' numbers'. **Ref 2:1**

How can I stop him waking in the night?

If you are lucky, by four or five weeks your baby will settle to a regular sleeping pattern which allows you time for relaxation in the evening and sufficient sleep yourself. But one of the commonest problems mothers of young babies have to suffer is the regular night waking of their infants.

The traditional view, which you will certainly hear and you may believe, is that night-waking is due to parental mishandling, or spoiling. Recently, there have been three carefully conducted studies examining this very point. It is worth looking at the results of one of the very recent examinations of a group of children over the course of a year.

59 children aged 15 months produced 13 regular night-wakers.

59 children aged 21 months produced 13 regular night-wakers.

57 children aged 27 months produced 16 regular night-wakers.

Nearly a quarter of all babies *are* regular night-wakers. They are likely to have been so virtually from birth and continue to be difficult to settle to sleep throughout their infancy. The study examined occasional wakers as well as regular wakers and it is interesting to see in the results that there are no convincing differences in the ways that parents of regular wakers set out to solve the problem – except that parents of regular wakers tend to try *more* methods. The main methods employed included:

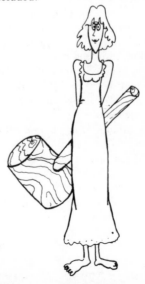

BABYSHOCK

Staying with the child

Taking the child to his parents' bed

Administering a bottle or dummy

Picking up and cuddling

Allowing to cry

Sedation

This study, and many others, lend no credence to the view that babies cry *because* they are over-indulged, stayed with or taken to the parents' bed. Further there are no differences between bottle and breast-fed babies nor between more intelligent and less intelligent children. Nor can it be shown that the wakers have fussier, more over-protective, or more neurotic mothers.

The one big difference that does show up is that wakers are far more likely to have suffered complications around the time of birth. How this provokes them into night-waking is unknown.

In some cases it may be related to enforced early separation between mother and child. See page 115.

If your child wakes a lot it is, therefore, unlikely that your doctor or health visitor will be able to tell you why. But it can be seen that it is very unlikely to have anything to do with the way you are handling him. Don't be afraid to try out all the methods suggested above, leaving sedation till last. Be consistent over a period. Breaking habits is harder than making them.

The problem of night-waking is worse for breast-feeding mothers as the father cannot take over. The best way to deal with this is to have the baby in bed at your side. It is possible to give her the breast while you sleep or doze. The baby is in no danger of suffocation. If your partner cannot sleep through the assorted gurglings, gruntings and snufflings then clearly one of them will have to go – temporarily or intermittently – into another room. If the father goes, there is no need for your sex life to disappear and set the stage for marital disaster.

Sedatives

Some babies are a desperate problem. Night after night of interrupted sleep would sap anyone's moral. It does not take a great feat for one to imagine that it might even provoke you into hitting your baby. In such a case, when all the other methods have been tried, it is perfectly reasonable to use a sedative. Doctors' babies are not uncommonly given gin or brandy, but there are more efficient drugs available. Most commonly prescribed are Promethazine (Phenergan) and Trichlorperazine (Vallergan). These are antihistamines designed for the treatment of allergies such as hay fever or itching from eczema or insect bites. All antihistamines have a sedative side effect and here the side effect is being used as the main purpose of the prescription. These drugs are safe. Some doctors prefer to prescribe them for two or three weeks only to break the habit while others are more generous.

Many women feel guilty or ashamed at sedating their baby, perhaps because of their belief that they must hold the key to the baby's behaviour somewhere in their own actions. But in fact, you may not be able to influence this exhausting habit in any other way.

Why do I sometimes feel like hitting him?

Post-natal stress is so well acknowledged in Britain that it is recognised under the law. Under the Infanticide Act of 1938, a mother cannot be found guilty of murder if she kills her own child within twelve months of the birth, provided *'the balance of her mind was disturbed by reason of her not having fully recovered from the effects of giving birth'.*

"When I said to my husband that I can understand women battering children, he came up with the classic statement that he was scared of leaving me with her during the day. Now that's hardly the way to bolster up somebody that needs help. Fortunately for me I have a very vivid imagination and every time I came near to tossing her across the room, I imagined the consequences – bones sticking out like this. So I never actually did it. Half the time I was just crying because I had thought of doing it."

"I lost control of myself once, and after that I'd lock him in his room for fear of what I might do to him. Then he began ripping up his bedroom, so I had a good excuse to go to the doctor because I had a delinquent child . . . although the problem was so transparent and all I really wanted was for the doctor to see what was going on in me. I felt so guilty, yet I was worried about admitting the hatred I sometimes felt towards my son. Then I began watching other mothers at the church coffee mornings and I began to notice that all was not well with them either. I talked with the others a bit about how I felt, and when I could see that I was not judged or accused and that they also had similar feelings, I began to feel better."

"One evening she had cried and shrieked and yelled, and I hit her and threw her in the cot, literally threw her in and slammed her bedroom door. Then I came outside into the front room and just stood there shaking and crying. Finally she just cried herself to sleep and I went back into the room, into the nursery, and she was just lying there asleep . . . but she was sort of crying in her sleep, you know, sort of sniff, sniff, and her face was wet. And I just sat there on the floor and held the bars of her cot and I thought I cannot do this any longer. I just loved her so much. I desperately wanted to pick her up and cuddle her. But I was just so frightened that she would wake up and cry . . . and then I knew that I'd just hit her again."

Any mother who claims never to have felt an urge to hit her child is either a liar or an angel. Tottering on the precipice

of violent action directed at your child is one of the most difficult and psychologically distressing experiences a mother can have. Combined with everything else, a woman's awareness of her potential as a batterer can and does start many women on a descent into depression and anxiety. It is extremely important therefore to consider three available facts:

Firstly, virtually all mothers, at one time or another, have felt like inflicting violence on their child. Few carry out the act.

Secondly, in every passionate relationship violence is never far from the surface. Part of the enjoyment of sex is violent just as feelings for a child can swing from protective love to absolute fury.

In conclusion, every battering requires three elements: a parent ready to injure; a child to provoke injury; and an event that provokes the final straw.

What can I do if I feel like hitting him?

Beware of the suddenness of the anger you feel – that is the thing to try to avoid. When you feel it happening, take stock of what is going on in your life. Are there too many outside pressures? Is the baby exhausting you by keeping you awake half the night? Are you bothered by conflicting advice? Are you getting as much help as you need from the baby's father?

If you are suddenly overwhelmed with anger about your child and are scared that you might hurt him, *telephone someone.* Alternatively, first go to a neighbour and cool down. It is better for yourself to rely on friends rather than medical treatment in sorting out conflicting ideas on emotions aroused in raising children. **Ref 2:1 Ref 2:2**

However awful you feel about every- 149

thing, someone will listen to you even if they have nothing much to say or offer; the contact with another person will be a life-line. Even better, if you have a friendly neighbour willing to care for your baby just for a few hours, take the opportunity to escape and do something totally non-domestic. This will help you get your problems into perspective.

There are other sources to turn to: **Ref 2:3**. It is through organisations such as those listed under the reference that a great deal of support and practical help can come. The chances are that you will meet someone else who feels as awful as yourself. In sharing these feelings you begin to understand the source of them. Once they are out in the open they do not fester in quite the same way as before.

At a Welfare Clinic in North East London for mothers of pre-school children, 40% of working-class mothers and 20% of middle-class mothers had been prescribed sedatives such as valium. Not only does this reflect the amount of stress women are experiencing, but also that drug prescription is the most common method of dealing with it. Sedatives are over-prescribed and condemned by many as the easy way out. But there is no escaping the fact that many people find them invaluable,

particularly people who have neither the time nor the energy to get to the bottom of their problems and really sort things out. In those circumstances, tablets are the best prescription.

If you find yourself becoming anxious, with unhappy memories of your own childhood coming to mind, admit these openly to yourself. An unhappy childhood is never forgotten, only temporarily suppressed and has an uncanny way of looming its ugly head when a child of your own is born. If you can find a way of accepting that these unhappy things did occur but resolving that they will not happen to your child, then childhood can be a happier time for you both. This may sound far easier to do than it really is, but you can find relief in writing things down privately and/or seeking a trained counsellor or therapist to help you sort things out. Seek such professionals through your doctor rather than responding to advertisements for therapists in newspapers or magazines. Some of those advertising are skilled; others are not. When you are upset, you are not in a good position to discriminate. However terrible or shameful things might seem to you, a trained person can help you see them in a different perspective – and it is unlikely that you will shock them, as they have heard harrowing stories before!

What happens if I have injured my child?

If you find yourself in the unhappy position of having injured your child, being suspected of having done so or being at risk of doing so, within a day or two a meeting will be convened between your doctor, health visitor, social worker and – if he is involved – the hospital paediatrician.

If other professionals have been involved with your family, for example a probation or NSPCC officer, they will be invited to the meeting as well. They will share the information that they hold and try to make four decisions:

Is the child at risk?

Should he be entered on a register of 'At-risk children'?

If he is at risk, is it safe for him to stay at home?

Who should have the job of helping the family?

At many such meetings, often after a 'tip-off', it is decided that there is really no case at all, no action is taken and *no file is kept*. If the baby is thought to be at risk he is entered on a list kept in the Social Services department which is then available to all hospitals. The majority of such children remain with their parents and a 'key worker' is appointed to help them through there difficulties. This is usually a Social worker, health visitor or a NSPCC officer. This person tries to be a friend and counsellor, to help with practical problems and be available whenever needed in a crisis.

No such meeting can remove a child permanently from a parent – *only a court can take such actions*. However, if a child is thought to be in serious danger, a magistrate may file a 'place of safety order' at the request of a social worker or police inspector. This entitles the agency to remove the child from home for a maximum of twenty-eight days. If the conference is convinced that returning the child home will put it in serious danger, a care order will be sought. There is a court hearing and the parents may be legally represented. Moreover, there is a right of appeal. It is scarcely necessary to point out that such action is uncommon. **Ref 2:2**

Why do hospitals treat my child as if he were battered when I take him in suffering from a simple accident?
If your child attends hospital after an accident you may become aware that questions are being asked which suggest the doctor is suspicious. But if he does not ask such questions, he is failing in his duty to your child. Unhappily, deliberate injury is so common that such questions are now virtually routine. Such an inquiry might even be in your own interest. If your child suffers an accident you should not feel insulted when the details are carefully explored with you. If you do feel angry, try to consider whether it was because there was a tiny hint of carelessness or distraction which allowed the accident to happen.

What can I do about feeling so isolated?
Feeling alone is, next to fatigue, the most commonly quoted problem of new motherhood. Possibly there has been a big change in your way of life involving the end of a career and a subsequent loss of acquaintances and friends. You are there alone with your baby and feel cut off from the outside world – life even. One mother described the feeling which for her manifested itself in a complete inability to communicate:

"When I came home I was on a tremendous high. I felt thin! I was high! Everything was a party mood for about two days. Then I went from that to an awful, curious, blank void when I couldn't communicate. I remember a friend coming round who has children, yet I shut myself off completely. I couldn't take conversation. I think I was just terribly tired. That went on for about three weeks. We'd always joked about 'PND' – but then I realised that I'd got it! I was having post-natal depression. And yet I could do nothing about it. Telephone conversations were completely one-sided. I couldn't remember what I had said. People would turn up (as arranged apparently over the 'phone) as a complete surprise to me.
"I really felt on my own – couldn't communicate to anyone. My poor husband. I 151

remember watching The Wild Bunch on television – it was a really good film, but I couldn't bring myself to talk about it; it was communication. I couldn't get the baby out of my mind; it was baby, baby, baby ... I was fine when I picked him up. I was always all right with him.

"Then one day, three weeks later, I got up and realised I wasn't feeling like that anymore. It happened as suddenly as that. I said to myself, 'Right, I'll go out today, talk to people.'"

The young mother felt a purposeful need to talk to other mothers, share her experiences and extricate herself from the gloom of the past few weeks. But she didn't know anyone in a similar situation, had lost touch with her old friends as she had moved house prior to the birth. As she explains:

"It's easy meeting other mothers when the kids are going to school. But if you don't know anyone, you don't know which school to go to, which shop to go to, anything . . . There's nothing more lonely. So one morning I thought the only way to meet someone is to go somewhere where there are mothers who have just had babies. So I went to the Clinic and I thought, 'I'll look for a mother! A mother my sort of age with a child of the same age as mine. I sat there in the Clinic for hours looking at other mothers as they came in. It's an awful thing to admit that you have sifted through people in this way, but I felt that it had to be someone I would get on with or there's no point.

"Finally, I noticed Carol. She came in, sat down for a while and went in to the surgery with her child. I couldn't get up the courage to say anything, couldn't think how to go about it. Then just as she was going out of the door I thought to myself, 'Well it's now or never,' and rushed up to her and blurted out, 'Excuse me, but I've just moved here. I haven't got any friends – will you be my friend?' She looked absolutely astounded and then said, 'Of course, come and have tea!'

"Through meeting her, I met somebody else and the ball started rolling. But if I hadn't done that, I'd still be sitting here wondering why no one was talking to me."

A priority is to get to know your health visitor. She will put you in touch with post-natal groups. Some women resent health visitors and think they are prying into their affairs, interested only in whether you are going to batter your child. It is worth taking space, therefore, to describe what it is that they do.

Health visitors
Health visitors have a statutory responsibility to visit all new mothers. One

will be notified when you leave hospital and should be knocking at your door within a matter of days. If she isn't and you feel you could do with some friendly, informal advice, ring your doctor's surgery or your hospital and tell them that you would like to see her. Health visitors are State Registered nurses with midwifery experience (six months' experience as a ward sister is desirable but not compulsory). They will spend one year at a university or polytechnic studying such subjects as sociology, psychology, law, the development of the individual, public health, paediatrics. Altogether the course of preparation will have lasted about five years. They are then employed by the Area Health Authority and attached to doctors' surgeries, health centres or child welfare clinics. One health visitor talked about her role and the kind of problems which health visitors are used to dealing with:

"First of all there is an introductory meeting at which I tell the woman what my job is about. I let her know what beneficial services are available to her, grants, allowances, etc. Then we generally settle down to some basic questions about feeding – how often, whether to breast or bottle-feed, whether one can overfeed, whether the child is getting enough – changing, etc. We discuss worries about weight gain, should a child be woken during the night feed, what are the 'normal' developmental stages, and other specific problems. I find there is a need to help structure new mothers' days – times for feeding, sleeping, when a mother can get out, when she can leave the child, what arrangements must be made, etc. But most frequently I will be called upon to counsel women in some stage of post-natal panic. If mothers ask definite questions, I can and will give definite answers. In general however, there is this woolly thinking, a sort of amnesia due to a combination of shock, exhaustion and a general failure to realise their extremely high expectations of themselves.

"I make three points:

1. All babies are different. Some cry and demand more than others and no amount of conscientiousness will change that fact.

2. Organisation is all-important in the sense that if a child is asleep between two and four o'clock, a mother must grab herself some sleep and not dash to the ironing board or look for alternative energy-consuming entertainment during this time.

3. I reassure women of their abilities to mother.

"More and more I find mothers complaining of a sense of dissatisfaction with their role, which may be as strong in some as a sense of post-natal panic. Frequently this leads on to the question of whether or not to go back to work. I encourage them to list their reasons and examine the list in the clear light of day. If asked, I advise where to find surrogate mothers and emphasise the need for consistency in the sense that au pairs who change jobs every so often are no good at all.

"Finally I warn mothers about the mountain of conflicting advice they will receive from well-meaning people during this period of their lives."

Post-natal groups

These groups may be invaluable for some, though they are not the answer for every mother's feelings of isolation since they can tend to foster competitiveness – the 'who has the brighter baby' syndrome.

There are all sorts of post-natal groups springing up in this country in answer to the pleas of mothers to meet other mothers and share their feelings and problems. Some strive to meet women's needs to get away from domestic chit-chat and meet lively like-minded people who enjoy intelligent conversation not limited to babies, babies, babies. **Ref 2:3**

BABYSHOCK

Here are some comments from mothers with experience of post-natal groups:

"I think there is a great need for post-natal groups, although I do think that the National Childbirth Trust type of group is a wee bit middle class – coffee mornings and teas. I think it is better to encourage small crèche groups where you can leave your child for a short while . . . But whichever you choose, it certainly helps at the beginning to know that you are not the only one whose baby doesn't eat or sleep."

"My National Childbirth Trust post-natal support group was very good indeed. In fact I think most post-natal groups are useful especially in the very early stages. I had a lot of help from neighbours, but for those who don't, a group which offers practical advice, shares feelings, reassures, and offers friendship outside the group is a very good idea."

"I would have liked to sit down and chat to someone about everything, but all they wanted to do was to talk about how fantastic their child was and what was yours doing now. I wasn't particularly interested in how their children were doing, so it sort of petered out for me."

"Anything like that, that's optional, has got to be a good idea as you'll only get people who need it."

10
Motherhood
-how do I know
that I am doing it
properly?

"The problem was, and I suddenly
realised it, that I wasn't giving any of
myself to the child. If I didn't give
any of myself to her, I'd never get
anything back.'

Motherhood - how do I know that I am doing it properly?

Is my child developing normally?

As parents, people are naturally concerned with the growth and development of their children.

Paediatricians use very exact charts which are drawn up strictly according to chronological age, but since no two children ever develop at the same rate, either before or after they are born, professional charts depend for their usefulness upon the professionals' ability to take into consideration a number of other factors.

When carrying out a test, the skilled examiner will try to relate all the results to a pattern and not reach his conclusions from individual passes and failures. He will make an allowance for the baby's feelings and the strangeness of the surroundings. Even then, a firm conclusion may be impossible. The range of normality *is* so wide that the examiner may be able to say little more than that later re-testing is necessary. In itself, this does not mean that your child is developing abnormally.

The following chart has been drawn up for mothers who are suspicious that their children are slow developers and want to know at what age they should seek advice.

BABYSHOCK

Problem	When to seek advice
"I think he may be deaf"	Immediately
"He doesn't seem to see things"	Immediately
"He shows no interest at all in his surroundings"	Immediately
"He can't hold his head up when lying on his stomach"	4 months
"He hardly makes any sounds"	5 months
"He squints"	6 months
"He won't take a toy from me"	8 months
"He can't sit on his own"	9 months
"He doesn't turn towards a hidden voice"	9 months
"He won't stand on his feet when I hold him"	12 months
"He can't get across to me what he wants"	18 months
"He has no words"	18 months
"He can't climb"	20 months
"He can't walk"	20 months
"He doesn't copy activities"	2 years
"He doesn't join two words"	2½ years
"He can't feed himself"	2½ years
"He can't name pictures in books"	3 years
"He still is wet during the day"	4 years
"He is still wet at night"	6 years

Competitive mothers
Because of this wide range of normal behaviour it will not help either you or your baby to indulge in being competitive about your child's abilities. It may be fun to delight in them and it is rare for a mother not to boast of them, but quite a number of mothers interviewed decided not to attend post-natal support groups because of this tendency to compare babies competitively.

Most attributes which may be the subject of competitive games amongst mothers bear no relation to long-term intellectual or physical development. Some, such as toilet-training – frequently an obsession of first-time parents – reflect parental expectation and coercion rather than the child's cleverness. The only conceivable use of such games may be to stimulate the mother of a backward child to seek professional advice, but the price paid is unnecessary anxiety in mothers of quite normal children.

When might a normal baby fail clinic tests?

If your baby was born prematurely, remember that he should be judged as though he had been born on his expected (not actual) date of delivery. But there are some other babies who fail to reach the usual developmental stages expected by 'screening' tests. They may inherit unusual developmental patterns from their parents. Some families are late talkers, some late at being dry at night, others late to walk. Amongst the last, are the babies who fail to make the usual progression from rolling over to crawling, pulling to stand, cruising round the furniture and finally walking – these are 'bottom shufflers', 'commando crawlers' and 'rollers', all of whom are late in walking but turn out to be normal in the end.

Amongst those who are late talking are a group who are also late writing, or awkward at fine movements and may have difficulty in catching a ball later on or tying laces. They may also not be sure whether they are right- or left-handed. While such children may be said to have a defect in their awareness of the position of objects in space and their own limits (so that their eyes and hands do not co-ordinate well with each other), most of them will turn out perfectly normal, although unlikely to play at Lords or Wimbledon.

During tests, some babies are just not very curious; they do not explore. If offered a toy, they just gaze at the examiner's face. If placed on the floor, they remain Buddha-like, contented and unmoving. Or they might simply be in a bad mood, 'sickening', or tired when tested.

Some babies are 'floppy'. Their muscles are soft and they are often double-jointed. Without any protest, they can be manipulated into a passable imitation of an advanced practitioner of Yoga or a Circus contortionist. Rest assured that the vast majority of these babies are normal, although in the first year they seem delayed in 'motor' power.

Can I hurry along my child's progress?

The answer lies in how much the particular task has to be learnt and how much it is innate. No child can walk before he has achieved the necessary muscle power and co-ordination, a sense of balance, and the correct 'saving' reflex movements if he begins to fall. Training is highly unlikely to speed these up in a normal child. Moreover, there is no evidence to suggest that the child who walks at nine months will be a better athlete or more intelligent than the later walker who sat on his bottom until he was two years old or was contented with pulling himself up on the furniture.

BABYSHOCK

Walking-frames and bouncers are great fun, but there is no evidence that they hasten a baby's ability to walk. Indeed some children may actually be delayed by them. A baby-walker inhibits the use of a child's buttock muscles, which are essential to keep the hips straight when standing and walking. Bottom-shufflers and 'floppy' babies, in particular, should not use walking-aids.

On the other hand, language and social behaviour are learnt and are most certainly encouraged by parental involvement. The more you talk to your baby, the more you read him stories, the more you point out shapes, colours, and pictures, the more advanced will be his intellectual development.

What might go wrong?
Accidents in the home

Between the ages one year and four, forty per cent of all accidents occur in the home. Every year in Britain, forty thousand children under two years of age – most of them boys – receive medical treatment for accidental injury. These statistics underline the importance for parents to accept, in practical terms, the difference that a child will make to family life. All parents, for their own peace of mind and their child's safety, need to modify their homes in such a way as to prevent or at least minimise the possibility of accidental injury.

If you think your home is a safe place, lie on the floor so that your eyes are on the same level as your child's.

Look for and replace or repair: Faulty electrical gadgets

Sharp-cornered furniture

Sharp-edged toys

	Uncovered electrical sockets which will admit objects poked at them
Avoid:	Slippery polish
	Glass which splinters
	Pots and pans which tip easily (consider buying pan guards)
	Unguarded fires and paraffin heaters
	Baby-walkers which topple
	Unlit stairways. Use stair gates and teach stair negotiation early
	Widely opening upstairs windows
	Using polythene bags (or confine to an inaccessible place)
	Cats
	Pillows for babies
	Nightdresses (pyjamas are less likely to set on fire)
Lock away or place out of reach:	All medicines, including iron tablets, liniments and skin preparations
	Cutting and mixing utensils with unprotected blades
	Household materials, such as bleaches, disinfectants, furniture polish, turpentine and paraffin
	Weedkillers and pesticides
	D.I.Y. tools
	Kettles and all hot liquid containers
	Matches and candles
Check:	Your hot water supply does not exceed 52 degrees C (125 degrees F)
Supervise:	Babies on beds and other flat surfaces above the ground
	Toddlers in the bath
	Children in swimming or paddling pools

Children should be taught what articles and activities are dangerous from infancy. You should make clear what is really unsafe and what is merely anti-social. Eating tablets must be absolutely banned, whereas eating slugs does not really matter. Children who are scarcely allowed to do anything soon realise that their parents' objections are unnecessary and are more likely to have accidents than those allowed some freedom. **(See also Appendix)** 161

A first aid kit

2 Crêpe bandages 5 cm × 2.25 m

12 Gauze squares 7.5 cm × 7.5 cm

Cotton wool

Eyebrow tweezers (for splinters)

Scissors

Elastoplast

Insect repellent

Sun-tan lotion

Zinc and castor oil cream (for babies only)

Witch hazel

12 Paracetamol tablets (older children only, see below)

100 ml Paracetamol elixir

100 ml Phenergan elixir
100 ml Kaolin paediatric mixture
4 Kwells (or other travel sickness preparation)

4 Piriton tablets

Dosages

Paracetamol 500 mg tablets
Age 6–10, 1 tablet, 6-hourly

Paracetamol elixir 120 mg in 5 ml
Age 4–6, 15 ml 6-hourly
    1–4, 10 ml 6-hourly
    –1, 5 ml 6-hourly

Paracetamol is for relief of pain or high temperature.

Phenergan elixir
5 mg in 5 ml for wakefulness due to acute illness. Also useful for travel sickness, ear ache, allergic reactions to bites or stings.

Kaolin paediatric mixture
Age 5–8, 15 ml 4-hourly
    1–5, 10 ml 4-hourly
    –1, 5 ml 4-hourly

Kaolin is used for diarrhoea.

Kwells (300 mg)
Age 3–7, ½ tablet

Kwells are for travel sickness.

Piriton (4 mg)
Age 2–5, ½ tablet twice-daily

Piriton tablets are used for allergic reactions to bites and stings.

AGE	TYPE	NOTES
0-1	TRIPLE i.e. DIPHTHERIA/ TETANUS/WHOOPING COUGH POLIO (by mouth)	3 doses starting at 3-6 months
1-2	MEASLES	
SCHOOL	DIPHTHERIA/TETANUS POLIO (by mouth)	
10-14	BCG (Tuberculosis)	skin test first
	GERMAN MEASLES	Girls only

Illness – immunisation

The table shows the immunisation programme currently recommended in Britain. It is normally carried out at an Infant Welfare Clinic.

Media reports, the establishment of an organisation representing 'vaccine-damaged children' and recent government legislation on compensation have created much anxiety in the minds of parents. Most of the anxiety has centred around pertussis (whooping cough) vaccine. Before discussing this, the effects of the other vaccines are dealt with.

Diptheria and Tetanus

These vaccines are extremely safe, the only problems being occasional redness and swelling at the injection site.

Measles

The vaccine produces a mild form of the disease, so that a rash, fever, sore eyes and throat, and a runny nose may occur five to ten days after the injection. Some children should not be given the vaccine, for example those known to be allergic to eggs and children with asthma or eczema. Your GP will advise you if you are in doubt.

Polio

Occasional side effects are diarrhoea and a rash.

Pertussis (whooping cough)

This disease still kills between five and fifteen children in Britain annually. It leaves dozens – and in an epidemic year hundreds more with lung damage. The illness may last for three or four months and is most severe in babies, who may turn blue and briefly stop breathing several times daily at the height of the illness.

There is not space to discuss fully the evidence concerning the possible dangers of this vaccine. The following points are worth noting:

A vociferous and well-organised pressure group has provoked Governmental acceptance that the vaccine may have been injurious.

The medical profession generally, and its experts on vaccines in particular, recommend that the vaccine *should* be given.

Thirty-five million doses of vaccine were given to British infants between 1964 and 1977. There were thirty-two reported cases of encephalopathy (brain fever) and one hundred and forty-two of convulsions.

Every day of the year, one in every fifty thousand children has a convulsion. The number of convulsions and cases of brain damage occurring soon after vaccination has not been proved to be more than would occur by chance on those days.

163

BABYSHOCK

Three in every thousand babies die unexpectedly in their first year and some of these, by chance, will happen after a baby is given vaccine. There is no evidence that 'cot death' is more common in the days or weeks after vaccine than at any other time.

Some of the children claimed to have suffered vaccine brain damage have now been fully examined and other causes for their disease found.

Since 1976, every children's specialist in the country has received a letter every month reminding him to report every child suffering inexplicable brain damage. Preliminary results have failed to show that this occurs more frequently after vaccine than at other times of the year.

Notwithstanding the above, it is possible that pertussis vaccine may cause brain damage in something between one in one hundred thousand and one in a million children. This is less than the incidence of such damage after, say, measles, between three hundred and three thousand times less than a 'cot death', and fifty to five hundred times less than dying from a household accident.

The vaccine should not be given to children subject to convulsions or those known to have pre-existing brain damage or those who have suffered an unpleasant reaction to a previous dose. As you may now realise, it is difficult to make a balanced, logical decision. It is easier to bear an 'Act of God' than an 'Act of Man'. Every time your child takes some medicine, crosses the road, plays in a room on his own, goes to the beach, breathes in smoke from your cigarette or develops tonsillitis, there is a risk of illness, injury or death. It is impossible to live without risk. It is no longer fashionable to automatically accept the advice of experts: in this case, the 'experts' have no particular axe to grind, but, with only a few exceptions,

well-informed doctors still recommend the full immunisation schedule.

Illness – when should I seek medical advice?

There are many excellent books which parents can refer to for advice about child illness (page 246). To forestall parental anxiety, here are occasions when if you do not seek medical advice problems could develop.

Any illness in a child under six months

Any illness that makes you exhausted, irritable, or at the end of your tether

Discharging ear

Shortness of breath or abnormally rapid breathing. Remember that in the first weeks, all babies breathe fast and irregularly

Croup – a noise when breathing that suggests obstruction to the flow of air, especially if the child's ribs are sucked in as he breathes.

Convulsions

Inexplicable drowsiness. Children are often drowsy when they have a high temperature and this is not in itself worrisome

Diarrhoea or vomiting for more than a day

An ill child whose colour becomes extremely pale or blue

Inexplicable bruising or bleeding

Stomach pain for several hours that he cannot be talked out of. The child in pain who lies still is likely to be iller than one who threshes about.

Less urgent problems which require you to take advice include:

Squint in a child over six months

Suspicion of poor hearing

Headaches in a previously well child

Hernia

Unexplained limp

What kind of mothering does a baby need?

Between your child's birth and the time when he begins to 'strike out on his own' as a walker and talker, an immense amount of physical and emotional growth takes place. In the past, books and experts stressed the dire consequences should mothers fail their children during this 'all-important' period. Emphasis was given to specific training practices such as whether to breast or bottle-feed, whether feeding should be 'demand' or 'schedule' or a mixture of both, when and how the child should be toilet-trailed, etc. Early motherhood was seen as a craft

which every mother must learn with the implication that there is a goal of 'perfect motherhood'. Some experts added further to mothers' burdens by stating that babies are born as 'clean slates' on which you have the sole responsibility to write your own impressions during the early months and years. It is not surprising that many mothers, inundated with advice from an unending stream of baby-care manuals, tend to experience feelings of inadequacy and guilt that they are not measuring up to apparently more successful mothers.

This 'good-versus-bad mother' ideal is a dangerous picture of what motherhood is really about. There are no pre-ordained clear-cut rules – 'You *should* do this; you *mustn't* do that'. Babies do not need perfect mothers, only 'good enough' ones. A perfect mother, if she existed, would hardly prepare her child for our imperfect world. Babies can and do tolerate their mothers 'getting it wrong' some of the time. Early mother-hood may be a full-time job, but there is far less likelihood than many suppose for a mother to 'get it wrong'.

What is a 'good enough mother'?

Adequate or 'good enough' mother-hood is a concept introduced by Winnicott, a distinguished paediatri-cian and child analyst. He noticed that far from there being a need for mothers to strive to measure up to high 'craft' standards in the early months, they are in a sense 'programmed' to meet their children's requirements. Further, it was shown that babies are born with certain innate dispositions and abilities which are not the result of the way their mothers handle them, but some of which are actually designed to promote closeness between mother and child.

To begin with, the baby's task is survival. Winnicott observed the unusual state of the new mother which predisposes her to provide an environment suitable for 165 the survival of the newborn. He called it 'primary maternal pre-occupation'. because he felt that this phrase helped explain her extraordinary sensitivity to her baby's needs. Most people, throughout their lives, are far more aware of their own needs than anyone else's, however generous they may be. A new mother usually displays a growing capacity to be more intensely aware of her child's need than of her own. She is 'tuned-in' to him, so that she notices the most subtle changes in his physical and emotional states and ponders what they mean. She gradually learns to interpret his facial expressions, his gurgles and cries, and uses her knowledge to respond to him in the most appropriate way. Because of her preoccupation with her baby, the mother becomes an expert in him; no one else knows or understands him as she does. As Winnicott said, it is not cleverness or specialised knowledge which the mother needs at this stage; the secret of her skill lies in her *devotion* to her infant. Today it is known that maternal love may take time to grow (page 114), but given reasonable support it will grow in the end.

It may be difficult to imagine the world of a newborn baby. Imagine suddenly finding yourself in another world, full of unbelievably strange objects. Everything is novel and unexpected, nothing can be taken for granted. An important part of early mothering is a capacity to empathise with the baby's experience, and to try to respond intuitively to his need for comfort and stimulation. The extreme helplessness of the human infant is terrifying unless there is, initially, some such sense of basic security.

How babies inspire mothering

Newborn babies are not born as 'clean slates'. From the moment of birth they are imbued with complex reactions which enable them to reach out and encourage communication with their mothers. Their eyes are like a fixed and focused camera lens set to see clearly at a certain distance – about eight inches, and this more or less coincides with the distance between the mother's and baby's face when he is feeding. So the newborn has, from the beginning, a fairly clear picture of one of the most important features of his environment. Babies also show clear preference for faces amongst the patterns within their view, and tend to focus on the eyes. In other words, babies are already programmed to pay particular attention to faces, which puts them in a good position to establish a bond with their caretakers. It also means that you, as parents, are quickly established as the most interesting part of his world.

Both taste and smell are well-developed at birth and these senses encourage a swift bond or attachment to the mother in particular. If the person who is the primary caretaker is not the baby's real mother then similar attachment will occur to him or her. A baby soon learns to recognise his mother's milk and will turn his head towards a pad saturated with her milk, in preference to a stranger's. By six to ten days, a baby can pick out his mother's smell. If a week-old baby is fed by his mother wearing a mask, he will become distressed and feed and sleep poorly.

We just don't get on – what can I do?

There *are* situations in which new mothers may find it difficult to meet their babies' needs adequately. There are also babies who find it hard to adapt to their new life.

Some of the problems may arise from incompatibilities of temperament. An energetic, high-spirited mother with a very sensitive baby, who does not like too much rough-and-tumble, may take time to develop a gentler style. While each is adapting to the temperament of the other, neither may enjoy each other's company very much. The baby may cry a lot and the mother get little reward for her care of him. He may ignore her or look away when she wants to play. If this happens, she may feel disappointed and quite possibly worried that all is not going well. She may blame herself or her child for spoiling everything, and this then gets in the way of resolving the problem.

It may help a mother to stand back and try to observe herself and the baby objectively. Maybe a close friend, preferably one with children the same age, can offer some useful observations. The opposite problem may arise at a later stage with a quiet, mild mother and a strong-willed, vigorous child. She may

easily become a doormat because she cannot stand her ground even when she knows the child wants something unreasonable. The child becomes more tyrannical in his demands, and also more unhappy and insecure because he is too

small to enjoy that much power. She may let things go on like this for a while and then realise it will not do, make a firm stand, and find that the child is actually happier for it.

Both mother and child influence their relationship and it is only in exceptional cases that one imposes their will in a one-sided way upon the other. They form a system which is regulated by them both, and which contains within itself the means of correcting mistakes, given an adequate environment. The mother is obviously the senior partner, but even a young baby has considerable resources to enable him to get what he wants, which is, above all else, a satisfying and pleasurable relationship with his mother. For example, just as she may be beginning to tire of the interrupted nights and arduous days of the very early stages, he rewards her with radiant smiles whenever she comes into view. At about six months, he begins to single her out as a special person whom he desires to be close to above all others. If she is absent-minded and preoccupied, he will increase his attempts to get her attention until she has to notice him. If she overwhelms him with attention, he will switch off and signal that he, like her, sometimes likes some peace and quiet. Given sufficient goodwill, these short-term failures to achieve a satisfying balance between the baby's needs and the mother's are just part of their developing relationship. All close relationships involve negative as well as positive feelings, hate as well as love, and it is sentimental nonsense to assume that mothers and babies are any exception. Serious problems only arise when a mother is unable to respond flexibly to the baby's signals, or the perhaps rarer situations when a baby is particularly slow at adapting to her. The most usual cause of such problems is maternal depression. Depending on his tempera- 167 ment, he may become so discouraged by his mother's lack of response that he gives up and becomes withdrawn and quiet. Alternatively, he may try harder to reach her, his friendly overtures becoming more and more aggressive until she feels bullied by him. There is a large body of recent research findings on the link between severe maternal depression and emotional disturbance in children, though it is not known exactly what the causes are or how permanent the effects on children. What is certain is that many women have brief periods of mild depression, and only if it is severe and persistent will it reach a crisis point.

Chronic anxiety may have the effect of making a mother interpret almost any change in the baby as a portent of disaster. She cannot distinguish between good and bad news from the baby. He also begins to pick up fairly soon a message from his mother that the world is a dangerous and nasty place where it is wise to expect the worst. He may later become the sort of child who is afraid to leave his mother, resists going to school, fails to make friends there, and generally finds life a frightening rather than an enjoyable business. Exceptionally stormy and hot-tempered people may also find child-rearing a problem. Mothers require patience, tact and good humour in abundance, and not everyone possesses these excellent qualities to the same degree.

However, if a mother can be aware that she is a worrier, depressed or short-tempered, which as the previous section showed can be helped, she will be able to avoid imposing her emotional problems on her baby. Children are disposed to love their parents, and can be marvellously forgiving of their faults if they have not been made to feel too guilty about them.

Initially, how much care does he need?

Many women worry that 'excessive care' can produce a selfish, conceited adult. How much should a baby be cuddled? What are the dangers, if any, of over-stimulation at this stage?

Babies in advanced industrial societies are held and cuddled less than in most traditional societies where, for safety, they are carried about by their mothers much of the time. It used to be assumed that the most important aspect of the mother/baby relationship was feeding. Now there is good evidence to believe that physical contact is even more important and that we have much to learn from traditional cultures about the care of young infants. The results of famous research studies by the Harlows was an important factor in changing opinions about cuddling. These studies were not of human babies, but of monkeys, who were reared apart from their mothers, with two surrogate mothers made of wire. One was fitted with a milk bottle, and provided food, the other was covered with soft fabric and provided comfort. When the baby monkey was frightened or distressed he ran and clung to the 'cloth mother' rather than the 'wire mother' with the milk. It may be that some of the crying in the early months which is so distressing arises from having too little of the kind of contact the 'cloth mother' provided, *because we do not realise that babies need it as much as they need food*. It is not practical for western mothers to carry their babies about all day. Wrapping them firmly can provide a similar feeling of safety and comfort many fretful babies immediately.

On the other hand, there are individual differences in a baby's response to cuddling. In one study, some babies actively protested at being cuddled, although they were strongly attached to their mothers. They preferred to be comforted in other ways, with food or by being carried about or, as they grew older, just staying close to their mother when upset. They were usually very active babies, and it seemed to be the constraint of being held which they disliked so much. Some mothers were upset at having babies who seemed not to enjoy being cuddled, but most changed their ways of handling them until they found the method which best suited their baby.

What about over-stimulation?

Part of a mother's role is to stimulate her children, to arouse curiosity, show how interesting the world can be and help develop a capacity for learning. In the very early period, when a baby is making the most elemental adjustments to being in the world at all, he needs just

a necessary minimum of outside stimulation. The quieter and calmer life is, the better. As he gets older, maybe two or three months, there are moments when he enjoys being talked to and played with, and these periods increase as time goes on. But there seems to be an optimum level of stimulation even then. A tickling game is great fun, yet can suddenly be too much if it goes on too long or is too intense. The baby may 'switch off' when he has had enough, by looking away or through the mother, and it may be that she does not notice his signal to stop. At a later point, a two-year-old with a very active, sociable mother, may so rarely have a quiet day at home that there is no comforting, familiar routine at all and he can never anticipate what is likely to happen next. *There is a balance between under- and over-stimulation which varies for different children at different ages* and a mother will discover which balance is right for her and her child only by trial and error.

What else is involved in 'good-enough' mothering?

In the end, it is the ability of parents, or substitute caretakers for that matter, to communicate with children and encourage their development through three aspects of care – **love, play and control** – that effects how well things go for both parents and children.
What you do in specific instances – when you stop breast-feeding, when you get him to stop wetting his bed, whether or not he sucks his thumb, a dummy, a blanket, or nothing, and so on – has very little to do with the way he will turn out in the end. Rather than over-concerning yourself with the transient fads and fashions of the wealth of baby-care advice available, you can communicate with your child in a way which will have a direct effect on his later development, and indeed your enjoyment of being a mother.

BABYSHOCK

PLAY

What do parents have to know about play?

The great thing about play is that children do it anyway. On the whole adults are bystanders. Common commands like "Go upstairs and play" from parents show this; they know the child will get on with it anyway. In one sense it would seem that the most important thing to know about children's play is that it gets them out of your hair. More than that is involved though. The wide range of activities called 'play' is vital to the child's physical, emotional, intellectual and social development. It is quite different to adult play. When adults play, be it football, bingo, dominos or flirting at a party, there are rules and they have to do as well as they can within their limitations. In pre-school play the limitations are not imposed by rules but by the child's own immaturity and most of the time the child is playing to find out how much he can do and enjoy the pleasure of being able to do it. Of course, the more he can do, the more the limits are pushed back and thus he develops.

Take a baby in a pram tugging at his feet with his hands in front of his face. He is

learning how to move his fingers to grasp objects and how to reach out for those things he wants to touch or pick up. He is doing two things at once: learning how to co-ordinate and regulate his own movements until they become practised and no longer require

great concentration; forming an idea in his head of how the various parts of his body fit together. Becoming more competent at both these tasks is pleasurable – there is a great desire in children to understand the world and to achieve more and more complicated tasks – and as he lies there *playing* with his feet, he chuckles.

A few months later the same child will endlessly drop things onto the floor whilst sitting in his high chair. He isn't seeking attention, he is playing, he is learning to let things go, to release his grasp. The reason he laughs when he does it (after you've replaced his spoon in his bowl for the third time) is because he is enjoying the mastery of letting go of things, NOT because he's got you round his little finger.

Throughout the pre-school years the child is learning how to co-ordinate his body: grasping, letting go, crawling, walking, running, walking backwards, skipping, hopping, climbing trees, piling up bricks, jumping and so on. Practising these achievements is not done seriously, like practising the piano, but with a sense of pleasure and amusement as his body's limits are explored – both alone and in competitive or admiring company.

The same is true for speech which involves talking, singing, rhyming and using nonsense words; for thinking which includes counting to huge numbers, puzzles and riddles for example.

What has been considered so far is play with the purpose of exploring, developing and perfecting accomplishments; in other words, developing *mastery*. This is the type of play which it is easier to see as more than just self-entertainment. It is possible to describe play under headings which, although they overlap, emphasise its different aspects. Three of them are:

**Mastery
Curiosity
Fantasy**

Mastery, illustrated in the two above examples, is learning *how*. Other activities are more difficult to recognise as being concerned with developing skills. Consider a mother and her baby daughter playing 'walking round the garden like a teddy bear' which gets repeated over and over again to everyone's delight. Here is a game involving two people taking turns – like all social encounters. Games like this are a first step in learning how to get on with people.

Not that all playful activities between parent and child in the first year or so of life are concerned with learning social skills. Hide-and-seek games enable a baby to learn that objects continue to exist even when out of sight – a revelation to the baby in the last half of the first year. Rough-and-tumble, at which fathers excel, exercises the reflexes which save the baby when he falls off balance and therefore is necessary for the first stages of learning to walk. Much of early play is concerned with the development of the body, its limbs and its sense organs in particular, and how to enter the social world of people whom the baby rapidly engages in playful activity. Serious business conducted in a non-serious fashion.

In the first year of life, other people and his own body are far and away the most important playthings for the baby.

After a child's first steps have grown into a more confident walk there is a continuous, fruitful extension into climbing, running, leaping and jumping. Body mastery brings a great sense of accomplishment: "Look Mummy, look at me, *look*." By and large, children discover or provide their own materials – stairs, chairs, beds and so on. How much further you encourage them is a

matter of taste. Children who live in large houses with spacious gardens get bought climbing frames, whereas it is the children of families living in high-rise blocks who need them. *In a sense, toys should provide what is not naturally available. a climbing frame substitutes for a tree.*

A basic collection of toys for developing and exercising body mastery over larger limb movements can be found in most houses containing children:

A big ball to kick

A small ball to throw – and, later, to catch

Something to push: a cart with an upright frame handle – best if weighted with telephone directories at first – or a wheeled rattle on a stick

Something to pull: almost anything on a string

A wheeled vehicle to sit on and scoot around with: e.g. a wooden 'tricycle' *without* pedals

171

Later, a scooter or small bicycle/tricycle with pedals

Mastery of finer movements, involving more intellectual and sophisticated social attributes and activities overlap so much with curiosity and fantasy play that it is described there.

On the whole, mastery is something in which parents take so much vicarious delight, that few children are deprived of the chance to develop their physical skills to a remarkable degree. There is only one such activity that is often neglected in the pre-school years and that is swimming. With the availability of inflatable arm-bands, and the provision by many local authority swimming baths of special classes for mothers and small children, pleasurable learning of survival skills in water is possible from the age of at least two (earlier if you have access to a specially warmed bath – it is the cold not the water that upsets babies).

Swimming is invaluable not only for safety's sake but for the confidence and enjoyment it can bring.

Curiosity

As seen earlier, growing awareness of their own bodies leads them to play with their own hands, their feet, their genitals and so on, exploring and discovering. Mouthing of objects is evident throughout the first year but once they can bring their hands to the mid-line in front of themselves, handling objects to discover their special characteristics becomes similarly absorbing. Experiments with monkeys have shown how intense the drives of exploration and curiosity are. Monkeys will perform complicated tasks for hours in exchange for the privilege of being able to gaze out of their cages at the outside world. Very young babies have shown how quickly they can learn to trigger light displays they can look at.

In the home, such complicated schemes are unnecessary, a hanging mobile above the cot, a string of beads across the pram and the act of placing the baby in a half-reclining bouncing chair – rather than leaving him lying looking at the ceiling – are constructive ideas.

At around six or seven months, about the time of learning to sit, babies become much more intrusive in their interest in material objects. Rather than *just* mouthing objects they poke with their fingers, bang with anything they can, squeeze and bite. This has the effect of discovering the *basic properties* of the object: how hard, how easy to tear, how squashy and so on. Within a few months this develops into an exploration of *function* and *relationships*: a spoon can carry food, or be banged on the table; it can go inside a mouth (but not right inside an ear). A box can hold something small but not something big; it has an opening in one side but not the other. It can hide things or be used to carry them around in. Everyday objects around the house are pressed into service in a curious exploration of how they are made, what purposes they can be made to serve in addition to their usual function, how they are bigger than some things, smaller than others, can contain a few things but not a lot and so on. A nest of boxes or cups is a very useful toy if you want to preserve your saucepans and crockery. Similarly, a set of hammer pegs may help deflect the somewhat anti-social habit of banging and clattering.

In the second year of life, attempts to build and make things demand the provision of bricks. With these, the laws of balance and support are discovered, the basic essentials of bridges and houses explored, and creativity becomes blended with curious discovery. As so many people have said, bricks are (after people) the most satisfying and engaging toy of all for many children. The important thing to remember is to buy enough. A big bag of plain wooden bricks will provide more satisfaction than a small number of coloured ones. Cloth bricks are useless.

In the same way, posting boxes, jigsaws and modelling clay or Plasticine have endless application in the development of fine manipulative skills as well as the discovery of how things are, and could be, put together. Curiosity about the structure and properties of objects can be satisfied not just by inspection but by creative attempts to build or portray the objects.

Fantasy

Fantasy is a convenient word for 'pretend' play where the child tries to make sense of experience, come to terms with impulses, and explore social relationships. Sometimes this is obvious: watching a child play 'schools' with dolls, or a group of children playing 'mummies and daddies'. You can hear the tones of the teacher or – embarrassingly – yourself as the 'mummy' threatening dire punishment for a minor transgression. Here the child is exploring what it is like to be the other person in a familiar relationship – the teacher instead of the pupil, the mother instead of the child. In playing at what it is like to be the other person, they come to some idea of how they themselves fit into the relationship.

Usually it is not quite so clear. Small children playing cowboys or Batman are not obviously exploring relationships; it would seem that they are identifying with powerful figures able to kill or punish 'baddies'. This may fulfil various moods: an opportunity to feel powerful instead of small and powerless; a chance to let rip with weapons and kill or be killed (but only for a few moments) thus starting to come to terms with the notion of dying; an opportunity

to leap and run in 'mastery' terms and so on. As usual, one piece of play serves various functions, but here the theme of fantasy predominates and serves the purpose of rehearsing inexplicable experiences and emotions.

With respect to emotions, there is no doubt that play can serve the purpose of helping overcome fears; one of the greatest benefits to children's hospital wards has been plastic disposable syringes with which dolls and teddies can be injected. The fear of injections, though by no means abolished, has been eased considerably. Similarly, children who have just been in hospital play 'doctors and nurses' for weeks afterwards, mulling over the experience, making sense of it and bringing it down to a less threatening dimension. Real feelings can be experienced but the scale is manageable. Between the ages of three and five in particular, children act out fantasised situations in a

self-centred, self-important but not very self-conscious way. Dressing up, especially as adults, doll-play, tea sets, 173

BABYSHOCK

Wendy houses and such items as toy guns enable a more lively approximation to the real thing. On a smaller scale, doll's houses, puppets and dolls can be used vicariously as the children themselves and as familiar figures or stereotypes which they know from their environment or, at second-hand, in books or on television. The common theme is that the toys should be components of a setting within which the child can 'play at' a possible (or impossible) situation and experience it without being overwhelmed. In a way it is a sort of thinking or even dreaming, but whereas adults can think to themselves – rather like reading silently – children have to act things out – like reading aloud.

Drawing and painting are special areas where the child can portray people, objects and scenes and, within his own abilities, illustrate not only his memory or observation of actual items but create a world of his own – once again to his own level and on a manageable scale. Although, to the adult eye, accuracy and realism are often the standards by which children's pictures are judged, it is the liveliness of the content and the relationship to the child's experience which is its value to the child as he attempts to explore possible situations and experience his responses to them. The child is in control – unlike in dreams where he can be overwhelmed and frightened. A point shown by an eager adult who plunges into make-believe and by virtue of his expert mimicry conjures up a situation that really frightens – and the play is over for the child. With fantasy-play the best rule is to provide what they need and keep out of it.

Consumer guide to toys   Ref 3:1

Children certainly cannot discern whether a toy is new or secondhand, and are even likely to love the battered old plaything more than the shiny new. Toys are absurdly over-priced – try attending a toy trade fair one day and see the wholesale prices as compared to the retail – and it is best, if you can, to try and make things for yourself, or improvise certain play principles with anything you happen to have at home.

A word about sex differences. It is certainly true that our culture dictates that girls play with dolls, boys with guns, girls help their mothers cook, boys fight and climb trees. Some people have reacted very strongly against this and insist on their boys having dolls, their girls guns. Various studies have confirmed that girls and boys show different play interests. Referring to such studies it seems that girls can behave in a tomboyish way and it makes no difference, but boys who *persistently* play with dolls *rather than anything else* are possibly (*not* definitely) at risk for developing an insecure sexual identity. Continued and exclusive doll-play or *persistent* dressing up in girls' clothes by a boy is something worth asking advice about. Occasional cross-dressing and doll-play alongside other boyish activities is perfectly healthy. Action Men or G.I. Men are not dolls for the purposes of these suggestions, which is not to say that one cannot see them being cuddled by brawny five-year-old boys! Children of both sexes should have the opportunity to look after a cuddly soft toy even if they do not make a big thing of it. In looking after it, they can experience at secondhand the pleasure of being cared for themselves.

Be guided by the child, not by what you expect of the child. Don't be tempted to give toys more suitable for a child of an advanced age: keep them in store if you receive them now. Remember that children vary enormously in their interests and rate of development. Suggestions concerning suitability can only be approximate.

Stick to the brand names you know, or look for the kitemark of the British Standards Institute. Safety of toys has improved vastly but with the under-threes you should still watch out for anything small enough to swallow (beads, marbles) anything attached by wire (cuddly animals' eyes), anything breakable that might have jagged edges.

See Appendix for guide to toys through the first five years

How much should I educate my child before school?

It is staggering how much muddled advice parents have been given over such topics as whether to teach their child to read themselves. Some of the alarms raised have been rather mis-leading, for example the fear that if you teach a child to recognise words on sight ('look-and-say') then if he goes to a school where letter sounds ('phonics') are taught he will be so confused that he won't learn. Similarly the idea among educationalists to wait for the child to demonstrate 'reading readiness' is now outdated. Don't be put off by any of this, the real question is not, 'Should I, as a parent, teach my child to read?' but 'What skills does my child need to master before he can read?' The answer to this is as follows:

Vocabulary. Make sure your child knows a wide range of words, not just nouns but the words for size (big, small, huge, etc.) names of colours, ideas of speed (fast, quickly, slow) and so on, so that his understanding and use of language is rich.

Clear speech. It is impossible to distin-guish between the sounds of the letters 'B' and 'P' if you don't distinguish between them when talking. The accent is not important but the sounds we use when giving them are.

Understanding the idea of written speech. Children do not experience speech as a sequence of separate words, they hear it as a string of sounds. The idea that one can have speech sounds written down on paper may be a little difficult to grasp. The notion that they can be broken down further into words and into letters is really quite complex. Just simply pointing out words on notices like 'Bus Stop' is worthwhile and should *long* precede teaching letters. Reading aloud to your child, perhaps in the form of a bedtime story, should be a daily event from at least the age of eighteen months.

Teaching visual discrimination. In order to tell the difference between letters, the child has to detect details that may be otherwise quite unimportant. A picture of a chair, after all, is a chair whichever way it is pointing but a 'b' is different from a 'd'. In other words the child has to unlearn some of the recognition skills he has previously learned in accepting that chairs can point various ways and look slightly different, but still be chairs. With print, though, the differ-ence between a 'd' and 'b' is crucial whereas the difference between a little 'q' and a big 'Q' is not – in a children's book at any case. Helping a child to find a picture exactly the same – as in a game of snap – is a profitable exercise.

If you attend only to the above areas, you will probably find your child reading in any case.

The same principles apply to number skills. Children learn to count quickly but they need help to understand that numbers are a way of labelling things (number 1, number 2, etc.) as well as a way of counting and a system of ordering (first, second, etc.). Counting rhymes are so much part of the nursery tradition they can be taken for granted, but other mathematical skills such as addition and subtraction for example 175 can be introduced informally in talking about saving or spending money, or sharing out sweets. Encouraging a child to develop new ways of sorting out a box of buttons or beads can help develop the notion of 'sets' or way of grouping objects – by size, by colour, by shape and so on. There is no need to set time aside for such activities, a better policy is to make a mental note of their usefulness and pounce when the time is ripe. Children have a nose for button-boxes anyway.

CONTROL

How can I stop him being so disobedient?

Mothers have to be tough as well as tender. As the baby grows into a toddler, they may feel they are not so much raising lambs as training tigers. Some mothers find this the most difficult part of the job. When this sweet, friendly baby begins to say 'no' to everything, even to things he really enjoys like his bath or eating, when he throws a tantrum in the supermarket and everyone around looks at her as if she is mistreating him, when he stamps and kicks and screams, she may wish she were a million miles away.

It helps to have some idea of what to expect and what the child's behaviour means at different stages of his development. A newborn, crying frantically because he is hungry or cold; a three-month-old, crying with evening colic; or a three-year-old crying because he has to stop playing and have his tea, can make you feel desperate; but they are different situations and need different remedies. They can arouse intense feelings of helplessness or sympathy, distress or fury. Emotions in small children are naturally sudden, violent and extreme, and few situations in ordinary life can produce such an immediate emotional reaction in an onlooker as a child in a state of extreme distress or rage. People may re-experience their own infantile misery and fury, and be overwhelmed with a flood of feeling which is quite unlike their usual grown-up composure. It can be frightening to feel so strongly. You may wonder if you're cracking up under the strain. Suppose he keeps on like this? Will you end up hating rather than loving him, or one day lose your self-control and do him an injury? Or will he end up dominating you and the rest of the household, and expecting the world to give him what he wants when he wants it for ever and ever? On page 145, coping with a young baby's crying and night-waking is dealt with, what about problems which arise later on?

The second year onwards

As the baby gets older and begins to make more sense of the world, the hungry one-year-old can see that his mother is preparing his lunch and knows that he will soon be fed. He does not need to keep on crying as he has already made his point and he knows his mother understands. A certain degree of regularity will help him to make such connections, so that fewer situations arise when the child gets frantic because he does not know whether his needs are being taken account of or not.

During this period he also begins to learn the meaning of 'no'. There are certain things which he cannot do because they are dangerous or destructive. He cannot pull out the wires in the television or turn on the gas taps, though to him these are just interesting tricks. First you might say 'no' and move him away over and over again; perhaps you divert him to other acceptable activities; maybe you even give him a gentle slap if he is very persistent. Finally, he learns that pulling wires leads to his mother looking cross and saying 'no' and moving him away. He wants to pull wires but he doesn't want all the bother that follows and he does not want to upset his mother to whom he is devoted. One day he goes over to the television ready to pull wires and then stops; he may hesitate, then look at his mother to see what she thinks. He may even say 'no' quietly to himself and go off to find something else to do.

Sometimes he tests her out by trying once again to see if she will relent, even though he clearly knows it is not allowed. He has *internalised* the rule and no longer needs it to be imposed from outside; he is learning the beginning of self-control though it will be many years before he no longer needs guidance from his parents as well.

At this stage, when the basic idea of rules and limits is being learned, it is helpful to keep them down to a reasonable minimum, but to be clear and consistent about those you do have. If you expect too much, life becomes a constant battle. Your child cannot distinguish between the important things which he must not do and less important things which do not really matter either way. If you expect too little or are vague and changeable about your rules he may feel there are no limits at all and he can do anything if only he pushes hard enough. It is also by this stage that a child can be spoiled. Lack of any rules, or rules which apply one moment and not the next, leave him confused and make him unnecessarily troublesome.

The negative phase
Around the age of two there is a change in the child's attitude to discipline. He is by now aware that there are boundaries beyond which he cannot go without being restrained. He may have settled down to accepting those limits with reasonable good humour, enjoying the many things he is allowed to do and not minding too much about the few he is not. If he is talking by this stage you may even hear him saying in a virtuous tone, "We don't do that, do we. Oh, no." (that being pulling wires or hitting babies or whatever). Over a few weeks he seems to change; he cannot be easily diverted. He digs his heels in when told what to do or not to do and refuses to budge; he will not stand still to have his coat put on for a walk; he refuses to sit at the table to wait for his pudding; if pressed he may scream and fight and finally get into such a rage that he is completely impervious to anything the adult does to calm him down.

What is going on? Does he no longer care about pleasing his mother? He does, but he is also beginning to develop 177 a sense of himself as a person with his own desires. He also has a will of his own and he has to defend it against the stronger and more developed will of the adults around him. Nevertheless, he cannot have everything he wants, however badly he wants it. Life is not like that. To live together, everyone has to make concessions and compromises; everyone strives for their own ends, but it should not be at the cost of exploiting or damaging other people. There is always some tension between the needs of the individual and the group but there need not be a fundamental conflict. The two-year-old needs his individuality to be respected but he also needs to respect that of the others in the family.

The strength of his bond to his mother makes the battle particularly intense. As a baby he was almost a part of her; he could not tell where he left off and she began. It was all one blissful whole. Now he knows he is separate and different and he must make sure everyone else knows it too, saying 'no' is one way of asserting your individuality and everyone does it at times if they feel their rights are not being respected. The problem with the rebellious toddler is that he seems to feel he can never say 'yes' or go along with anyone else's suggestions without putting up a fight first. He is overstating his case. Once he has made the point that he is an individual, he can afford to be more generous and give ground more gracefully. He will grow out of it in time.

Old enough to know why

As he gets older and more articulate it becomes easier for you to reason with him. He can make his wishes known in words and his parents can explain their necessary restrictions on his freedom. He will still get angry when frustrated, either by adults or by his own incapacity to carry out his intentions, but it is a more manageable anger. He is more aware of the effects of his behaviour and has a better memory for events and is therefore more susceptible to reward and punishment.

A great deal of psychological knowledge has been built up over the last half century on the principles of learning. The central finding is that behaviour which is rewarded or 'reinforced' is likely to be repeated. If there is no reward it is less likely to be tried again. Punishment has a more unpredictable effect, it may stop undesirable behaviour for good but it may cause such frustration that aggressive and destructive behaviour are actually increased. In some cases, the only time a child gets any attention from his mother is when she slaps him. The rest of the time he is largely ignored. His need for communication is greater than his fear of a painful smack – indeed paradoxically the smack can become rewarding.

Most of the basic research has been carried out on animals, involving, for example, rats running races for food rewards. Although human learning is vastly more complex, the fundamental laws still apply. A toddler who learns that his temper is rewarded with a bag of sweets and a suddenly obliging mother will work himself up into a temper more often. If tempers do nothing except to wear him out, they will slowly diminish in number. A very common pattern is for tiresome behaviour to go unrewarded for a period, only to be rewarded in the end. He goes on and on demanding something and is told he cannot have it until the mother is worn out and 'gives in' to him. He has therefore learnt that it is worth going on a long time before giving up. If you then decide that you should stand firm next time, you will need to be very determined and persistent.

If there are still a lot of tantrums at this age, it may be that it is not clear to the child what is desirable and what is undesirable behaviour. If he is constructive and reasonable, no one may seem to notice. If he only gets what he wants when he is difficult, it is obvious he will go on being difficult. If you would like your child to be generous or kind, you should let him know how pleased you are when he shares a toy with another child or comforts a younger one who is crying. In more technical terms you *reinforce* good behaviour by rewarding it and *extinguish* bad behaviour by failing to reward it. For most children, their mother's attention is a reward in itself. If she is very busy, the child may only get attention when he is naughty. So, if he is naughty quite a lot, she can reverse the situation by noticing him when he is doing well and praising him and ignoring his more negative behaviour (unless it is really dangerous). If you watch an experienced mother or playgroup leader, they are intuitively acting on this principle much of the time. Playgroups which encourage parent participation provide a valuable educational experience for mothers. Observe for yourself what works and does not work with children at different ages. You can also get a fund of new ideas for play activities at home. If he has sufficient scope for play, which need not involve the expense of toys, there are fewer disciplinary problems arising from the boredom of having too few outlets for curiosity and constructiveness.

What should I do with my child in the event of . . . ?

Temper tantrums

Though the accusing looks from other women at the supermarket check-out might make you think otherwise, tantrums are a normal part of child development and not a reflection of your inadequate skills as a mother.

Although you cannot stop them altogether, you can usually reduce the frequency of tantrums, even with an exceptionally vigorous and independent toddler. If his needs and wishes are already being taken into account he will not have to fight so hard to have them attended to. When a full-blown tantrum does occur it can be very frightening for him. In extreme cases it can also be frightening for the mother as some children hold their breath during a bout of screaming and even turn blue in the face. If this happens, hold him gently but firmly until it is all over and he comes back to himself again. He may *feel*

very destructive, but it would probably distress him if he were allowed to be destructive. He needs to know that his mother is strong enough to prevent him, but also that she does not desert him in his struggle with his feelings and, particularly, that she does not mean to retaliate in kind and attack him back. This would only teach him that destructive feelings really cannot be controlled even by mature adults. Equally, he needs to learn that he cannot coerce others by his fury. Alternatively, you can leave him lying on the floor and watch, waiting until the storm blows over. Smacking may make you feel better, but usually makes the tantrum worse. If you have decided that he 179 should not have a bar of chocolate just before lunch you should hold your ground. If you feel like giving in, it probably means it was not a vital issue in the first place and you could have avoided confrontation by saying 'yes' at once. None of these things is easy; anger produces anger or fear in others and it is natural either to attack back or surrender. The small child cannot cope with his mother doing either; the first makes him fear for himself, the second for her. Almost all toddlers have tantrums, and most mothers lose their tempers or 'given in' from exhaustion at some time or other. But life will be easier for you both in the long run if, as a general rule, you remain calm and firm in the face of provocation.

If tantrums are becoming a real nuisance, it is a good idea to talk the problem over with your husband, with friends who have had children, or with your doctor or health visitor. Your husband needs to be involved because it is important that he takes the same approach as you. A few minutes talk when all is calm, will probably save a blazing row between the two of you at the same time as the 'little angel' is throwing a tantrum.

Refusing to eat

Food can become a source of conflict between mother and child. You may feel hurt if he refuses his dinner when he may just have a temporary gastric upset and honestly not feel hungry. If feelings run high and eating or not-eating provokes emotional turmoil in the family, the stage may be set for 'an eating problem'. Sometimes he may appear not to be eating enough for his health's sake. In fact, if he is otherwise healthy you can rely on him to eat enough for his needs. It may be that he is refusing meals but eating enough in snacks to keep him going. Make mealtimes as pleasurable as possible; sit down together and make it a social occasion. If food is refused, take it away without fuss. He will make up for it at the next meal and will most certainly not starve (disturbed adolescents suffering from the serious condition known as *anorexia nervosa* sometimes do, but this does *not* occur in small children).

As soon as he shows an interest in feeding himself, allow him to do so even though he makes more mess. Being fed is an uncomfortable business and the drive for independence will make him want to do it himself as soon as he can.

Almost all children have some food fads – foods they particularly dislike or like. Take them into account as you might those of other family members, but not at the cost of providing a different dish for every person. It is also a good idea to keep snacks down to the minimum; a mid-morning snack for an adult can be the equivalent in calories of a whole meal for a small child, but is unlikely to provide the other nutrients he needs. Give him small amounts of new or less light foods so that he does not feel he is being 'force fed' but, at the same time, he does gradually get used to a fair variety of foods.

Not wanting to sleep

Individual differences in the amount of sleep necessary vary widely even in newborn babies. Small babies can be assumed to take the sleep they need (although some seem to have difficulty in relaxing enough to drop off even when they are tired). Rocking may be very helpful and soothing for babies like this. Some appear to appreciate soothing music. Being put to bed in the same special place also helps. For older children, sleep may become a focus of emotional conflict just as food is for others, and for similar reasons. Falling asleep requires a basic trust that you will be protected while you are asleep and not abandoned by everyone. Toddlers going through a negative phase or tense, worried children may feel too anxious to sleep easily – just as most adults sleep badly during periods of anxiety.

Some difficulty at bedtime is very common in the second and third years. This is probably because of the conflict between the child's continuing dependency on parents and his growing need for independence. These needs occur simultaneously and are therefore deeply confusing.

Many children have an elaborate ritual for bedtime. They may start with a bath

then a ceremonial goodnight to everyone, a warm drink, cuddly toys in the bed, a bedtime story and a last cuddle and kiss. The more calm and unhurried the process, the likelier they are to fall asleep and make your evening more peaceful. Problems may be expected before an evening out – when you are hoping to get baby to bed and yourself ready before the babysitter arrives. Perhaps *you* may be feeling frayed by six or seven o'clock, possibly with older children to attend to and an evening

meal to cook. If your husband can get home in time to help with the putting to bed *or* the cooking, he will benefit by having a quiet household later in the evening. If there are cries, even after the settling down routine, it may be better to go up for another reassuring 'goodnight', than leave your child to become frantic and then possibly get up and come looking for you.

If an older child of three or four is refusing to go to bed at a reasonable time, or repeatedly coming down and interrupting your time together, he may be not so much frightened of being left alone as enjoying the extra attention or getting a kick out of coming between you. He may be tired but will not allow himself to sleep. It is usually possible to guess his motive, and if you feel it is the latter, you should be firm and insist on his staying in bed with a night light and toys to play with if necessary. It is now 'grown-ups' time' and he must get used to it. After a few nights of protest, if he is sure you really mean it, he will give up moaning and begin to fall asleep at an earlier hour.

Lack of co-operation in every day routines

Independent toddlers dislike having their occupations interrupted by demands for them to stop for meals, for washes, going out shopping and other everyday routines. If he is deeply absorbed in his play he can be given several warnings that it will soon be time to stop. He can then prepare himself for having to give up something he is enjoying and which is important to him. Having given him plenty of time to get used to the idea, it should then be carried through with firmness. As you do so, you can chat him up about the pleasures of the new activity, talking about the interesting things you may see on a walk while struggling with his coat and gloves, or the games he can soon

181

play in the bath as you undress him. Such ploys are part of the maternal art, and not to be despised.

Constantly wanting to be the centre of attention

It is much easier for someone else to see whether your child is demanding attention because he is genuinely not getting enough, or because he is getting too much. People are not usually as aware of how they are affecting others as they are of how others are affecting them. If you keep an eye on your child as you work or chat with a friend, you can observe if he needs some assistance with a toy, or is at a loose end and needing a new occupation before he gets too bored. He is then less likely to make angry demands for attention and if he does, you can justifiably point out that you also have important things to do at times. One significant fact is that the more securely attached the child, the more independent exploration and play he will be capable of, without being clinging and demanding. Problems arise when an insecure child provokes you to push him away because he is wearing you out and irritating you with his constant demands. He will then feel more insecure and make more demands so you are more worn out. Again it is usually possible to tell whether a child needs attention or is just enjoying his power to provoke, and should have more definite limits set for him. If you cannot see it, your friends probably can, if they are brave enough to tell you.

How do I cope with a hyperkinetic child?

This condition is a source of much discussion amongst doctors, most of which has hitherto appeared in American medical journals. In that country, up to 4% of all children are said to suffer from hyperactivity, compared with the usually accepted figure in the UK of one child in four thousand (0.025%).

Hyperkinetic means over-active, but in Britain the terms is used by doctors in a special sense so that every highly active child is by no means hyperkinetic. The fact is that the definition of hyper-activity has largely depended on the view of the observer.

Hyperkinetic children are intensely restless, mobile and distractable, often irritable and unhappy too. There is some dispute as to whether the condition has a psychological or physical basis.

When what British doctors regard to be a hyperkinetic child comes into the surgery or consulting room, he will rush from one side of the room to the other, turn on the basin taps, pull books from a shelf, open drawers, climb onto a window still – all within a few minutes of arrival.

At home, he may wear his mother out with his need for long walks and vigorous activity, and his incapacity to settle down to quiet constructive play. Sometimes, if there is plenty of space to run about, it may not be too much of a problem until the child starts school, when his distractability gets him into endless trouble, and prevents him getting down to formal school work. Some paediatricians and child psychia-trists prescribe stimulant drugs like amphetamine for hyperkinesis, which seems a paradoxical thing to do, but it often works very well. Other ways of helping a hyperkinetic child include reducing the amount of stimulation when he needs to concentrate, e.g. turning off the radio or TV if he is playing; or taking him off to a quiet room is you are helping him with his reading. You can also build up his capacity to attend by rewarding him when he does it, with praise or sweets. His restlessness is exhausting and can be very irriating to adults so the danger is that he is *always* being told off, and *never* patted on the back when he does settle for a few minutes. It looks so easy, but it is very hard *for him*, and his effort should not go unnoticed. The condition tends to improve in later childhood and adolescence, but by then, without careful handling, he may be so discouraged by his many failures that he has given up trying. He may even get quite depressed and need some counselling if he is to feel happier about himself.

11
Motherhood
-what about me?

"(Working) should at least protect
you from ever feeling that you are
stagnating, or wasting your life, or
becoming a cabbage."

"What's the point of having children?
You don't have them because you
want to leave them behind with a
nanny."

Motherhood
-what about me?

How much of my child's development is up to me?

For convenience, the caretaking person throughout this book is usually referred to as 'mother', implying the biological mother. Although in the majority of cases they are one and the same, the psychological mother and the biological mother do not have to be the same person. The natural mother has a number of advantages in undertaking the role, but they may be outweighed by other factors in particular cases. She has the advantage in that pregnancy and childbirth prepare her for a close relationship with her baby, and she is the only one who can feed him at the breast which gives her a *unique* relationship with him.

Fathers

As has been seen (page 139), mothers should not always be in the front line of motherhood, and it is up to you and the baby's father to work out the extent of his practical involvement. If you want to swop roles completely, you may

encounter ill-informed friends, neighbours or even social workers, shocked because you are living differently. There is no basis in fact for frightening stories they may tell you about harm they think your decision will have.

Initially, some men find it more difficult to be of direct use. It may be that in your case financial support of the family, and emotional support of you, are considered by both of you to be the essential ingredients of his role.

"He leaves early in the morning and works at weekends. But when they see him, it's like a breath of fresh air. He does special things with them like skating. I can see how this can annoy some mothers, but I think it is important for the children to have someone with that role."

But as the child grows, it is vital that he participates more directly. There are special ways in which any father can involve himself in his child's development.

"He didn't make many allowances for me. He never came home in time to give her a bath . . . What upsets me so much is that my husband has missed so much! He loves her all the time, but he doesn't have a lot of time for her. He's so busy; he has so much else to do."

In play, as already described in that section, he is an important feature. Often fathers' play is more physical and imaginative than mothers' quieter style, though it is probably the latter that generally gives a child his basic security. In discipline too, he has a characteristic role.

187

BABYSHOCK

It has been pointed out that it is often difficult for you to disentangle by yourself, what is going on between you and your child. Are you provoking him or he you? Are you demanding too much or is he? Because you are so close to him, you have no perspective on the problem. A father who cares about you both is uniquely placed to make a judgement. It has also been observed that some mothers just do find it difficult to keep discipline, though they may have no trouble with the tender side of parenting. The father's different style and greater detachment are apparent to the child, and he will often respond quicker to his commands than his mother's. For

all these reasons, the father's role in discipline is a central one. If he opts out by refusing to get involved or undermines your authority by reversing your previous decisions, you have a problem on your hands. On all major issues it is vital that there be a common policy between you and anyone else involved in his upbringing. Your child should know that he cannot play one off against the other. Your husband should be made aware of his role in maintaining order, and that you need him to fulfil his part if you are to carry out yours, successfully. (Some modern fathers may be so

concerned not to appear chauvinistic that they prefer not to exert their authority, and the family suffers).

Other help

Some children have always been mothered by people other than their natural mother. Upper-class children had wet-nurses or nannies, so their mothers could give their full attention to what was seen as the vastly more important task of social life. Poorer children, whose mothers had to work out of necessity, were looked after by grannies or babyminders. However, they were always in a minority and most children have been mothered primarily by their natural mother, aided by other female relatives and the father. Mary Ainsworth studied mothering among the Ganda tribe in East Africa and found that even in a culture which provides a choice of caretakers, babies tend to have preferences and mostly attach themselves to their own mothers. In the West, grannies and other relatives are still very important in providing care for the baby which complements rather than substitutes for the mother's care. Au pair girls can also provide support and company for a mother, if there is space and money available for such a luxury. But they are not really suitable for *full-time* caretakers; they are usually too young for such a heavy responsibility and they rarely stay longer than six months or a year. By the age of five, a child could have had a dozen au pairs speaking a variety of languages and he may have given up getting attached to anybody. The question of substitute care is dealt with in detail on page 200. As well as enabling you to get some time to yourself, it is vital to encourage your child's interaction with others – children as well as adults – particularly if he has no brothers and sisters. This can start as soon as he can be propped up, but is important once he starts to walk.

over, unaware that she is making her daughter feel useless. Most women, however, think that they are doing just a little bit better than their own mothers and that seems healthy for everybody. Uncles, aunts, and cousins may also be significant figures in the child's world and family visits and outings can be increasingly important events for him as he gets older.

Children who are used to relatives and friends visiting and sometimes looking after them, learn something very important. They learn that there are other friendly interesting people in the world beside their parents. They learn that separations can be pleasurable occasions, where you can make up for the temporary distress of losing mother by having a good time with granny who also loves him very much. Her food is a bit different, her talk and games are a bit different but that's alright. Sometimes the modern nuclear family can be claustrophobic and imprisoning and give a developing child very little idea of the immense variety of human personality and life-styles which are acceptable.

Grandparents are often much loved by their grandchildren and they may also be able to give practical support to the parents, particularly during the early years. A woman's relationship with her mother may change radically when she in turn becomes a mother. She may become closer to her than she has for years and find her an invaluable source of knowledge but, occasionally, she feels so inexperienced that she almost hands over to her mother, afraid that she can never be as competent. If the grandmother enjoys this she may take

A developing child who is both sure of his parents' love and surrounded by a network of relatives and friends feels more secure and can afford to be more open and trusting than one in an isolated family who has only itself to depend on. When there is a family crisis, like a confinement or illness, there are other people to turn to for help and when they have a crisis in their turn, as all families do at some time, they know they can rely on the same degree of support. The old-style extended family provided an insurance against personal disaster and we have not yet developed a substitute for it, despite our elaborate welfare services. Each neighbourhood or district could, in theory, provide it but we are only beginning to develop ways of bringing people together so they can help themselves and each other. Groups like pre-school playgroup associations have led the way in showing how many resources there are in every local community, but we have so far barely begun to use them.

What about other people beside the parents becoming involved in disciplinary questions?

Consistency is important in discipline, but everyone has different ideas about it. It is often difficult enough for parents to agree between themselves. If a child has other caretakers as well, it is impossible to have identical policies about everything. A good general plan is for people caring for your child to be informed of the house rules, and abide by them. If he is in their house, he should go along with their rules, where that is more convenient for them, rather than trying to stick to yours. There is otherwise no limit to the variance which can be played on the 'Granny lets me do this' or 'Mummy never makes me do that' game, which can reduce all the significant adults in a child's world to a state of helplessness.

Day care for the under-fives

There is no doubt that playgroups are an excellent thing. For 'only' children they are an opportunity to learn how to get on with others in a setting where mother is, initially at any rate, at hand and where there are not large frightening bands of much older children. Learning how to survive in a playgroup is good grounding for entry to school later. There are other advantages: opportunity to play with different or bigger toys compared with those at home; a chance for mothers to meet other parents and children.

It may help to define a few terms. When it comes to the provision of day care for the under-fives there is one basic distinction that parents should bear in mind: day care falls into two separate groups. There is day care that is

basically set up in *your* interests – day care that is there to look after your children while you work. And there is day care which is set up in your child's interests. It will have a great deal to offer him but it is not, and never was, intended as a custodial service for working mothers. The first group includes childminders, crèches and day nurseries. The second includes, playgroups, one o'clock clubs, nursery schools and classes.

Playgroups
They tend to be run largely by mothers themselves and a high degree of involvement is expected from parents. In 1975, a third of a million children went to playgroups and their success is a reflection of the way they meet the needs of many mothers and small children.

The average playgroup costs about as much as a bar of chocolate for a morning session. The biggest organiser of playgroups in the country is the Pre-School Playgroup Association although other organisations such as the Save the Children Fund are also very active. The Pre-School Playgroup Association is an educational charity which exists primarily to encourage the setting up of playgroups and it offers invaluable help and information to mothers and others who want to set one up in their area.

Two booklets are especially informative and cover every aspect of a new playgroup from finance and registration to management and staffing.
  'PPA' and its playgroups.
  Starting a playgroup.
Both from the Pre-School Playgroup Association **Ref 3:2**

All playgroups have to be registered and approved by the local Social Services department, so to check whether there are already playgroups in your area, contact them.

One o'clock clubs

One o'clock clubs tend to be found in the public parks of London and larger cities. They are staffed by trained playleaders and are open to mothers and pre-school children from one p.m. till mid-afternoon as a place for children to play and mothers to meet. As a local authority provision they are generally free.

Nursery schools

Although nursery schools and classes are legally allowed to take children from two years old, in practice they usually start at three. The potential clientele for nursery school places is much greater than the number of places available – the best local education authority can only offer places to just over twenty per cent of its three to five-year-olds.

Nursery schools and classes come under the aegis of the local education authority and the bias of the nursery school is educational. This doesn't mean that your child will be taught to read and write. He will spend most of his time in play but he will be supervised by qualified teachers and the play will teach him a lot about handling play materials, colours, shapes, numbers and the social skills of getting on with other children.

Nursery education in state schools falls into two categories – firstly, the nursery school, which exists as a separate entity and which children leave at the age of five in order to go on to primary school. Secondly, nursery classes, which are attached to an existing school so that in most cases children stay within that same school from the age of three until they leave it to start secondary education. There are also private nursery schools. Ask among your friends and neighbours or look in the Yellow Pages for a list of those in your area. For state nursery places contact the local education authority.

Choosing playgroups and nursery schools should be straightforward. Are you and your child welcomed? Are the children already there well-occupied? Is there a wide range of toys and activities and are the toys in good repair? Consider how easy it is to get to and fro and so on.

A good playgroup leader will let you know how your child is getting on in your absence. Don't be too surprised if some of the things you hear about him are unlike the way he behaves at home; children's behaviour can vary tremendously in different settings.

Play and mutual discovery of his surroundings is important to a young child's cognitive development, and can also be one of the most enjoyable aspects of motherhood. For most parents, one of the rewards of child-rearing, to be set against the drudgery, sleep disturbance and lack of freedom, is to watch a baby learning to cope with the world. As adults, it would take years to learn as much as babies learn in a few months, if it were possible at all. They have a way of opening our eyes again to much that we come to take for granted. *But are these rewards sufficient to satisfy today's parents who want greater freedom than did their own parents?*

"I'd meet my ex-boss and he'd say, 'When are you coming back to work?' and I knew the job would be open to me if I wanted it. It just became apparent that I knew I never would, couldn't possibly leave the child. I have this incredible love for her which I find difficult to explain and quite took me by surprise as it creeped up on me."

How much of my time can be spent looking after my own wants?

Whether or not returning to work is in question, striking a good balance between looking after your child's needs and your own is often the subject of argument, prejudice, and sometimes feelings of guilt.

It is now clear, from case studies, that it is the *quality* of the relationship with the child which fosters the bond between mother and child rather than the sheer *quantity* of time spent together. The single mother who has to work, or the career woman who returns to her job when her children are young, may sometimes feel that they are depriving them. They may also fear that the children will become more attached to their other caretakers than to themselves. The evidence suggests that this is not so. Kibbutzim children who are cared for by nurses of 'metapelets' and only see their parents for a few hours in the evening for play and conversation, are almost always fonder of their parents. It is the person who is most sensitive to the child's needs, and who has the most affectionate relationship with him, who is most significant in the child's emotional life and to whom he will become most attached.

It follows that a father who is warm and expressive with his child may be more significant than a mother who cares for the child all day, but who is less responsive to him or who is more irritable or moody. In fact, by the third year, many children show a preference for their father's company, rather than the mother's, especially when it is a question of play and having fun. Mother may still be more important when the child feels unhappy or unwell.

The key issue in attachment seems to be the intensity of the interaction rather than its duration, so if you only have a few hours together each day they should be as mutually enjoyable as possible. It may mean spending some of your income on domestic help or labour-saving machines so that you are not trying to do too much at once, or sharing the household work more equitably between both parents, so neither is

overburdened. It may mean not being too fussy about the house and giving the children top priority, especially in the early years. Above all it means not feeling guilty about the times when you are not there, so that it spoils the time together when you can enjoy each other's company to the full.

What is maternal deprivation?

Dr John Bowlby, a psychiatrist and researcher at the Tavistock Clinic in London, has been a major influence in child-care practice and research. He was the first writer to draw attention to the effects of early separation from their mothers on children's development and he and his co-workers have continued to develop his ideas. His starting point was the observation that some children and adults with severe personality problems had a history of separation from their mothers in the early years. They may have been illegitimate and brought up in a series of foster homes or in an orphanage. They had either never had the opportunity of forming a secure attachment to one person or had lost their attachment figure through death or desertion. In extreme cases, the person may have become incapable of forming a close relationship with anyone, trusted no one and cared for no one. He is an 'affectionless character'. As a result of researches, Bowlby concluded, *'what is believed to be essential for mental health is that the infant and young child should experience a warm, intimate and continuous relationship with his mother (or permanent mother substitute) in which both find satisfaction and enjoyment.'* In Bowlby's view, a child who does not have this experience suffers from 'maternal deprivation', as a child who is badly nourished suffers from physical deprivation.

For a time Bowlby's ideas were so influential that they affected government policy. For example, in cutting back on day nursery places and nursery schools, though he himself had never said that children needed their mother's care for twenty-four hours a day and should never be separated from them, even for a few hours. Partly because they had been exaggerated and misunderstood, a reaction set in against his theories. Other researchers criticised his findings and produced evidence that in many cases separation from the mother during childhood did not produce the disastrous effects he predicted. For example, children of working mothers are no more likely to be disturbed than other children. It was, however, generally accepted that separation from mother and home in the early years was a distressing experience for a child. Part of the evidence came in the form of films made of young children briefly separated from mother and home. The films were produced by John and Joyce Robertson who were colleagues of Bowlby at the Tavistock Clinic. The most common reason for brief separations in the normal family are hospital admissions for the child or the birth of another child in the family. The Robertsons filmed children who were in hospital or in children's homes or foster homes for brief periods. They showed very clearly the intense grief of the separated child and the stages through which he passes, coming to terms with his loss. Bowlby has defined these as 'protest, despair and detachment'. At first the child cries desperately and struggles to get back home, then he gives this up and looks deeply unhappy and withdraws from everyone. Finally, he appears to recover and begins to take an interest in what is going on around him. When he is finally reunited with his mother, he may appear not to recognise her or may angrily reject her for deserting him. In some later films, the Robertsons also showed how these effects could be diminished by providing a good foster home for a child who has to be taken into care for a short period. They fostered children themselves and showed that though they still missed their mothers and homes, a substitute mother who would be constantly available to comfort and play with them could relieve much of the distress. They also talked to the children about their home and family and kept the mother's image alive by looking at photographs and mementoes of her.

After decades of research, the consensus of opinion is that between the ages of about six months and three years, separations can be distressing and disturbing for children especially if there are already problems in the family, such as disharmony between the parents. *But much depends on the quality of the care he receives while separated and on how the parents cope with any difficult behaviour he shows on his return.*

If you are a mother having your second baby, you may miss the first very much while you are in hospital, and look forward to seeing him again. If he ignores you or pushes you away, and continues to be angry and defiant for some time after your return, you may feel hurt and rejected just as he felt hurt and rejected by your going away. He may be too young to understand that you had no choice and that you missed him too. Some children also become exceedingly clinging and demanding, refusing to let their mothers out of their sight, even to go to the lavatory, in case she disappears again. It can be very exhausting for a mother who is also coping with a new baby, to have a formerly independent toddler regress to being so babyish again. If you are a mother it is sometimes difficult to remember just how significant you are to your child. You may not feel like a VIP, but to him you are the most important person in the world, and everything you do affects him deeply.

His anger at separation is a sign of how great is his dependence and need for you, not of rejection or indifference.

What about going on holiday with or without my child?

It is advisable, if you are going to leave a young child with someone, to have a dummy run. If you intend taking him to a childminder, introduce the idea to him by degrees. Let him see that the childminder is someone you know and like. Leave him for an hour the first time and then return. If you intend leaving the child with relatives for a week or so, try an overnight stay first and see how it goes. Impress upon him, that you will be coming back. And start from an early age as you mean to go on. There is bound to be unhappiness if you wait until the child is four or five years before you leave him for the first time. Far too many parents give up all hope of wider horizons when children are small because they think travelling with them presents too many problems. Travelling with small children does take planning, but unless you are happy being housebound it is worth taking extra effort to organise a trip.

There is no such thing as the ideal holiday for a family with children. If you are rich enough to travel with your own nanny, presumably you could book into the Ritz with impunity. But the best bet for most people is a holiday which allows maximum freedom for all of the family and freedom for you to carry on your children's routine undisturbed. Most families with small children find that some form of self-catering accommodation in the country or at the seaside provides the best combination of freedom and space at a price they can afford.

The right equipment makes all the difference. The shortest journey may need a baby sling, a pram, or a push chair, or a back pack. Long journeys require iron rations, changes of clothes and nappies, a bag of toys and a travelling cot. Here is a basic travelling check list for anyone going far with a baby or a young child. You may not need all of it.

More disposable nappies than you think you will need – especially on air journeys. The all-in-one pants with lining are by far the best.

Tissues.

Plenty of cotton wool.

Plastic bags for disposing of rubbish, dirty nappies etc.

A damp flannel in a plastic bag or jar of baby wipes.

For small babies take extra Babygrows or other changes of clothing for inevitable accidents.

A packet of non-crumbly biscuits, savoury as well as sweet.

A selection of good portable food – bananas are ideal.

Bottle or mug.

An emergency bottle of milk or squash.

Dried baby foods and dried milk or powdered orange are easy to carry and only need added water to convert them into meals.

Entertainment will depend on the age of the child: a portable selection of small toys, books, pencils and paper.

Essential comfort objects like teddies or dummies. Carry a spare dummy if your child uses one and pin it to him on a piece of string. Hang the look of the thing – you will not want to be grovelling for dirty, dropped dummies on plane or car floors. Dummies, or sweets or a bottle are useful to give children on aircraft take-off for sucking to counteract the effects of pressure on their ears.

A carrycot, or later, a folding, travelling cot makes all the difference to your child and your self-sufficiency on the move. A travelling cot, in particular, can double as a playpen, and saves all those problems about borrowing cots or persuading hotels to instal them for you.

Travelling on planes
Airlines demand a medical certificate once the mother is past the seventh month of pregnancy and you may find, if you intend going on holiday in the last two months of pregnancy, that insurance companies will not insure you.

One of the great ironies of air travel is that although all airlines charge ten per cent of the fare for babies under two they give no baggage allowance. All mothers know that ninety per cent of the luggage they carry belongs to the baby, not them. The answer is to take as much of it into the cabin with you as 195 possible, where it will travel free. Over two years old and the fare rises to fifty per cent of the full fare.

The secret of successful air travel with small children is to be assertive, even selfish and ruthless. On all but the most crowded planes there is usually the odd spare seat. Make sure that you get it, even though you are not legally entitled to it, because every square inch you can grab will help. Most airlines put parents with small children onto the plane first so that they can settle – usually in the front seats. The bulkhead seats have the most leg room. If you are travelling with a small baby, ask when you book your ticket for a Skycot. These are portable carrycots provided by the airline which clip onto the cabin walls. The baby will sleep peacefully in its Skycot while you have a free lap left for eating your meal . There is usually no shortage of liquid refreshment on planes and small children can drink lots of water and fruit juice. Cabin staff will theoretically heat babyfoods for you, but while some are marvellously helpful, others turn a blind eye to mothers with small children.

Be warned that changing nappies in aeroplane lavatories is hell because there is no surface big enough – in most planes – to lay the baby down. Another reason for commandeering an extra seat. If the plane is not at all full, make sure that you get a row of three seats to yourself and then your journey will be easy. You and your child will have room to play, eat and sleep in comfort. Plane travel does no harm to small children and babies. The worst parts are the inevitable delays in strange airports when you run out of orange juice and nappies . . .

Cars

The British are not highly safety-conscious in cars, and especially not where children are concerned. On the continent it is illegal to allow children in front seats. In Britain you often see parents using small children as personal safety barriers on their laps. Who goes through the windscreen first if there is an accident? Never let children travel in front, and make sure that they are adequately secured on the back seat – not standing up breathing down the driver's neck, vulnerable to being thrown all over the car in an accident. Babies travelling in carrycots should always be secured by special safety straps available in any baby department. An unstrapped carrycot easily slides off the back seat with even a quick stop, and deposits its contents upside down on the floor. As soon as they can sit up, bigger babies and toddlers should have their own safety seat, secured to the car floor by garage staff with special safety straps. They must always be well strapped in. Older children should sit on the back seat secured by a lap strap. There is a kind of safety barrier available for children which doubles as a safety break and a table for them to play games and read books on as they travel. If your children are car-sick, ask your doctor to provide you with suitable travel-sickness medicine. Proprietary brands of travel-sickness medicine are prefectly suitable for children provided you stick to the stated children's dosage. Ask your chemist for his advice. Avoid letting them travel on too full or empty a stomach and always make sure that you have plastic bags for them to be sick into and the cloths to mop up if accidents occur. **Ref 4:2**

Taking a child abroad

If you are taking your children abroad you may be needlessly worried about the possible hazards to health. It is a fact that even the most under-developed and disease-prone countries continue to produce millions of children who somehow thrive. It is equally true that the well-nourished western children who go there often resist local infections better than their parents. It is essential not to be put off by well-meaning people who think that Britain is the only safe place for children. If you are worried about taking a child abroad, consult your GP. If you want the most up-to-date expert advice on health precautions and innoculations – especially in tropical countries – The Ross Institute of the London School of Hygiene and Tropical Medicine operates an excellent advice service. Apart from publishing their own booklet – *Preservation of Personal Health in Warm Climates*, they also provide a phone-in service to anyone with queries about health problems abroad **Ref 4:1** . You will be put through to someone who will help you. One of their experts is a paediatrician with particular experience of children in tropical countries who will be able to answer a parent's specific queries. **Ref 4:3**

To work or not to work?

The working mother
Advantages to you
Financial reward
Increased independence
Personal fulfilment
More intense interaction with your child when you are at home

Disadvantages to you
A sense of guilt at neglecting your child
Dissatisfaction because of dual responsibilities
The resentments of full-time mothers
A sense of isolation from support of other mothers in the community

The full-time mother
Advantages to you
Personal fulfilment
A sense that you are performing a worthwhile job
Increased involvement in a community
Avoiding a job that you didn't enjoy

Disadvantages to you
Less independence
Less money
A sense that not working leads to stagnation
All the problems that accompany bringing up a child

BABYSHOCK

All the arguments for and against full-time or working motherhood will not necessarily apply to you. You may be fortunate enough, if your husband's salary is sufficient, not to feel it is necessary to bring money into the family on your own account. As a working mother, you may not feel guilty that you are neglecting your child if you are able to provide him, like the Kibbutzim children, with adequate substitute care.

Financial reward

"Money is quite simply the only reason why I would consider working while the children were young."

What financial benefit will your absence bring? A recent book that took the view that all mothers of under-fives should stay at home – being state-subsidised to do so if necessary – concluded that most British working mothers actually bring home no more than £15 or £20 a week after they have paid for fares to and from work, taxes, and substitute care. This cannot be the final word, however, if it implies, as the author does, that this is a negligible sum in a modern family since for many it is a *crucial* sum and could be the total food bill, a sizable contribution to a mortgage, etc. Whatever your salary level, the important point is that you should weigh up whether the benefits *in your case* make the disadvantages *in your case* worthwhile.

"I did in fact go out to work part-time after she was born. I did it because of the money. I wouldn't have done so for my own sanity, because I really do believe that if you have children you should look after them. I enjoyed working to start with, but the job mushroomed and they asked me to work for them full-time. I held off. Then, after I'd been there nine months, the matter was taken out of my hands completely because they took on so much work

that not only did I have to go full-time, they had to employ someone to help me. So, I worked full-time for about three months and then stopped. It simply got to the point where I couldn't do both satisfactorily. I was always late for one or the other, and the money didn't compensate for the effect it was having on her. She became clingier, but it was possibly due to my hang-up. If you are happy with a situation then your child will also probably be happy with it. But I wanted to see more of her."

Independence

For some women, it is not enough to know that you can go back to work later. As has been seen, the sudden loss of independence particularly if it is accompanied by resentment that the child's father's life-style has not changed an iota, can in some cases lead to misery. There is absolutely no doubt that a new mother is not as free to satisfy her own needs outside the home if she takes on her motherhood role full-time.

"I am actually considering working freelance outside the home mainly because I find it extraordinarily exhilarating to be away from him for a few hours. I appreciate him much more when I come back to him. I could never work though if I felt that the child was not properly cared for in my absence."

Personal fulfilment

The wish for independence by itself is a fairly pointless reason for wanting to work unless a measure of personal fulfilment will result. In fact, it would be tantamount to admitting that you should never have had the child. Very many full-time mothers cannot understand how women can make a decision to have children and not look after them – as if it were a contradiction in terms. The argument has a great deal of force. Personal fulfilment was listed as an 'advantage' in both tables, however, and it is of course possible to achieve it from a number of different sources. You

198

may agree with the mother who said: *"At the very least it's a worthwhile job, and the highs you get from children are better than anything else."* You may, on the other hand, be drawn to the view from a successful working mother: *"(Working) should at least protect you from ever feeling that you are stagnating, or wasting your life, or becoming a cabbage."*

Resentment

Said one working mother, *"If you do make the decision to go back to work before your child is at school, you will need . . . a specially thickened skin to cope with the remarks and the resentments of traditional full-time home-maker mothers around you, who may try to make you feel you are failing in your duty. You are effectively cut off – if you actually leave the house every day to work – from the maternal club that exists in every neighbourhood. You cannot take your turn with the droppers at nursery school, or pickers up, or helpers with the nursery class. You cannot swop a weekday's care with another mother so that each of you has a free shopping day – although you may be able to do your bit at weekends . . . But be consoled. If you are single-minded about carrying on working as the right course for you, and manage to organise successful substitute care, you will be the object of unadmitted jealousy among those other mothers. You will quickly find that their babies will be no better behaved, no cleverer or happier than yours. And there is much personal gratification to be had out of managing two distinct modi operandi – your professional and your domestic life."*

It happens, probably less frequently, that full-time mothers feel guilty about *their* decision on the matter – usually if it is a mother's first child which has followed a personally successful career. This may be due to the impact of rousing arguments she has listened to before becoming a mother or reasoned now by childless women or indeed working mothers.

Generally the arguments turn on the stultifying aspects of motherhood, the importance that women take their rightful place in the world of work alongside men, or the common confusion that rearing a child is in the same category as washing up, cleaning the house, etc. The last argument is categorically wrong but perhaps excusable – the emphasis on baby craft as the essential ingredient of good motherhood has over the years reduced the art to the level of a housewifely chore.

In the end, if your mind has not been made up for you by circumstances beyond your control, you must make your own decision. In doing so, and particularly when considering the argument of the working mother above, look carefully at the real issue – the standard of substitute care available to you.

"What really got to me about leaving her was the idea of my daughter being looked after at a nursery by somebody during the term time and somebody else during the holidays when most children are spending time with their parents. I remembered coming home to an empty house from the age of six – always being first in. I'd come into the house and it was dark and cold and nasty. I really didn't want that for my children."

Can I work from home?

This does sound the ideal solution, but be wary since working at home does take a special sort of commitment. It is, simply, too easy to put off unless you are capable of a degree of self-discipline or the job itself has its own attractions which will draw you to it, irrespective of how much ironing, washing, etc. is piling up. The clear advantage of working at home, however, is its flexibility. **Ref 4:4** may give you some ideas for earning money at home.

What substitute care is available?

Employing nannies in your home is the most expensive form of child care but 199 probably the most satisfactory. Your child stays in the familiar home environment, there is no problem about having to work fixed hours (if the help lives in) and all you are really doing is extending the family network to one other person who is building a close relationship with the child. They are available on a daily basis or to live in at least from Monday to Friday. Either way she will have to be someone who will become part of the family and will genuinely love this type of work. The usual way of finding the right person is by advertising (in *The Lady*, *Nursery World*, or your local paper) or visiting domestic employment and nanny agencies (look under Babysitters in the Yellow Pages), or by word-of-mouth. Nannies invariably know other nannies who are thinking of changing jobs.

Really grand, upper-class nannies will expect a whole floor of your house as their base with a proper nursery, children's bathroom and good quarters for themselves with colour television thrown in. They will also expect a good salary. In return for this very large outlay you will have a properly qualified, highly experienced nanny who will take the entire job of child care and rearing off your hands – if that is what you want. She will not do any other jobs in your house because, of course, you will have other domestic staff to do that for you. A younger, well-qualified but less grand nanny will still expect reasonable accommodation, a good salary and a high degree of autonomy with your children and she will not expect to do housework either. One nanny agency in London **Ref 4:5** operates a system called Share-A-Nanny. The idea is that two families in the same neighbourhood get together and share the cost of a nanny who looks after both sets of children. The idea is a good one but is difficult to make work in practice. The chief difficulties lie in

exactly matching the needs and time-tables of the two families and sometimes the system breaks down completely. However, if you have a friend in the same position as you and you think you can make it work, it is an idea well worth considering. It is still not cheap.

Mothers' he'lps

If you want someone who will combine child-care with hoovering the floor and peeling the potatoes then you need a mother's help. They will come to look after your children but they will do housework as well. They may well be less qualified than a nanny – they may not have done specialised NNEB training – but they might be just as experienced. If they live in, then you can expect to pay them anything between £25 and £35 a week. If they come in daily then they will expect from £35–£45 a week – and in both cases we are talking about a salary after-tax. Mothers' helps are found through the same sources as a nanny although it is often worth advertising locally.

In the case of both mothers' helps and nannies you can knock anything between £10 and £15 a week off their salary if you also provide their accommodation and meals.

Could you stand having a substitute mother in your house?

This is a hard question to answer until you have tried it. But it is true that to appoint a second mother, and to work at making the three-way relationship with you and your child successful, you have to be both adaptable and tolerant. You have to recognise that your nanny's needs are as important as yours.

What should I look out for when choosing a nanny/mother's help?

First, she should strike you as a loving and caring person, and as someone you could get on with. Usually you will know this instinctively, but in brief interviews it is horribly possible to make regrettable misjudgements. Observe how she reacts to the baby on first meeting. Establish from the beginning how long you would like her to stay with you (usually six months at least) and precisely what her duties and hours will be (usually a five and a half day week with a long weekend off once a month; evening by arrangement). Some nannies will help with housework, others won't; some cook, some sew. In return they usually expect a room to themselves, preferably with bathroom and their own television. And when you consider the vital importance of the work they are doing for you, these are extremely reasonable expectations. When you arrange salary, talk about how many meals she will have with you, and whether she will be expected to pay for her own telephone calls.

For her sake also, you should be honest about the way you live. No point in saying, "I'm always home by five-thirty" if you aren't, or "We don't go out much in the evenings" if you plan to change all that, with her help. Get it all straight from the start. If you say she can use the car on her nights off, or watch television any time, you have to mean it. If you do not want her to smoke you must say so; nanny agencies ask employers to specify this.

There are great difficulties about providing care for small babies *outside* the home; they require very personal care from a small number of people who know them very well. Outside the family these are not easy conditions to fulfil. Nurseries for babies need to be small and well-staffed so that there is plenty of time for cuddling and playing with them, as well as the routines of physical care.

Local Authority Day Nurseries
You can find out about these from the Social Services Department of your Local Authority. Although these exist to offer full-time day care to the children of full-time working parents, your chances of finding a place for your child are minimal. Because day care is so thin on the ground, places in nurseries like these are reserved almost entirely for the children of problem families and of single parents. They are not always ideal places.

Whereas nursery schools come under the aegis of the local education authority, day nurseries come under Social Services and are traditionally staffed by nursery nurses under the eye of a formal matron. Their approach to the children in their charge is custodial rather than educational. In other words they see their role as keeping the children fed, watered, changed and in one piece rather than as giving them anything extra in the way of stimulation and play. Often the way a nursery is run means that staff do not have the time to spend with individual children, especially as day nurseries are practically the only child-care facility which will take small babies as well as toddlers and pre-school children. Unfortunately, this lack of stimulation and affectionate attention from adults often only compounds the damage done by poor home circumstances.

BABYSHOCK

Crêches and private nurseries

Although day nurseries, public and private, are the only form of outside day care that offer a full day to the working mother, it has been estimated that the total number of nursery places available cater for less than a quarter of the children of working mothers who need the services. Private crêches and nurseries hardly fill the gap, partly because there are not many of them and partly because they are usually expensive. Charges in local authority nurseries are nominal because they are subsidised. Charges in private nurseries have to be more commercial, although often they are subsidised by the employers of the people who use them. Unfortunately, despite constant campaigning for crêches, there are still almost more campaigns than there are actual crêches. The best way to find out what is available in your area is to contact the local Social Services Department. All nurseries, public or private, have to be vetted by the local council and their premises must comply with the law. Staff ratio requirements differ, but an average is one member of staff to between six and eight children.

But it is essential to vet them yourself. In the meantime, NALGO has produced a booklet called *Workplace Nurseries: NALGO Negotiating Kit*, which advises employees how to go about campaigning for child care at their place of work. It draws heavily on real experience of crêches set up by the National Health Service and academic institutions, deals in detail with the actual cost of setting up crêches, and is a mine of useful advice about maternity and paternity leave, re-training etc. **Ref 4:6**

In terms of outside care, a good childminder is probably the best substitute for her although it is almost impossible to manage more than one small baby at a time, especially if there are toddlers to look after as well.

Childminders

A childminder is a person who takes your child into her own home and cares for her, for a wage. A great deal of controversy has surrounded childminders recently, largely because they vary so much in quality. A childminder is the traditional solution to the problems of the working mother and one estimate says that some three million children are looked after by childminders, registered and unregistered. The advantage of a good childminder is that your child will be looked after in an ordinary home as opposed to institutional surroundings. Provided that the childminder is only looking after two or three other children, your child can find himself in a family atmosphere and be able to develop a steady relationship with the minder, much as he would with an aunt or grandmother. **Ref 4:7**

The disadvantages of bad minders are many. Unregistered minders may have inadequate premises. They may take too

many children simply to make extra money. They may neglect the children physically – leaving them to cry, changing them infrequently, feeding them inadequately. They may neglect them mentally and emotionally – offering them no affection, not playing with them, never taking them out. Children who attend such minders become, at best, very silent and subdued and can fall drastically behind other children of their age.

So the first precaution to take is to make sure that the minder is registered with the local Social Services Department. They will give you a list of registered minders. Inteview the minder thoroughly. Your child's health and happiness are at stake. What you are looking for is not necessarily an immaculate and tidy home – sometimes a bad sign – but any indication that the minder is affectionate to and plays with the children in her care.

Are there lots of toys, books, small chairs and a table for drawing and painting, stimulating colours? How many children does the minder look after? How many rooms are the children permitted to use? Do the children get out in the fresh air, to play in a garden or walk in a park?

Watch out for the large and centrally-placed television set. If you suspect that the children are just plonked in front of the set for a large part of the afternoon, look elsewhere. Brian Jackson's recent book, *Childminder* opened our eyes to the sometimes horrific conditions that certainly do exist in minders' homes in many working-class urban areas where the mothers' need to return to the factory to work is often desperate. But good, responsible, affectionate and caring minders do exist – women who talk to the children in their charge, take a real interest in them, cook them wholesome meals and positively enjoy their company. The observation of these key attributes is up to you.

If she seems the kind of person you are happy to have care for your child, return frequently, if necessary, to check that all is well. A good minder will understand and apreciate your concern. A childminder can cost anything between £10 and £18 a week depending on the area, but £12 is a reasonable average. Childminders, conscious of the bad image given them in the past, are making more effort to raise their standards and some councils arrange courses and facilities for their minders. A good minder who is plugged into this wider network of expertise and play facilities may be the best child-care solution for a working mother.

The choice is fairly limited, and for most working mothers the best care is out of reach. In Britain the situation cannot be said to be dramatically improving. If public opinion can be gauged at all by the popularity of recent books, and recent political manifestos, then the tide is turning in favour of full-time mothers once more. That in itself does not bode well for the future of care facilities for working mothers. Having discussed what care a child needs in these important developmental years and seen what alternative care facilities are available, the frankest conclusion has to be that not all children of working mothers *can* be receiving adequate care – and it is interesting that the Liberal Party has reached the conclusion that some sort of State funding should be introduced to support financially deprived full-time mothers on the basis of statistics available on delinquency.

Only as children get older are they able to cope with more change and variety in their caretakers, and begin to enjoy the company of other children more. Two-year-olds do not really play with each other but they enjoy playing alongside other children and watching their games and activities. By three, they are usually speaking quite fluently and are beginning to be capable of genuine co-operative play. Playgroup or nursery school is not a way of relieving the 203 mother but a most enjoyable and valuable experience for the child.

If you must seek substitute care of some kind, it is your responsibility to ensure that the caretaker you choose is capable of looking after your child *as you would yourself*. That necessitates a consistent attitude towards the three aspects of care which have been discussed. Remember that it is your own happiness for years to come as well as your child's that is at stake. Pursue the 'investigation' with unqualified thoroughness, not failing to take up references or talking to other mothers because you think it unkind or untrusting of the caretaker herself.

If you do decide to work, and can find adequate substitute care, the most vital aid to life as a working mother – even before you get to the choice of a mother-substitute – is an understanding partner. More than understanding, he will have to be tolerant, equality-minded, positively helpful and encouraging, not likely to be irritated at the inconvenience of having a working mother for a wife. He will need to be as flexible about your working hours as his own. He will need to help on Sundays so that you too can have a day off. He will understand that working all week and mothering all weekend takes its toll on you. He will never sneer at your work or belittle it. He will realise its importance to you and your self-esteem.

Blessed with such a paragon, the other half of your battle as a working mother is over. There are lots of husbands who *say* they don't mind their wives working, but actually take it out on her by expecting her to catch up on domestic chores in the evenings without helping her at all.

It is incumbent on all fathers to realise that bringing up children is a joint responsibility from the start, and it is never more important than in a two-career family. To learn to share parenthood equally, not only has the father to take an increased part in child care, but the mother has to relinquish the conviction that she is naturally better at it. She has to be able to trust her husband to share her traditional role to do it equally well – as of course, he probably can.

What about the special problems of the single mother?

An increasing number of families is being brought up by one parent. A few are fathers, struggling against the odds to bring up their children single-handed, when the mother has deserted or died, but most are mothers. A few may have chosen to have a child on their own, but most have not and are simply making the best of a bad job. The future consequences of raising so many fatherless children have yet to be faced, but in the meantime single mothers have to work out new ways of organising family life, so that they and their children have the best existence possible. There is no denying that a child without a father is disadvantaged, though the disadvantage might well be greater if the parents decided to stay together in an atmosphere of hostility and distrust.

The single mother has to be both mother

and father and many women find it takes a major adjustment to develop the more 'masculine', decisive, authoritative side of themselves while continuing to be accepting and tender to their children. Whenever possible, the children's relationship to the father should be encouraged and protected, so that they do not feel he has left home because of them. The mother then has to consider herself and how she is to preserve her emotional and physical well-being. She will probably find that she needs her own family and her friends more than ever before, and she will also need new sources of support to make up for the loss of a permanent partner. Gingerbread groups and other organisations such as the National Council for One Parent Families **Ref 4:8** provide a new social life and the comfort of knowing that other people have faced the same problems and survived, as well as useful information about tax, insurance, housing, day care, etc.

Gingerbread is a well-organised pressure group which operates 300 local self-help groups. Not only can they help individual parents and their children with practical problems and queries but they can put them in touch with their local group who will provide both practical and moral support. Gingerbread organise day care schemes and have arranged holidays for one parent families. They produce booklets and information on all the problems affecting one parent families

Both economic necessity and loneliness may make it imperative that the single mother returns to work, to as interesting a job as she can find. The better she makes life for herself without actually neglecting her children, the better mother she will be. A depressed, despairing mother, creates enormous problems for a child; he feels he has to make it all right for her and it is too much for him to cope with. He may either become prematurely responsible and adult or realise he cannot do it and give up trying to achieve anything at all. On the other hand, some children in single parent families feel justly proud of their achievements in having managed well in difficult circumstances and they may develop stronger characters than other children who have never had to face any problems in life at all.

The single mother is soon aware of being in an unusual social position. She is neither unattached like her single friends nor securely attached like her married ones. She may experience a considerable conflict between her desire for a new sexual partner and her sense of responsibility to her children. If she meets a likely new partner should she bring him home to meet the children, or to spend the night when it may not last for very long? It is tempting to have someone move in to replace the lost husband and father as quickly as possible. If it does not work and there is a series of stepfathers in and out of the house, the children may become disturbed and unhappy. They have to cope not only with the mother's distress as each new relationship breaks down but also with their own because they may have become attached to him too. It pays to be discreet and, where possible, conduct affairs away from home until some definite commitment has been made.

12
Parents as models

Parental conflict has been shown to be the single most potent cause of child psychiatric disturbance.

Parents as models

Before he crawls, a child usually begins to copy his mother for instance in peek-a-boo games, and throughout his development he will look to his parents as models for his behaviour. The most consistent attitude towards his care will be undermined by his parents displaying a contradictory stance in their own relationship or in relationships with others. The demands of 'good enough mothering' do not end with direct communication with your child.

What harm will rowing in front of the children have?

Every married couple has occasional rows. If they don't, one or both are bottling up their natural feelings of occasional anger and exasperation. No two people live closely together without some conflict, and rows are a means of resolving that conflict and getting the relationship on to the right footing again. Constant rows or a continuous state of hostility between parents are another thing entirely. When there is more hate than love in the relationship,

children infer the obvious – hate must be more powerful than love, and love does not stand a chance. *In study after study, parental conflict has been shown to be the single most potent cause of child psychiatric disturbance.*

The disturbance is usually of the 'acting out' kind, involving difficult behaviour, aggression, truanting and later delinquency, rather than the more neurotic type of emotional disturbance. It is not clear exactly why children are so badly affected by marital discord, but the lack of an harmonious relationship at home on which a child's own emotional stability is based is the most obvious explanation. Seeing his parents insulting and criticising each other, mistrusting each other, and sometimes physically assaulting each other, reduces his trust in both of them. How can they be relied on to love and care for him when they treat each other so badly? The example they set him for relationships is not one of generosity, co-operativeness and warmth, but of meanness and hostility. It is, therefore, not surprising if he relates to other 209 people in the same way, fighting and arguing with parents, siblings, teachers and schoolmates. He lives on the edge of a volcano, not knowing when the next eruption will take place, and taking out his misery and anger on the world at large.

Quarrelling parents are also often so pre-occupied with their battles that they have little time or energy for anything else, and the care of the children may suffer. If your rows become more acrimonious and frequent, it is time to take stock of the situation and try to work out a better basis for the marriage. Even if the children have been upset by it, they will gradually settle down again if you sort out your relationship. Stop criticising each other and try a little honest self-criticism instead. Are you really so blameless, and is only your partner responsible for all your troubles? If you cannot resolve the situation on your own, despite all your efforts, don't be ashamed to talk to friends. If this doesn't help, look for expert advice, from a marriage guidance counsellor, priest, social worker or other appropriate professional person. Once you are caught up in a relationship of conflict it can be very difficult to see what is going on, and an objective third person can help to untangle the threads.

Is 'staying together for the children's sake' harmful?
Some embattled parents feel they must stay together for the sake of their children, even when they have tried and failed to resolve their marital difficulties, and it is clear to them and everyone else that they will never be happy together. As has been made clear in the preceding section, if you are in this position you are not doing your children any favours. If you are concerned about them, then you should either try harder to resolve the problems, or agree to differ and separate. The problem is that the real reason for

staying together may be nothing to do with the children, and places a totally unnecessary burden of responsibility on them. Many couples in conflict need each other despite the awfulness of it all. Who would they have to blame when things went wrong without each other? This is a likely pattern where both partners are insecure and prickly individuals who have a lot of problems coping with relationships in general. Painful as it is to be unhappily married, it can be even more painful to face up to one's own faults and inadequacies. The fighting may therefore serve a function for you but it does not for your children, especially if they feel you are putting up with such an unhappy life because of them.

What are the effects of separation or divorce on children and how can the situation be best explained to them?
Despite the many disadvantages suffered by single-parent families, their children are probably less likely to be adversely affected than are the children of deeply divided parents. Obviously, a happy, intact home is better. Children brought up in one-parent families are more likely to be disturbed or delinquent, especially when separation or divorce has been the cause, rather than the death of a parent. This fact suggests that the conflict preceding the break-up is more significant than the actual loss of the parent. It is also possible that however desolated a child may be by a parent's death, he does not feel *rejected* in the way he does if the parent chose to leave the family. He can therefore come to terms with his loss more easily, after a necessary period of grief and mourning.

Divorce is therefore not a light matter if there are children involved. It may be better than chronic family hostility but it is not better than resolving the conflict and living together in harmony. It involves the child in a division of loyalties, and if he is deeply attached to both parents he may find it painful to have to live with one without the other. If divorce is inevitable, the conflict can be lessened by explaining the situation to him as objectively and with as little malice as possible.

He should know that although his parents no longer love each other, they still love him and both will continue to care for and accept responsibility for him. They may no longer be married, but they are both still his parents, and they should co-operate together for the welfare of the children. The marital battle should not continue to be fought using the children as ammunition. Disputes over access, or the continued denigration of parents by each other will give the child no opportunity to settle down to a peaceful life with one parent or the other. There are very rare occasions when the parent is so disturbed that he or she is a destructive influence on a child, in most cases it is better to keep in steady and predictable contact. Young children particularly can only maintain a relationship if they see someone frequently and regularly. Dropping in occasionally, and out of the blue, can be very disruptive to the child's security. If he is very fond of the parent (it is usually the father, so for convenience will be referred to as 'he') he may be constantly tensed up and waiting for him to appear. It also helps to have a regular place in which to meet, preferably the father's new home where ordinary family activities like games and meals together can continue. Cafés and parks may be fun on occasions, but their delights soon pall compared to the comfort and privacy of home. If the father lives too far away for the children to be taken there, or if he has no settled place of abode, it may be better for the meeting to take place in the family home while the mother goes out for the day, or evening, or weekend.

One of the unresolved – and perhaps unresolvable – problems of divorce is that the remaining parent (usually the mother) has to carry a much heavier burden of work and responsibility than in an intact family. She may easily become over-strained and edgy because she has too little time for rest and recreation. If the plans for access are made in a spirit of generosity and genuine concern for the children, it can provide a much needed respite for her, as well as maintaining the children's relationship with the father on a more solid and realistic basis than if it only involves treats and joy-rides. Otherwise he may become a very peripheral figure to his children, and their affection for him may dry up for lack of sustenance.

If the mother re-marries, and the children acquire a stepfather, and possibly new sisters and brothers as well, the family structure becomes exceedingly complicated. Step-parents have a difficult role, as the many folk tales of wicked stepmothers testify. The lost parent may become idealised in the child's mind, and the step-parent has to put up with all his negative and destructive thoughts about parental shortcomings. For young children he may 211 simply become the father, with all the respect and affection a natural father would receive. Older children may feel it would be disloyal to transfer their affections too readily, and may take some time to adapt to the new household.

If the children react at first by being critical and difficult, the couple may be anxious that their new marriage will not stand up to the strains. Doing justice to both the marriage and the children is something of a balancing act, and there will probably need to be more discussions about contentious issues than in an ordinary family, where more can be taken for granted. Professional help may be needed at some stage to find out how the family can live together more contentedly. The advantages to the children of their mother's remarriage may only be felt later, when they are growing up, and can then get on with their independent lives without worrying about leaving her too much alone. **Ref 4:8**

We hear a lot about the importance of the early years. Once there are serious problems with a young child, will they affect him for much of his life? Fortunately not. The message from most research and clinical experience is that it is never too late to make a fresh start. For example, the research on maternal depression has found that if the mother gets better so does the child, and the same applies to other psychiatric disturbance in parents. Many families go through periods when life is difficult for all its members. A young child may be ill and everyone else is exhausted and anxious so the other children get shortshrift. An elderly parent may have a terminal illness and their spouse may need a lot of extra care from their grown-up children while they themselves are in the midst of child-bearing and child-raising.

A child may have to go into hospital and come back angry and insecure as if he felt that it were his parents' fault that he became ill. A parent may go through a period of emotional crisis, perhaps after losing a job or because temporarily estranged in the marriage. Any of these situations could be a starting point of life-long problems for a child in the family, but none of them need to be.

Children are acutely aware of the emotional state of their parents and sensitive to their irritability or preoccupation with other problems and they may react by disturbed or difficult behaviour. They may sleep badly, become very fearful, get into tempers easily and so on. To the hard-pressed parent coping with some external crisis, the child's behaviour may seem the last straw and he or she may feel very angry about it. Once the crisis is past there is time to reflect on what has happened and the opportunity to make up to everyone for the time and attention they have been missing out on.

As children get older, it is possible to discuss with them what has been going on and this may be a great relief. It can be done in a very simple and restrained way. For example: "I'm sorry I'm so grumpy today, I'm a bit worried about Granny not being well." Young children tend otherwise to think it is really their fault if their parents are unhappy or upset. They feel bad and guilty and will react by becoming tense or behaving in a disturbed way. The evidence seems to suggest that it is not the rare traumatic event or acute crisis which causes later emotional illness but the chronic repetition from a disturbed pattern recurring relentlessly during the years of childhood. Frequently, being blamed or disparaged, always having to support an anxious or depressed parent, consistently being neglected or ignored - these are the real scourges of childhood which leave their mark.

13
Looking to
the future

Re-adjusting at year five

Looking to the future

"You have to sort yourself out a whole new philosophy when they are more or less off your hands. Bringing up children takes you over so much – not just in a practical sense, but mentally too. Over the last two years, I have had to adjust to just this change. Perhaps I could have prepared myself for it earlier, but that might have deprived the children in some way. I like to think that the fact that I didn't work when they were growing up was justified, and I feel good about it being selfless . . . But that hasn't helped me much now."

The day that your last child starts school heralds a new stage in the continuing process of change which began with the conception of your first child. How you approach it depends on what you have been doing and thinking while your children were small. If those years have been spent simultaneously caring for your own needs beyond child-centred activities, you are far less likely to find yourself standing at the school gates a lonely and empty person.

Playgroup or nursery school does in part prepare you for this novel independence, but at that stage the day's routine still revolves around your children. When your youngest child is five years old and at school, there is a *real* sense of change. Some mothers miss the fraught times as much as the good times, and the silent home has a way of making a mockery of comments like,"I bet you're glad to have them off your hands."

Although the fifth year of your child's life is the limit of this book's undertaking, his development and yours as his mother do not of course stop there. But caring full-time for another human being evokes qualities few other activi-

ties summon, and there may be a real sense that never again will you utilise the qualities which brought both you and your child through the first five years.

Because the highs you get from full-time motherhood are unique, it is tempting to shelve the problem of what to do now, and some women indulge in what has been called 'neurotic creativity' – they simply have more children.

Having children for selfish reasons, whether conscious or sub-conscious, is at best a shaky basis for your future happiness, not to mention your child's. However experienced a mother you are, if your partner is not really interested in another child the repercussions could be problematic for the whole family.

The other more positive way to look at this new stage in your life is to ask yourself how you can actually benefit from your experience as a mother. If it was a fulfilling experience, how can it be harnessed to help create a more fulfilling 'public' life than you enjoyed before you became a mother?

"Motherhood prepares you to cope with life far better than any sort of work. For a start it is more difficult than most jobs and certainly more creative. The only problem is that you are unlikely to be satisfied with the kind of job you did before becoming a mother. You are older, and having run a home and brought up children, you don't feel prepared to do anything as menial as a secretary, for example."

The first thing is to set about changing your self-image – something which 215 tends to be characterised by the way you think about yourself as much as the way other people think of you. Because motherhood has for years been associated with housewifely chores, this is no easy feat. However outspoken you were about the virtues of full-time motherhood while you were engaged in it, you will have to come to terms with the fact that it rarely does much for your *curriculum vitae*. The changes that are involved are similar to the changes you had to make when first becoming a mother. They have to do with self-confidence and determination to succeed despite apparently over-whelming odds.

"For a long time you hide behind your children, and suddenly you have to go out and make new relationships again, unbound by anything to do with having children. There is no easily pin-pointed common denominator between you and the other people you are now rubbing shoulders with. You forget what it is like after eight years at home. It's actually very good for your self-confidence, and it gives you another dimension which people respect you for."

As before, you will need all the support your partner can provide.

"I had no idea how much was going to be involved in going back to work. I love it, but there were terrible rows at home. After eight years, my husband actually found it harder than I to come to terms with the fact that things were going to change. It wasn't just a question of whether or not he approved of my going back to work. He was going to have to change a few things in his life too. I decided I would train to teach dress-making and that meant a three-year City and Guilds dress-making course. It was only a question of his being home in time for me to go out and study on a few evenings a week . . ."

Some husbands, particularly if the family is not in need of extra money, may resist the idea of wives taking on commitments elsewhere. If this happens to you, ask him why, what worries him about your going out to work? There really is no reason for him to hang on to the tired, old-fashioned precept that your place is in the home – and there are probably very few husbands today who would admit to believing it anyway. Make it plain to him that you need to keep up with the changes that the rest of the family is going through and that your absence from the home is not going to cause irreparable damage to the family, provided he understands that he too is going to have to adapt to change along with everyone else. Inevitably, when taking on something new, there is a shift in priorities. Through discussion with him alone or in the company of friends who have made a similar transition, it should be possible to work out a path of compromise which will not cause the family to fall apart. Because your freedom is actually what is in question it may be tempting to make your points forcibly. Psychologically, it may not be the best course of action. As in becoming parents in the first place demanded changes in both of you, so now changes are occurring which are best handled together.

Then of course there are the practical problems of what to do. If you decide to take up your career where you left off, your contemporaries of say ten or twelve years ago may have left you far behind. Will you be able to 'get back in'? Employers are unlikely to welcome you with open arms. Although, in many jobs, employers do prefer to employ women who have had children simply because they feel secure in the knowledge that they will not suddenly leave.

See page 244 – there is a list of training programmes and organisations which recognise the difficulties women face in returning to work. **Ref 4:9** It is particularly worth considering work which utilises knowledge you have acquired in the process of bringing up children. If you have enjoyed assisting in the development of your child's personality there are short training courses – for which academic achievement is often unimportant – that will enable you to pass on your knowledge.

Appendix

BABYSHOCK

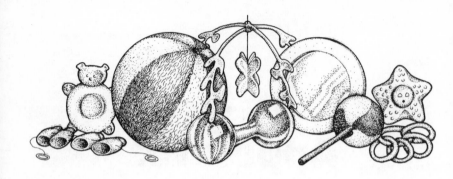

Birth to six months

Hang mirrors.

Bells (e.g. a cane ball with bell inside, or any soft furry ball with rattle or bell inside it that will hang in a cot).

The Fisher Price Bluebird musical box with pull ring is indestructible and, later, is easily operated by the baby.

Mobiles, suspended from the ceiling above the cot. But keep out of reach and securely fixed.

Nursery friezes, bright pictures can also be hung on the walls near the cot.

The family cat, dog or budgie will be as fascinating and popular as any of the aforementioned articles. Prop your baby in a cradleseat and leave the pet to do the rest. The Mothercare bouncing cradle – a seat of canvas and wire – can be used as soon as head control is developed (i.e. around six weeks on).

Rattles, such as the Mothercare Rumba and the Kiddicraft plastic triangles, which have been going strong for thirty-five years, come into their own at this stage. At about five to six months start to prop your baby up with cushions on the floor or wedged in a high chair so that there is a surface to play on. A dropped object can then be retrieved without adult assistance.

A playpen is a useful safe place to put an increasingly mobile baby while you answer the phone or the doorbell. It is also a useful device if there are older brothers and sisters around who are playing with swallowable marbles or Lego bricks. But more than this, it provides a stable framework for the baby to pull himself to standing.

A cradle-play of swivelling rattles on a string made by Kiddicraft can be strung across a playpen or elsewhere, within the baby's reach. This sort of play helps hand-eye co-ordination and is a source of entertainment at the age of four to five months before he can sit up properly.

Six months to a year

Most of the toys in the previous section continue to be appropriate. Within the playpen, certain toys can be usefully attached to the bars – the best playpens have bars.

The Fisher Price Happy Apple and other floor toys come into their own now.

The Fisher Price Activity Centre is also a good bet.

During this period your baby will learn to sit unaided, releasing his hands to pick up objects and, inevitably, put them in his mouth. This is the normal way for babies to learn about shape, texture and so on, and should not be discouraged.

A ball is fun now. The Mothercare First Ball, which can be clutched, or even a large lightweight plastic beachball will do – as will anything that squeaks when squeezed .

Small cuddly toys, and Duplo Lego or Sticklebricks are fun to finger at this stage. The Fisher Price Floating Family is perhaps better played with out of the bath now.

One to two years

A busybox – home-made and of all-consuming interest at this age. Collect together thirty or forty small objects that can be felt, thrown, touched, examined, things of different colours, shapes and textures, anything to excite curiousity, and put them in a large bucket, basket or reinforced hardboard box. The idea is that your baby sits on a blanket on the floor and gets on with it – Start by emptying all the contents of his busybox onto the floor. Almost anything will do – velvet pieces or fur fabric, a pingpong ball, a small jar filled with rattling lentils, a defunct bunch of keys, cotton reels, bright labels or 221 packaging pasted on thick card, a set of animal picture cards, or small furry toys.

Pushalongs or pullalongs encourage mobility now. The Galt wooden truck is an idea. Fill it with telephone directories for balance, and if you do not choose Galt, make sure it has a stable supportive handle. Among pullalongs, the Fisher Price chattering telephone and the Kiddicraft Clatterpillar (a bright orange and yellow plastic, very robust rattling centipede) are favourites.

Another mobility toy, which will be used for the next two years is the pedal-less tricycle, or equivalent sit-on-and-scoot vehicle.

One to two-year-olds like action toys triggered by a simple action.

Jack-in-the-box.

Musical box.

Mothercare Trigger Jigger pop-up toy.

They are also fascinated by relationships between objects.

Hammer pegs are good fun.

The Galt posting box.

Kiddicraft beakers.

Duplo Lego.

Before any representational artwork comes amusement through copying you draw or mould shapes.
Thick jumbo-sized crayons are good.

Plasticine (but keep it away from the carpet).

Home-made play dough could also be introduced.

Fantasy play brings a number of household objects into their own now.
Pots and pans (but keep the bleach out of reach).

Also dolls, teddies, toy telephones, toy hammers are useful now.

Colourful picture books are enjoyed as much for turning the pages as looking at the pictures. Rag books rarely work.

Two to three years

A blackboard, easily painted on the back of a door with special blackboard paint or bought mounted on an easel.

Finger paints.

Colouring books.

Rocking or riding animal.

Jig-saws (simple six-piece now, but getting more advanced as the year progresses).

Bean bags for learning to throw and catch.

Humming spinning top.

Beads, large and brightly coloured to string onto necklaces and bracelets.

Cookery set with miniature pots and pans.

Baking set with cut-out shapes for pastry. 'Helping' you in the kitchen now can be a mutually enjoyable pastime.

Glove puppets.

Dolls accoutrements, such as prams, cots, buggies.

Dolls that you can do things with.

Non-pointed scissors for cutting out pictures.

Scrapbooks for the cut-outs.

Coloured stars and gummed paper shapes.

Dominoes, the large junior type.

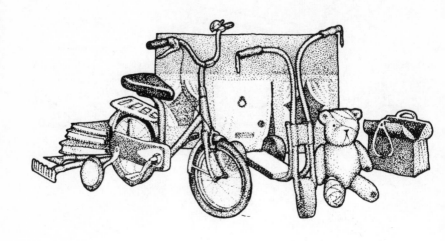

Three to starting school

Tricycle.

Climbing frame.

Scooter.

Garden swing.

Miniature adult tools, such as rake, trowel, watering can.

Make-believe toys, such as hospital or nurse's set, post office set with lickable stamps.

Clicking toys, such as an old typewriter or Palitoy Tutor Typer, which has keys which click but writes words itself.

Printing set (needs patient supervision).

Puppet theatre (improvise one for glove puppets to encourage dialogue and invention).

Shop (again improvise this with plenty of old jars, packets, boxes, etc. for playing at buying or selling).

Clock (big and plastic, but with hands which can tell the time).

Tea-set.

Snap cards.

Nursery records. The ones by Three Four Five Publishing are especially good. Rhymes are sung by small piping voices of children themselves. Tapes are recommended for long car journeys.

Build up the busybox with the kind of items the wizards on BBC TV's Playschool use to fashion ingenious things with – lavatory roll middles, milk bottle tops, pipe cleaners, yoghurt cartons, Squeezy bottles, glossy magazines, round-edged sweet tins, etc.

Collages. Three-to-fives enjoy cutting out bright pictures from magazines and Christmas cards, and make a collage using a simple flour and water paste. Other things to cut and stick on might include scraps of material, bits of wool and string, raw spaghetti and rice, pieces of egg-shell, feathers, milk tops, flowers, leaves, spent matches, coloured tissues, used stamps, glitter powder. For paste, mix half a cup of flour with enough water to make it creamy; boil slowly, stirring frequently.

Play dough. To make, add a quarter cup of salt and a little cooking oil, plus enough water to make a pliable dough, to each cup of flour. Food colouring or powder paint can be added. Kept in a plastic bag in the fridge, it lasts several days.

Sand. The best sort of sand for children's play is builder's washed river sand which can be bought in a bag from a builder's merchant. Why not use a lorry tyre from a garage as a basis for a sandpit? Sand play tools are the same as you might take to the beach – buckets, spades, plastic flowerpots, yoghurt cartons, spoons, etc.

Water. If you are tolerant enough, this could be organised at home. Use a waterproof sheet under a washbowl or near the sink. Fill either with para-phernalia such as plastic beakers, Squeezy bottles, cartons, some with holes in to make pouring more interest-ing. Also corks, pebbles, ping pong balls, toy boats, floating lolly sticks, straws, tubes, balloons. Water, like play dough, can be coloured with any food dye.

Paper and pencil play is absorbing at this age. Leave the child with paper, crayons or felt-tips and let him get on with it. It is a good idea to leave plenty of pictures or alphabet books about for inspiration.

Domestic chore play. This may be the answer when you have to get on with something in the house. Your toddler may not let you alone – he wants to stay and help. So, set aside certain tasks which can be done with the child around – cleaning large areas of paintwork, for instance, or washing a car, polishing a big table or clearing out a cupboard. Only with small meticulous tasks should a child be a hindrance.

Dressing up. All children adore this. Why not make up a collection in a trunk, basket or cupboard of clothes nobody cares for any more. Hats and old wigs are especially important. Hats trans-form identities – cowboys, policemen, bakerboys, Red Indians, brides, busi-nessmen all wear hats which tend to end up in local jumble sales. Eye masks,

parasols, shawls, lengths of old fur, old handbags, discarded spectacles, false beards, moustaches, and gaudy jewellery are all popular. You could also add musical instruments – a drum, tam-bourine, recorder, triangle or xylophone. Christmas tinsel, pieces of old lace, glittery sandals, even chain mail can be made by spraying a string vest silver, as can space men's boots by spraying old wellies. Sit back and watch the fantasies flow.

225

BABYSHOCK

Playing house. It is a fortunate and popular child who has a swing, slide, sandpit, trampoline or climbing frame, but most popular of all at this age is the summer house or tree house. An enormous cardboard box (such as a fridge or washing machine or chair might arrive in) makes a superb Wendy House. Cut out a door and a window, paint on flowers and trees and bricks, cut a hole and stick in a chimney ... But in fact, any confined space into which a child can climb and nest-build, stick up a self-painted picture, simply sit on a miniature chair and serve make-believe tea, serves as well. Converted playpens might be used, even the space under a table, sealed off from the grown-ups' world with a curtain, and furnished with cushions.

Building and collecting. The pre-school and early years can be the time when a child begins collecting things. Building systems, for example, like Lego and Fischer-Technik, or items like stamps, buttons, shells, pebbles, postcards, matchboxes, leaves, coins, scraps or labels.

Books. Possibly the most important and often most absorbing pre-school toy. After the age of two, many children start deciding for themselves which books they prefer. In Britain, public libraries are an excellent source of books from the earliest ages, and the local library can be a useful and enjoyable regular outing.

First aid

Is he in a dangerous place?

If so, move him without delay. If in contact with an electric current, switch it off or break the victim's contact with the source with a wooden object.

Is he breathing adequately?

Noisy breathing suggests obstruction. Check that his mouth and nose are not blocked by blood, vomit, debris or a swallowed tongue.

Get him on his side, tipped slightly head down, clear out his mouth with your finger and hold the lower jaw forwards. If the airway is clear but he does not breathe, take a deep breath and place your mouth over the victim's mouth and nose, sealing your lips over his face. Breathe out. Move away and let the victim breathe out on his own. Repeat ten times a minute. A child does not need a full lungful. A baby needs only the contents of your puffed-out cheeks. You can tell if you are doing enough if you can see his chest move with each breath. If there is a hole in the chest wall, seal it with whatever comes to hand – clothing will do.

Is his circulation adequate?

If the child is not breathing and is very pale or blue, feel or listen for the heartbeat just to the left side of the mid-chest.

If nothing or very slow (below 40/minute), clear the airway and give six breaths as above. If there is no improvement, hit the lower breast bone sharply three times with the fist. If there is no improvement, raise the child's legs in the air, lay him on his back then rhythmically compress the lower end of the breast bone sixty times a minute. A small child needs only three fingers, an older child the lower part of the flat palm. Do not do this unless you are sure – it can fracture ribs and damage internal organs.

If you are single-handed, give five breaths to fifteen chest presses.

If the lips go pink and the pupils are or become small, you are doing well. Continue until the patient's heart beat returns or skilled help arrives.

Is he bleeding?

Stop the bleeding by direct pressure on the bleeding point. If you haven't a clean dressing, bare fingers or a fist will do. If bleeding is from an arm or leg, hold the limb upright.

Is he unconscious?

First, act as above. Then lie him on his side, head slightly down and legs and arms half bent.

Prevent chilling but do not deliberately warm him.

Whatever has happened

Do not give any food or drink.

Has he taken poison (or drugs)?

If lips or tongue are burned, do not make him vomit but give him milk to drink. Otherwise, hold him head down and tickle his throat with your protected fingers. Do not give salt water (or anything by mouth).

Has he been burned?

Put out flames.

If the skin is not blistered, relieve pain by running cold water over the burn. 227

BABYSHOCK

If blistered, just cover with a clean dressing until skilled attention arrives. Do not remove burned clothes or adherent matter such as tar.

Allow a drink only if the journey to hospital will be more than an hour. Chemicals should be washed off the skin with water.

Has he a broken bone?

Await skilled attention. If unavoidable, simply provide comfortable support to the limb.

Foreign bodies

In a serious wound – leave them unless loose.

In the eye – stand behind the child and part his lids while he looks in all directions. If you can see it, wipe it off with a tissue. If not seen, turn the lid back and look again. If you cannot turn the upper lid back, go to a doctor or an Accident Department.

In the nose – ask him to blow while you compress the opposite nostril with your finger.

If it does not come out, seek medical aid. In the ear – do not remove anything jammed in the earhole. An insect can be floated out with (cold) cooking oil. Do not do this if the child has had an operation on his eardrum.

Nose bleed

Do not panic.

Sit him with his head bent a little forwards.

Put a cork between his teeth, let the blood dribble into a bowl.

Forbid sniffing and swallowing.

Leave for ten minutes.

Poisoning

One in one hundred pre-school children are accidentally poisoned every year. Almost any prescribed drug, and many agents used in house and garden, are poisonous to small children.

If you find your child with a half-empty bottle of medicine or sitting amongst scattered pills, do not panic.

1. Save the container and all the pills or medicine to show your Doctor.

2. Contact your GP immediately. Attendance at hospital is not necessary or even desirable in every case and your GP may prefer to deal with the problem at home.

3. If your GP is unavailable, take the child (and tablets) to the nearest hospital with an Accident and Emergency Department.

4. If the journey will take more than thirty minutes and the child has *not* swallowed parafin, turps, petrol, furniture polish or corrosives and is fully conscious, make him vomit by putting a finger to the back of his throat. Do not give him salt water to drink.

Animal bites

Rabies does not exist in the UK but any parent whose child is bitten by an animal should seek medical advice. Tetanus immunisation may be necessary. If bitten by an animal in a country where rabies still exists, (which means most of Europe, parts of the US, all of Asia and Africa), immediate medical attention should be sought and, if possible, the animal captured for examination.

Snakebite

Adders are the only poisonous British snake. It has a dark zig-zag band along the centre of its back. However, there is always the remote danger of a bite from a pet exotic snake. Therefore, the reptile should be captured, if possible, or killed for precise identification.

The bite should be covered with a clean cloth or handkerchief and a firm but not tight tourniquet tied above the bite and the limb held immobile. The tourniquet is too tight if the foot or hand becomes very pale or blue. If in doubt, release it. The child should be taken to hospital, the tourniquet being released for ninety seconds every fifteen minutes.

Almost all patients recover unharmed.

First aid for fever and pain

Fever and pain accompany most infection your child is likely to catch. Any child with a high temperature should be cooled down. Fever is uncomfortable, may produce severe headache, and in 3% of children provokes a convulsion. Never wrap up a feverish child whatever your instinct or your mother tells you. Call a doctor if the baby is under six months, but before doing so for an older infant, first do the following.

Turn off all external heating

Strip the child to pants or nappy only

Remove all blankets (use only a sheet)

Add enough clothing to prevent shivering

Give paracetamol four-hourly as recommended on page 162.

If the child is extremely hot to the touch (39 degrees C or 103 degrees F, if you have a thermometer in the house) he should be tepid sponged. Make all of his body, *except his head*, wet with lukewarm water and do not dry him.

Studies by the US Army on volunteers showed that the body needs to be kept wet for twenty minutes, and that lukewarm water is better than either cold water (which produces shivering) or alcohol, which the volunteers probably drank. This treatment will lower the gemperature 1.5 degrees to 2 degrees C (3 to 4 degrees F).

The drugs mentioned above can also be used for pain.

Abortion

In what circumstances should I consider abortion?

This is an extremely personal and individual question, and really cannot be answered in a general way. It has been stated that a planned pregnancy does not necessarily entail happy and successful parenthood. Equally, an unplanned pregnancy cannot preclude happiness for parents and child. But an unwanted baby may cause hardship and much unhappiness which will certainly reflect in the unfortunate child's developing personality.

It may be useful to look at the reasons given by women who requested abortion in one private clinic. Half the women were single, the other half were married, separated, widowed or divorced.

Single women

Too young to cope
Still studying
Parents don't know
Boyfriend left her
Raped
No financial support
Harmful effects to the foetus (infection, X-Rays, drugs)

Married women

Too old to cope
Cannot afford another child
Husband doesn't know, not his
Husband or boyfriend left her
Casual encounter
Husband unemployed
Harmful effects to the foetus (infection, X-Rays, drugs)

Who should I go to for help?

Most women go to their general practitioner. In 1967 and again in 1970, a survey of GPs showed a substantial change of attitudes towards abortion. Generally, you will be a good judge of whether your doctor is approachable and likely to be sympathetic. Common reasons for avoiding GPs include fear of parents being told (or husband, if the woman is married), fear of upsetting the doctor/patient relationship and losing respect in the eyes of their doctor, or fear of the abortion appearing on her medical notes for all-time.

Normally, her GP will refer a woman to a gynaecologist, but if there are none in the patient's area, the doctor may advise a private clinic. There is a waiting list at hospitals which may involve a lapse of three or four weeks before being seen by the consultant gynaecologist and counselled by a social worker. For this reason, and because it can be a humiliating experience to be interviewed in the midst of a busy outpatient clinic in front of students and nurses, many women willingly pay for the operation to be carried out.

If you would rather avoid both GP and local NHS hospital, you have the choice of approaching a registered pregnancy advice bureau or a licensed nursing home or clinic. Be absolutely sure that the organisation you choose is approved by the DHSS. Addresses may be found in telephone directories or evening newspapers.

What formalities must I undergo before abortion is agreed?

The abortion Act 1967 insists on the patient being seen and examined by two doctors who will then sign the green form 'A'. If a woman is under sixteen years of age, parental consent is sought. The examining doctor will ask about previous medical illnesses and operations and whether she has any allergies or takes any medication or drugs. Pregnancy is confirmed by a urine test. The doctor or a counsellor explores the patient's feelings about the abortion and in this way determines whether grounds for termination of pregnancy exist. The wording of the law allows for freedom of interpretation by the signing doctor and his decision may or may not concur with a woman's request.

The majority of women who discover they are pregnant make up their mind quite quickly whether they wish their pregnancy terminated or not and usually present a 'fait accompli' to their general practitioner. There remain a few who are undecided because of fear of the unknown, religious reasons or simply because they are not sure what they or their partners really want. In counselling, the doctor or counsellor explores why a woman wants the abortion, her knowledge of what is going to happen to her, her fear about future pregnancies and finally helps her to cope with the future. Most patients are so nervous, tense, full of remorse and guilt at what they are about to do, that a compassionate counsellor can be a great help in clarifying decisions one way or the other, and in overcoming any post-operative physical and mental stress.

In the UK, abortion is justifiably performed under one of the following clauses:

Continuation of pregnancy would involve risk to the patient's life greater than if the pregnancy were terminated.

Continuation of pregnancy would involve risk of injury to the physical or mental health of the patient greater than if the pregnancy were terminated.

Continuation of pregnancy would involve risk of injury to the physical and mental health of any existing children in the patient's family greater than if pregnancy were terminated.

There is a substantial risk that if the child were born it would suffer from physical or mental abnormalities so as to be seriously handicapped.

Most pregnancies are terminated under the loosest of these clauses, clause 2.

How is abortion performed?

Provided the pregnancy is less than twelve weeks termination can be performed safely either under a general anaesthetic or local anesthetic and the method generally used is by vacuum aspiration and/or curettage. Some gynaecologists do perform vaginal terminations up to twenty weeks but this is rarely carried out in NHS hospitals because hospital consultants feel that the dilatation of the neck of the womb – the cervix – could result in more difficulties in future pregnancies.

The above procedures generally require a twenty-four hour stay in hospital or clinic. However very early pregnancies could be discharged after about four hours, provided the clinic has a licence from the DHSS to discharge patients the same day.

Pregnancies over sixteen weeks can be terminated by inducing a miscarriage with an injection of prostaglandine. The patient undergoes a full labour and may require further treatment the next day – a D & C – to clean out the womb and prevent haemorrhage from any retained products. Most women do not like this method of termination as they are afraid of suffering contraction pains and tend to prefer private clinics where a vaginal termination can be obtained at eighteen weeks under a full anaesthetic and without unnecessary suffering, even at the risk of an incompetent cervix later on.

Will I be able to have more children later?
What will I feel like after an abortion?

These two questions are heard repeatedly from women seeking terminations. Stories about women becoming sterile and feeling very ill and dying are relics from the past when abortion was illegal and the backstreet abortionist thrived on the suffering of frightened women. Due to the Abortion Act of 1967, all that has changed. In expert hands abortion nowadays is almost the same as having a scrape (D & C) and due to improved techniques such as suction termination, and improved lighter anaesthetic, most women feel no worse than having a tooth out.

In terms of your physical and emotional health, abortion is much less upsetting than childbirth. If you have carefully considered your decision and talked it over with the father, one might imagine that you will simply experience a sense of relief when it is all over. Very probably, you *will* feel relieved, but for a any number of personal reasons, and public reasons too such as the emotive status accorded abortion by campaigners, politicians, and the media, a number of far less positive thoughts and emotions are likely to flood across you. How a woman feels may depend upon the reasons why she opted for an abortion. If conception arose as a result of rape, the patient is likely to feel rather different to the woman who had to have an abortion on account of a damaged foetus. Regret, sadness, even guilt may follow a maturely made decision to have an abortion. And the antidote is likely to be a mature reaction to the negative thoughts. Tell someone close to you just how you feel; don't bottle up your emotions, or worse, go along with your partner's jubilation when you don't feel it. Make him understand just how you feel. If you do not share your feelings with him, he is less likely to be sympathetic and supportive.

There is absolutely no doubt that you will, in time, come to terms with the abortion, however much you may doubt it now.

Pregnancy Advisory Service,
40 Margaret Street,
London, W1
(01-409 0281)

British Pregnancy Advisory Service, local phone book, London Victoria branch, 2nd Floor, 58 Petty France, London, SW1
(01-222 0985)

Infertility

How do I know whether I am infertile?

Many women, and men too, worry unnecessarily that they may be infertile (i.e. that they cannot become or cause their partner to become pregnant). In fact only 10% of marriages in the UK are involuntarily childless and until you have had regular intercourse without comtraception for a period of six months or more, there is no need to consult your doctor.

There are various different reasons why a couple could be unable to conceive and there is certainly no sure test which you can carry out yourself to find out whether you are infertile.

The temperature test. Ovulation (the process by which the egg is released from the ovary) is an essential condition of becoming pregnant and by calculating the time in your monthly cycle when it occurs, you can isolate the most fruitful time to have intercourse. In some, but by no means all women, ovulation is followed by a slight increase in weight, ovulation is followed by a slight increase in weight, soreness of the breasts, or a thick 'tacky' vaginal secretion. Perhaps the most widely used method to fix the time of ovulation is the simple temperature test. The actual rise in temperature is, however, very low (between 0.5 and 1 degree centigrade) and could as well be caused by any mild illness, or even psychological factors, as by ovulation.

Who do I go and see?

You *and* your partner go to your local GP. It is sad that in very few instances do both partners go along to discuss the question of infertility, although it is as likely that the male is infertile (if anybody is) as the female. Some men prefer not to accept this statistical fact because fertility in the male has been linked in mythology with masculinity. Legends and myths are responsible for more unhappiness, distress and dissatisfaction than any reality. Ask your GP to refer you to a clinic which specialises in infertility, indeed many family planning clinics run infertility sessions. Alternatively, you can refer yourself.

What will the doctor do?

First of all you will be asked some questions, for example:

How long have you been having intercourse without contraception?

How regularly do you have intercourse, and is it painful?

Does he ejaculate inside you?

Do you experience any sexual difficulties? It is very important for *both* partners to satisfy this question. So often one partner may deny that there are difficulties, while a discussion between the three of you might uncover a case of impotence (the inability to maintain erection, which could be due to any one of a number of factors, such as tiredness, stress, drugs, excessive alcohol, or the ageing process), or improper penetration.

Do you wash after intercourse? Excessive washing may reduce the chances of conception.

Do you know when ovulation occurs? The time of ovulation may shift a day or 233 more in either direction from one month to the next, but we have seen why it is important to know when it occurs.

How regular are your periods? Irregular or prolonged menstrual cycles will reduce the number of ovulations and, therefore, the chances of conception.

What form of contraception did you use to use? Temporary infertility has sometimes been discovered in women who have taken the pill for a long time. The IUD (or coil) can lead to infection which in turn could hinder conception.

What infections have you had? A case of mumps could be the cause of infertility in the male. Other infections may result in a blockage of the reproductory tubes.

Only when the GP is satisfied that your answers do not point to a likely root cause will he carry out a vaginal examination to exclude any anatomical abnormality or blockage, such as an ovarian cyst.

What tests will the doctor carry out?
In your doctor's attempts to isolate the cause of infertility (the first step towards a cure) he might carry out any of the following tests.

Tests for a woman
To establish that ovulation occurs
The simple temperature test involves monitoring a woman's body temperature every morning before getting out of bed over a period of two or three menstrual cycles. Just after ovulation there is a slight rise of between 0.5 and 1 degree centigrade. The temperature will stay up for about 2 weeks then gradually dip towards the menstruation date.
About one week after ovulation your doctor may well wish to confirm this test with a blood test. He will be looking for a high level of the female sex

hormone progesterone, which will confirm that ovulation has in fact occurred.

To establish that there is no hostility to the male sperms
This is known as the post-coital test. Within eight hours following intercourse the doctor will take a sample of mucus from the top of the vagina. If the mucus is discovered to be scanty, he may prescribe a small dose of the female sex hormone oestrogen three to four days prior to ovulation to boost the chances of conception.

To check that the reproductory tubes are functional
Your doctor will refer you to a gynaecologist (a specialist who deals exclusively with women) who will establish whether the reproductory tubes are obstructed. This can be done either by special X-ray or by Laparoscopy. Laparoscopy, performed while the patient is under a general anaesthetic, involves the insertion of a very small telescope into the interior of the abdomen, and permits the gynaecologist a view of your ovaries, tubes and urteris.

Tests for men
The simplest and most likely test involves analysing the seminal fluid produced by masturbation or withdrawal. Since sperms remain alive for only about eight hours, it must be delivered to the doctor shortly after production.

If one or other of us is infertile, what then?
The answer depends upon why you are unable to conceive.

If ovulation is the problem, fertility drugs may be prescribed. The stories you may have heard about multiple births should not scare you. Provided the drugs are used carefully, and the resultant oestrogen is monitored, the chances of multiple birth are greatly reduced.

Your gynaecologist may advise an operation to unblock the reproductive tubes so that the egg can move down the tube and meet the sperm.

If the vaginal mucus has been found to be hostile to the male sperms, your doctor may advise a sodium bicarbonate douche to make the vaginal mucus more alkaline, and more favourable to the male sperms.

Male fertility problems respond less readily to treatment. If his sperm count is too low, he may be advised to bathe his testicles in cold water daily, and the sperm count repeated in one to three months. If this fails, artificial insemination may be considered. Sometimes this service is available on the NHS, but finding a donor may be a problem. Artificial insemination involves inserting properly matched spermatic fluid into the neck of the womb either fresh from a third party or a sperm bank, where it can be stored for up to four years.

The National Association for the Childless and Childfree, 318 Summer Lane, Birmingham, specialises in cases of infertility.